Experiencing Narrative Worlds

YALE UNIVERSITY PRESS

Experiencing Narrative

On the Psychological

NEW HAVEN & LONDON

Worlds

Activities of Reading

Richard J. Gerrig

Designed by Deborah Dutton.

Set in Bembo type by Rainsford Type, Danbury, Connecticut.
Printed in the United States of America by BookCrafters, Inc.,
Chelsea, Michigan.

Library of Congress Cataloging-in-Publication Data
Gerrig, Richard J.
   Experiencing narrative worlds : on the psychological
activities of
reading / Richard J. Gerrig.
       p. cm.
   Includes bibliographical references (p.) and index.
   ISBN 0-300-05434-3
   1. Books and reading–Psychological aspects.   2. Narration
(Rhetoric)   I. Title.
Z1003.G45 1993
418'.4'019–dc20   92-41688

A catalogue record for this book is available from the British
Library.

The paper in this book meets the guidelines for permanence and
durability of the Committee on Production Guidelines for Book
Longevity of the Council on Library Resources.

10   9   8   7   6   5   4   3   2   1

For my parents

There is no Frigate like a Book

To take us Lands away

Nor any Coursers like a Page

Of prancing Poetry—

This Traverse may the poorest take

Without oppress of Toll—

How frugal is the Chariot

That bears the Human Soul!

—Emily Dickinson, c. 1873

CONTENTS

ACKNOWLEDGMENTS

This book has evolved over the past several years with kind help from a broad array of friends, students, and colleagues. I have been fortunate to have had a large number of opportunities to present and discuss this work in both formal and informal settings. Its final form is very much a product of this near-constant stream of feedback. I am grateful to all the individuals who have listened and offered questions and critiques.

The book has been much improved through the efforts of Robert Crowder, Steven Greene, Gregory Murphy, Timothy Peterson, Deborah Prentice, and Robert Sternberg, each of whom read full drafts of the manuscript and provided invaluable assistance in sharpening my arguments and clarifying my conclusions. I will surely come to wish that I had followed their advice more diligently.

I thank David Allbritton, Allan Bernardo, and Aimée Surprenant for providing moment-by-moment assistance on briefer stretches of the book. They made themselves available on nearly a daily basis to help me formulate my ideas more precisely. I also thank the larger group of people who have provided advice at critical junctures: Mahzarin Banaji, John Boswell, Herbert Clark, Wendell Garner, Raymond Gibbs, Joseph Gordon, Helene Intraub, Donna Kat, Suzanne Lovett, Letitia Naigles, Laura Novick, Bradford Pillow, Arthur Samuel, Michael Schober, Jerome Singer, and Michael Tarr. At Yale University Press, I thank Gladys Topkis for making this whole process much easier than I ever thought it could be. Thanks also to Karen Gangel and Eliza Childs for shepherding the manuscript through production. Further afield, I am grateful to Diane and Alexandra Levitan for the remarkable and joyous ways in which they have changed my life.

Finally, I would like to thank, in each case for a second time, the people who have contributed most steadily to the course of my research. Herbert Clark remains the inspiration for all I undertake. Arthur Samuel has proved himself at every opportunity to be a great friend and insightful colleague. Gregory Murphy has contributed considerable wisdom and humor toward helping me shape my work. Deborah Prentice has been a collaborator of extraordinary intellectual vigor. Timothy Peterson has provided the comforting context in which this project could thrive.

Experiencing Narrative Worlds

Two Metaphors for the
Experience of Narrative Worlds

O̲ur lives overflow with experiences of narrative worlds. Even a brief story told in response to "What did you do last night?" can swiftly remove us from our day-to-day reality. At another extreme, we can disappear for hours into the narrative worlds of books and movies. Some narratives are created out of fact, some out of fantasy. Some are intended to communicate serious truths; some communicate pure joy. Some narratives are deeply memorable; some make only a fleeting impression. I am concerned in this book with explicating a common core at the heart of the various experiences of narratives. My goal is to understand the repertory of cognitive processes that give substance to this variety of worlds.

I approach this goal largely through close analyses of phenomena that figure prominently in readers' reports of their experiences. Scholars in a number of traditions have provided observations on the interaction of readers and narratives. I use many of those observations to show how current psychological accounts of narrative understanding must be extended and refined. At the same time, I describe how psychological theories can be used

1

to capture regularities of experience that have often been over-looked within competing traditions. My overarching aim will be to construct a theory that is equally respectful of the effects authors can achieve and the mechanisms by which they achieve them.

In this chapter, I present two metaphors that are often used to characterize experiences of narratives: readers are often de-scribed as *being transported* by a narrative by virtue of *performing* that narrative. My evocation of these metaphors will enable me to refer concretely to otherwise elusive aspects of readers' ex-periences: conceptual metaphors often function in just this way to structure domains of experience that cannot be accessed through literal language. Lakoff and Johnson (1980; see also Lak-off, 1987) cite an abundance of examples to support their theory that most such metaphorical mappings are nonarbitrary. Ex-amination of the target experiences can make evident the profound appropriateness of the metaphors; analysis of the met-aphors, in turn, can reveal important insights into psychological structure. I adhere to this philosophy in introducing the two metaphors of being transported and performance. These two images will serve both as shorthand expressions for what it feels like to experience narrative worlds and as touchstones for gen-erating research questions about those experiences.

On Being Transported

Andrew Parent, the hero of Paul Theroux's novel *My Secret History,* has been through some rough times. At a particularly low point, he picks up his travel journal and begins to read:

> I laughed out loud. Then I stopped, hearing the echo of the strange sound. For a moment in my reading I have been transported, and I had forgotten everything—all my worry and depression, the crisis in my marriage, my anger, my

jealousy. I had seen the Indian sitting across the aisle from me in the wooden carriage, and the terraced fields on the steep slopes, and the way the train brushed the long-stemmed wild flowers that grew beside the track.
It was half a world away, and because it was so separate from me, and yet so complete, I laughed. It was a truthful glimpse of a different scene. It cheered me up. It was like looking at a brilliant picture and losing myself in it. (p. 402)

In these paragraphs, Parent twice invokes the metaphor of being transported to a narrative world: once explicitly, "I have *been transported,*" and once by family resemblance, "*losing myself* [in a brilliant picture]." This metaphor, in fact, goes a long way toward capturing one of the most prominent phenomenological aspects of the experience of narrative worlds. Readers become "lost in a book" (see Nell, 1988); moviegoers are surprised when the lights come back up; television viewers care desperately about the fates of soap opera characters; museum visitors are captivated by the stories encoded in daubs of paint. In each case, a narrative serves to transport an experiencer away from the here and now.

Before I elaborate the metaphor of being transported more fully, I will use this first glimpse as background to sketch out informal definitions of *narratives* and *narrative worlds*. A classic definition of *narrative* comes from the work of Labov (1972), who gathered a large corpus of naturalistic narratives to support his analysis: "We define a narrative as one method of recapitulating past experience by matching a verbal sequence of clauses to the sequence of events which (it is inferred) actually occurred" (pp. 359–60). Against this background, Labov sets as a "minimal narrative" a "sequence of two clauses which are temporally ordered" (p. 360). He goes on to identify six structural components that storytellers may use to move beyond this minimum to create a fully formed narrative. Labov's account of the structure of narratives has proven to be valuable in the description of the storytelling behavior of both adults (Polanyi, 1989) and children (McCabe and Peterson, 1991).

Labov's definition will enable me to draw a contrast between narratives and the experience of narrative worlds. Consider this exchange from Peter Smith's novel *Make-Believe Ballrooms:*

> "Where are you calling from?" I said as I switched off the tape recorder.
> "Texas. Yippee. Bore me, I mean. Bore me. Just kiddin'. Aagh, I've just taken some poison 'cause I can't stand to be here. Oh, no, I'm commitin' suicide. Just kiddin', Bob, Texas is fine—" (p. 115)

Although no part of the reply, which is uttered by the character Mary-Ann, would match the structure even of Labov's minimal narrative, it nonetheless provides the potential for a visit to a narrative world. Even had Mary-Ann's reply been limited simply to "Texas," she would have given readers the opportunity to be mentally transported to Texas. If we define the experience of narrative worlds with respect to an endpoint (the operation of whatever set of mental processes transports the reader) rather than with respect to a starting point (a text with some formal features), we can see that no a priori limits can be put on the types of language structures that might prompt the construction of narrative worlds. If Mary-Ann's rich evocation of Texas transports readers to Texas, then it matters little that the utterance "Texas" looks nothing like a formal narrative.

Note that I am ignoring issues of aesthetics in this broad (and hazy) definition of narrative worlds. Bruner (1986), for example, asserts that "narrative deals with the vicissitudes of human intentions" (p. 16) largely to create a context in which he can examine what makes a narrative effective or ineffective. He goes on to describe some of the methods by which good stories draw their readers in. For one method, Bruner implies that texts which

require readers to fill in gaps—by forcing " 'meaning performance' upon the reader" (p. 27)—will, on the whole, be better
stories (that is, higher-quality visits to narrative worlds). Bruner
might be correct in the connections he hypothesizes between
content features of narratives and aesthetic experiences. Even so,
some core set of processes is likely to allow readers to experience
narrative worlds even when the stories themselves are poorly
crafted. In fact, as I argue in later chapters, one of the most
profound aspects of the experience of narrative worlds is how
very hard it is *not* to show some features of being transported,
whatever the quality of the narrative. "Texas" may not constitute an elegant entry into a narrative world nor sustain a lengthy
visit, but it has as much right to invoke the processes that constitute "being transported" as the best passages of the literary
canon.

Not all readers, of course, would take up the invitation to
visit Texas. Once we identify a narrative world as the product
of some set of processes, we must acknowledge that the experiences of narrative worlds will be optional: a text cannot force
a reader to experience a narrative world. Even something that
optimally qualifies as a narrative with respect to Labov or Bruner's templates will on some occasions fail to bring about the
type of participation that ensures the creation of a narrative
world.

A similar claim is captured in the distinction that has been
drawn between *propositional* representations of texts versus
situation models (van Dijk and Kintsch, 1983) or *mental models*
(Johnson-Laird, 1983). Early research on comprehension demonstrated that readers begin the analysis of a text by extracting
basic units of meaning, or propositions (see Kintsch, 1974, 1978;
Ratcliff and McKoon, 1978). We might imagine, for instance,
that Hal (who Mary-Ann mistakenly believes is someone else,
named Bob) might initially represent the reply to his question
as "The caller is from Texas," or *from (caller, Texas)*. As Hal

takes in more information, he might begin to pull out larger units of meaning, or *macropropositions* (see Kintsch and van Dijk, 1978; van Dijk, 1977, 1980). He might begin to gather together information about life in Texas or the people who live there. For readers to carry out complex reasoning with respect to a text, however, they typically must construct more elaborate models, situation models, which integrate information from the text with broader real-world knowledge (Johnson-Laird, 1983; van Dijk and Kintsch, 1983). (I use the term *situation model* because, as Garnham [1987] suggests, the term *mental model* is used ambiguously in the psychological literature.) Readers do not inevitably create such situation models: sometimes the text is too complex (Perrig and Kintsch, 1985) or insufficiently determinate (Mani and Johnson-Laird, 1982) to allow readers to construct coherent representations of the full situation. On the other hand, if readers need to perform certain types of judgments with respect to the text, situation models are essential. In Perrig and Kintsch's experiments, readers were required to read texts describing the spatial layout of a fictitious town. Only when the readers were able to construct a situation model could they easily verify true but previously unpresented statements about aspects of that spatial layout.

Empirical aspects of the dichotomy between propositional representations and situation models thus map onto the distinction I wish to draw between narratives and the experience of narrative worlds. Although readers might inevitably extract basic units of meaning from a narrative, the narrative itself cannot require that a situation model be constructed (though features of the narrative can rule out this type of representation). Although I believe that *narrative world* and *situation model* circumscribe similar theoretical claims, I will use the expression *narrative world* because, by calling to mind the metaphor of being transported, it better suggests the complexity of the experience of narratives. As we shall see, *narrative world* belongs to a broader theoretical agenda that examines the diverse consequences of constructing situation models.

By refocusing attention from narratives to the experience of narrative worlds, I am not trying to undercut the force of structural analyses like Labov's (1972). He was pursuing the quite different goal of explicating how experience is transformed into narrative structures. My aim, by contrast, is to make evident exactly how pervasive the experience of narrative worlds can be. It is a rare conversation among adults that does not depart from the here and now. All such instances allow a journey to a narrative world to begin. Clearly, we enjoy many activities that are explicitly designed to prompt experiences of narrative worlds: novels, newspapers, movies, television programs, history books, representational artworks, and so on. In each case, I suggest, we should be able to find some common core of processes that are the implementation of being transported. For the sake of convenience, I will continue to refer to *narratives,* but I will be using the term quite promiscuously. In particular, I intend *narrative* and *narrative world* to be neutral with respect to the issue of fictionality. Although many of the theoretical statements I cite were framed specifically around the experience of fiction, I suggest that they yield insights that apply to the experience of all narratives.

Note that I almost always refer to the experiencers of narrative worlds as readers. I hope that much of what I say would remain true regardless of how the experiencer is prompted to construct a narrative world (for example, as a listener, as a viewer, and so on). Even so, most of my examples are from the printed page; I am therefore most comfortable using *reader* to stand for the range of possible experiencing roles.

The Phenomenology of Being Transported

Characters in novels, as well as people in real life, often testify to being transported when they have been astonished by the depth of an experience. Such is the case with Andrew Parent who was surprised by how reading his travel journal had allowed him to forget all his "worry and depression, the crisis in [his] marriage, [his] anger, [his] jealousy." Such is also the case with the hero of E. L. Doctorow's novel *Billy Bathgate*. Billy has become the protégé of the mobster Dutch Schultz. In a scene revisited throughout the book, Billy watches over another mobster, Bo Weinberg, who will soon be pitched into the ocean, his feet encased in a tub of cement. In the final moments before he is drowned, Weinberg tells Billy about one of the murders he has committed, and how he got rid of the "hot piece" by slipping it into the pocket of a gentleman waiting to catch a train in Grand Central Station: "Can't you see it, hello dear I'm home my God Alfred what's this in your pocket eek a gun!"

> And he is laughing now, tears of laughter in his eyes, one precious instant in the paradise of recollection, and even as I'm laughing with him I think how fast the mind can move us, the way the story is a span of light across space. I know he certainly got me off that boat that was heaving me up and down one foot at a time through an atmosphere rich in oil, I was there in Grand Central with my hand delivering the piece into Alfred's coat pocket. (p. 159)

In this instance, although the here and now is especially compelling (particularly for Bo Weinberg), the narrative serves momentarily to transport both Billy and Bo to some imagined world in which they both can have a good laugh. Only minutes later, Billy is helping to kill the man who has so amused him.

What is additionally compelling is the challenge the passage provides for readers: those who are also transported by Bo's story are actually several cognitive layers deep (see Bruce, 1981;

Clark, 1987). In this part of the novel, Billy is telling the story
of the immediate circumstances surrounding Bo's execution.
Within that context he recounts the story Bo told him. All of
this, of course, takes place in the context of a novel. In metaphorical terms, each reader (given a certain level of skill from
Doctorow) will have been transported initially to the world of
the novel. From that world, the reader is transported again to
some new location by Billy's story. And within that story, we
are transported by Bo's story. The observation that readers can
be multiply transported strongly suggests why theorists often
select texts as a locus for illuminating complex cognitive processes. *Billy Bathgate* as an experience *feels* unremarkable: that is
the challenge to an adequate theory of being transported.

These first two anecdotal evocations of being transported
come from works of fiction. I suggest that Theroux and Doctorow have lodged this image in the thoughts of their characters
because it accurately captures the authors' own experiences (that
is, I suggest that we can trust the phenomenological reports of
most characters in realistic fiction as accurately reflecting the
types of mental experience real people have). Nonetheless, I offer
some additional evidence from a nonfictional source, one that
concerns responses to paintings rather than to written or oral
stories. Schama (1989) quotes a report from the *Journal de Paris*
on responses to Jacques-Louis David's *The Oath of the Horatii,*
painted in 1785:

> One must absolutely see [this painting] to understand how
> it merits so much admiration. . . . In the end if I am to
> judge from the feeling of others as well as my own, one
> feels in seeing this painting a sentiment that exalts the soul
> and which, to use an expression of J. J. Rousseau, has
> something poignant about it that attracts one; all the attri-
> butes are so well observed that one believes oneself trans-
> ported to the earliest days of the Roman Republic. (p. 174)

Schama quotes an additional testimony to the power of paintings to immerse eighteenth-century Frenchmen, if not others, in narrative worlds. Here Charles Mathon de La Cour is commenting on Jean-Baptiste Greuze's painting *Girl Weeping over Her Dead Canary* (1765):

> "Connoisseurs, women, fops, pedants, wits, the ignorant and the foolish," he [de La Cour] claimed, were "all of one mind about this painting," for in it "one sees nature, one shares the grief of the girl and one wishes above all to console her. Several times I have passed whole hours in attentive contemplation so that I became drunk with a sweet and tender sadness." (p. 151)

What both quotations reveal is how powerfully we can be transported to narrative worlds even under unfavorable circumstances. Studying these static paintings in a (presumably) crowded gallery, these two viewers were nonetheless transported to the world of the early Romans or to a world in which it would be possible to console the grieving girl.

In addition to characterizing experiences of narrative worlds, the metaphor of being transported also serves as a schema with respect to which theoretical questions can be framed and developed. In particular, we can sketch the features of the source domain of being transported to see what types of research have been undertaken in the past and what types may be called for in the future. Roughly speaking, here are the elements of a literal experience of being transported:

1. Someone ("the traveler") is transported

2. by some means of transportation

3. as a result of performing certain actions.

4. The traveler goes some distance from his or her world of origin

5. which makes some aspects of the world of origin inaccessible.

6. The traveler returns to the world of origin, somewhat changed by the journey.

Someone ("the traveler") is transported. One of the hoariest bits of advice with respect to travel is "When in Rome, do as the Romans do." In essence, we are admonished to refit ourselves for for local customs. Certainly if we plan to travel in good faith, we must be sure we are willing to behave as Romans do for the duration of the trip.

Literary theorists have suggested that narratives also call on us to adapt willingly to local conditions. Gibson (1980) wrote, "The fact is that every time we open the pages of another piece of writing, we are embarked on a new adventure in which we become a new person. . . . We assume, for the sake of the experience, that set of attitudes and qualities which the language asks us to assume, and, if we cannot assume them, we throw the book away" (p. 1). Prince (1980) similarly argued that the real reader should not be confused with the "narratee" (see also Bruce, 1981). To illustrate the distinction, Prince quotes from *Le Père Goriot,* in which the narrator tells the "reader": "That's what you will do, you who hold this book with a white hand, you who settle back into a well-padded armchair saying to yourself: perhaps this is going to be amusing" (p. 9). "It is obvious," Prince asserts, that few, if any, readers will resemble the armchair-bound character with a white hand evoked by the narrator: "The reader of fiction . . . should not be mistaken for the narratee. The one is real, the other fictive" (p. 9).

This suggests that the traveler assumes certain new characteristics (as called for by the narrative) as a consequence of undertaking the journey. This idea is virtually unexplored in cognitive psychology, which has emphasized the way the reader constructs the narrative world rather than the way the narrative world reconstructs the reader. The issue looms large, however, when we take up (in chapter 6) questions of how experiences of narratives affect real-world attitudes and beliefs. In this context, we can wonder whether narratives, by causing us to collapse the distinction between reader and narratee, might change our views of what sort of people we are. Gibson (1980) offered an instructive example: "Recognition of a violent disparity between ourself as mock reader [the term Gibson uses to mark the contrast with the "real" reader] and ourself as real person acting in a real world is the process by which we keep our money in our pockets. 'Does your toupee collect moths?' asks the toupee manufacturer, and we answer, 'Certainly not! My hair's my own. You're not talking to *me,* old boy; I'm wise to you.' Of course, we are not always so wise" (p. 2). Gibson's admonition that "we are not always so wise" is a compelling invitation for psychological research.

Travelers avail themselves of some means of transportation. The means of travel, in this case, are novels, anecdotes, movies, and so on. This is Emily Dickinson's explicit image when she begins, "There is no Frigate like a Book." I suggested earlier that little is formally required to bring about experiences of narrative worlds: the means are quite diverse and sometimes mundane. Great artistry might facilitate the journey, but the only a priori requirement for a means of transportation is that it serve as an invitation to the traveler to abandon the here and now. (In terms of our metaphor, I'm claiming that a pickup truck isn't as elegant as a Cadillac, but it will still get us to Texas.)

Travelers perform certain actions. Nested within the overarching metaphor of being transported is the second image—that readers *perform* narratives. In the next section, I describe the performance metaphor in some detail. Let me note briefly here that a major flaw in relying on being transported to organize my discussion is that the phrase projects an aura of passivity. I have used it even so because it accurately encodes readers' descriptions of their experiences. The disparity between the passivity of the metaphor and the active complexity of the processes that make the experience of narratives possible suggests that an adequate theory in this domain must concern itself with the illusion of effortlessness.

The traveler goes some distance from his or her world of origin. There are two senses in which we can interpret the distance a reader is transported as a consequence of experiencing a narrative world. The first captures the intuition that the world of "Star Trek" is somehow more distant in both time and place than the world of "All in the Family." The second captures the intuition that, nonetheless, we are equally prohibited from intervening in either world.

One of the frequently discussed properties of narrative worlds is that many of the truths intended to prevail within them are not explicitly stipulated by their creators (see, for example, Crittenden, 1982; Eaton, 1976; Lewis, 1978; Margolin, 1987). Thus, we would be reasonably willing to take it for granted that the majority of characters mentioned in narratives have livers, although the liver is rarely mentioned in ordinary narratives. Differences among narrative worlds on the first sense of distance partially represent our intuitions about the extent to which assertions true in the real world would remain true in the narrative world. Ryan (1980) articulated a *principle of minimal departure,* which states that "we reconstrue the world of a fiction . . . as being the closest possible to the reality we know. This means that we will project upon the world of the statement everything we know about the real world, and that we will make only those adjustments which we cannot avoid" (p. 406; see also Walton on the "reality principle" [1990]). (Note that "minimal departure" implicitly alludes to the metaphor of being transported.) The greater the departure from the real world—the more adjustments that must be made—the greater the perception of distance. This sense of distance presupposes, of course, that readers participate in the construction of narrative worlds, an assumption I embrace in the analysis of performance. Whatever the degree of overlap in propositional content, however, we are strictly prohibited from affecting the course of action in narrative worlds. This is the conclusion Walton (1978a) reached in his essay entitled "How Remote Are Fictional Worlds from the Real World?" There is no sense in which, by leaping to our feet and calling out, "Don't believe Iago!" we can save Desdemona from her fate. We know as soon as we redistance ourselves from the narrative world that Desdemona's fate is sealed and, in any case, that the woman about to be smothered is only an actress who will rise again to take a curtain call. Walton recognizes that, although we solidly maintain our real-world belief that fictional worlds are inaccessible, our behavior when experiencing a narrative world often gives the appearance of uncertainty. We are willing, for example, to argue about Iago's motives as if they exist in the real world. Walton suggests, even so, that "except in the rarest of circumstances, readers and spectators are not deluded. Tom Sawyer and Willy Loman are neither real nor believed to be. Instead, appreciators are fictional. Rather than somehow promoting fictions to the level of reality, we, as appreciators, descend to the level of fiction" (p. 21). I consider Walton's range of issues at greater length in later chapters. My major modification will be to remove "fictional" from his formulation. Walton's arguments in favor of being transported, I argue, apply equally to both fictional and non-fictional narratives.

Some aspects of the world of origin become inaccessible. When we leave our place of origin behind for a real-world trip, it is incontrovertible that certain elements of that place of origin become inaccessible: trivially, we must briefly do without our most comfortable armchairs or most reliable weather forecasters. In chapter 5, I take up the somewhat less trivial claim that the experience of narrative worlds also makes certain aspects of the real world inaccessible. Here, I offer an anecdote to sketch out what I mean by such a claim.

Edgar, the young hero of E. L. Doctorow's novel *World's Fair*, reports on many wonders, including one performed by his uncle:

Uncle Willy sometimes did tricks for us, and I remember one trick in particular that was my favorite and that he did very well. He'd stand in the doorway to my room and make it appear that a hand belonging to someone else just hidden from view was grabbing him by the throat and trying to drag him away. He would choke and gasp and his eyes would bulge and he'd try to tear at the claw-like hand; his head would disappear and reappear again in the struggle, and sometimes it was so realistic that I'd scream and rush to the door and beg him to stop, jumping up and swinging on the arm of the malign killer hand, which, of course, was his own. It didn't matter that I knew how the trick was done, it was terrifying just the same. (p. 57)

What is most remarkable about Edgar's description is his awareness that he should not be frightened—he "knew how the trick was done"—but he was frightened anyway. Edgar's experience, which I suggest in chapter 5 should be accepted as representative of nonfictional experiences (see Gerrig, 1989a, 1989b), demonstrates a clear dissociation between what he knows or believes in the real world (how the trick was done) and what he knows or believes in the narrative world (that his uncle was in danger). The cognitive psychological puzzle is how this dissociation is accomplished: Why is it that the real-world knowledge, which ought to be readily accessible in the repeated situation, fails to undermine the thrill of the trick? Edgar's experience provides evidence that immersion in narratives brings about partial isolation from the facts of the real world. In chapter 5, I return to this and related phenomena and describe experimental evidence that will make this claim less mystical.

The traveler returns to the world of origin, somewhat changed by the journey. For the majority of narratives, we would be surprised if some mental structures were not changed as a function of their experience. At a minimum, we would expect to have created memory representations to encode the actual propositional information in the narrative. Such minimal types of changes, however, need not have much effect on whatever it was the reader knew or believed before visiting the narrative world.

In chapter 6 I discuss the ways information from narratives can have a more profound effect on preexisting knowledge and beliefs. This issue is controversial largely with respect to fiction, where theorists have been troubled by uncertainty about what people *ought* to do about information or attitudes tendered in fictional worlds. Authors openly invent the details of fictional worlds: in many analyses, it is simply nonsensical to be influenced by information that has no real-world verifiability. If we *know,* for example, that we cannot meet Sherlock Holmes walking down a street in London, we should not be influenced by his opinions, as if someone might really hold them.

Anecdotal evidence suggests that we are not nearly so pristine in our use of fictional information. Consider a phenomenon reported on July 28, 1975, by both *Newsweek* and *Time* magazines, which *Newsweek* labeled "Jawsmania": "Its symptoms are saucered eyes, blanched faces and a certain tingly anxiety about going near the water" (p. 16). Fear of shark attacks inspired by the movie *Jaws* kept vacationers out of the water despite the most responsible efforts of the popular press to correct mistaken notions: "Shark attacks are statistically far more remote a death threat than, say, bee stings or lightning bolts; the great danger in going to the beach, says John Prescott of Boston's New England Aquarium, is the drive there and back" (p. 17). The (non-)swimmers were not persuaded by such demonstrations of the fictional worldliness of their beliefs.

The burden of chapter 6 will be to make sense of viewers' seemingly nonsensical reactions to *Jaws* by situating them in a richer context. I examine reactions to fictional information as a special case of general reactions to narrative information. Along the way, I reject simple "toggle" theories of fiction which have suggested that readers perform some mental act called "the willing suspension of disbelief" that eviscerates the effects of fiction. Whatever the effects of narrative worlds may be, they will arise because of strategic actions that experiencers do and do not perform with respect to those worlds.

Performance

In many respects, the task of the reader is much like the task of the actor. Consider this excerpt from Constantin Stanislavski's classic volume, *An Actor Prepares:*

> We need a broad point of view to act the plays of our times and of many peoples. We are asked to interpret the life of human souls from all over the world. An actor creates not only the life of his times but that of the past and future as well. That is why he needs to observe, to conjecture, to experience, to be carried away with emotion. (p. 181)

Readers are called upon to exercise exactly this same range of skills. They must use their own experiences of the world to bridge gaps in texts. They must bring both facts and emotions to bear on the construction of the world of the text. And, just like actors performing roles, they must give substance to the psychological lives of characters.

Most cognitive psychological research on the experience of narrative worlds has clustered, at least implicitly, around the metaphor of reading as a type of performance. Researchers have directed their efforts toward detailing the mechanisms by which readers actively contribute to the experience of narrative worlds. One important focus of research, initiated by Bartlett in 1932, has demonstrated that readers' memories for texts represent a merging of textual information with elements of preexisting knowledge. In his original research, Bartlett asked English readers to recall a story called "The War of the Ghosts," which he had adapted from a translation of a North American folktale. Bartlett found that his readers' reproductions of the story were often greatly altered through a process he called *rationalization,* the sources of which were both cultural and idiosyncratic. Some alterations reflected the readers' general tendencies to bring details of the story into line with English norms. Thus, at a lexical level, "boat" might replace "canoe" and "went fishing" might replace "hunt[ed] seals." At a plot level, Bartlett's readers often changed the story to eliminate evocations of supernatural forces. Within these general trends, however, there was great individual variation, which interested Bartlett as well: "The fact of rationalisation was illustrated in practically every reproduction or series of reproductions, but, as would be expected, the way in which it was effected varied greatly from case to case. For the particular form adopted is due directly to the functioning of individual special interests . . . or to some fact of personal experience, or to some peculiarity of individual attitude which determines the salience or potency of the details in the whole material dealt with" (p. 71). Bartlett thus concludes that individual performances— influenced by the general tendency toward rationalization—dictated the final forms of the reproductions. In chapter 2, I use the research that has followed Bartlett's lead to work toward an analysis of performance as an activity that is shaped by both shared and idiosyncratic cognitive structures.

Note that there are other types of individual differences that can be subsumed under the performance metaphor but are not the particular focus of this book. If we think of readers as actors, Bartlett's catalog of individual differences can be likened to the various interpretations equally skilled actors might give to the same role. The types of individual variation I will largely ignore are akin to the distinction between the Othello of Sir Laurence Olivier and that of a high school student. In parallel to the differentiation of good actors and poor actors, we can identify more and less skilled readers (and, thus, presumably people who are more or less skilled in interpreting stories in on-going conversation or in following the details of a movie, and so on). These differences are, in fact, nontrivial because less-skilled readers find it harder to become thoroughly immersed in narrative (Nell, 1988). In any event, I go forward with the assumption that, within certain broad limits, all readers are capable of performing the cognitive activities that enable them to be transported to narrative worlds.

Bartlett drew one other conclusion that is important for putting the performance metaphor in a proper perspective. Although he illustrates a variety of rationalizations, he maintains that "rather rarely this rationalisation was the effect of conscious effort. More often it was effected apparently unwittingly, the subject transforming his original without suspecting what he was doing" (p. 68). Just as I was concerned that being transported projects an undue aura of passivity, the performance metaphor appears to presuppose too active an involvement of conscious attention. Although some aspects of performance make explicit claims on attentional resources, a great number of "performance" acts are sufficiently routinized to take place outside of awareness.

Within cognitive psychology, the performance metaphor can be used to bring coherence to a variety of research programs.

Within literary criticism, the performance metaphor has more regularly emerged as a vivid corrective: theorists have invoked "performance" as a way of forcefully reinserting readers into the process of deriving meaning from texts. Wimsatt and Beardsley (1954) made what stood for several years as a strong case in favor of excluding the reader when they identified "The Affective Fallacy": "The Affective Fallacy is a confusion between the poem and its results. . . . It begins by trying to derive the standard of criticism from the psychological effects of the poem and ends in impressionism and relativism" (p. 21). Over the past few decades, however, literary critics have increasingly rejected the pejorative equating of "psychological effects" with "impressionism and relativism." Their research has been directed toward demonstrating the regularities of performance (see Benton, 1982; Kermode, 1983; Maclean, 1988; Suleiman, 1980; Tompkins, 1980a; as well as the essays in Suleiman and Crosman, 1980; and Tompkins, 1980b). In this section, I have elected to describe the work of three critics, Wolfgang Iser, Norman Holland, and Stanley Fish, all of whom have adduced types of evidence that remain largely unknown in cognitive psychology.

Iser has consistently characterized reading as having "the quality of 'performance'" (1978, p. 61). Two types of observations support his conclusion. The first is wholly in character with Bartlett's program of research—Iser is concerned with the way readers must fill the gaps authors leave in their texts. In a quotation from *Tristram Shandy,* Iser (1980) credits Laurence Sterne with the observation that it is often the author's intention to leave such gaps: "No author, who understands the just boundaries of decorum and good breeding, would presume to think all: The truest respect which you can pay to the reader's understanding, is to halve this matter amicably, and leave him something to imagine, in his turn, as well as yourself. For my own part, I am eternally paying him compliments of this kind, and do all that lies in my power to keep his imagination as busy as my own" (p. 51 in Iser; p. 79 in Sterne). Even so, Iser demonstrates (1989) that different works require different amounts of gap-filling performance. He discusses a phenomenon that amounts to a thought-experimental proof of the dissociation of text and reader in the experience of a narrative:

A second reading of a piece of literature often produces a different impression from the first. The reasons for this may lie in the reader's own change of circumstances, but all the same, the text must be such as to permit this variation. . . . The increased information that now overshadows the text provides possibilities of combination that were obscured in the first reading. Familiar occurrences now tend to appear in a new light and seem to be at times corrected, at times enriched. But for all that, nothing is formulated in the text itself; rather, the reader himself produces these innovative readings. (p. 10; see also 1980, p. 56)

In Bartlett's original experiment, he had his readers recall "The War of the Ghosts" with various time delays to see how the act of re-recalling changed their productions. Iser's analysis suggests that we should also observe readers reexperiencing texts to see how prior representations of the text come to wield their own influence on the course of comprehension.

The second type of evidence Iser presents parallels my evocation of Stanislavski. Iser observes, "In order to produce the determinate form of an unreal character, the actor must allow his own reality to fade out. . . . The reader finds himself in much the same situation. To imagine what has been stimulated by aesthetic semblance entails placing our thoughts and feelings at the disposal of an unreality, bestowing on it a semblance of reality in proportion to a reducing of our own reality. For the duration of the performance we are both ourselves and someone else"

(1989, p. 244). (Similarly, Poulet [1980] characterizes reading as "the strange invasion of my person by the thoughts of another, I am a self who is granted the experience of thinking thoughts foreign to him" [p. 44].) Once again, cognitive psychologists can wonder what mental activities enable readers to "reduce [their] own reality" and achieve the duality of inhabiting the real and narrative worlds as a real and narrative character. I discuss aspects of this problem in chapters 4 and 5.

Norman Holland specifically champions the "metaphorical family LITERARY PROCESS AS PERFORMANCE" (1988, p. 159). He argues that the "traditional metaphors" that have been used to describe the experience of literature, such as "LITERATURE IS FORCE, LITERATURE IS CONTROLLER, LITERATURE IS PERSON" (p. 117), "image people as passively being hit or poured into. I would trade them for language that expresses the craftsmanship, skill, dexterity, mastery, artistry—or clumsiness—that we bring to reading and (more obviously) writing. We even bring a craftsmanship to moviegoing and television watching" (p. 159). Holland supports this conclusion by demonstrating great differences *among* individuals in interpreting the same works of literature but great consistency *within* each individual in his or her interpretation of various works. Holland builds his most elaborate case with respect to the mental life of Robert Frost. By examining Frost's poetry, his critical responses to others' writings, and his general analyses of societal concerns, Holland extracts what he terms Frost's *identity theme:* "I was able to read Robert Frost as managing his fears of the unlimited and unmanageable by manipulating limited, knowable, symbols" (p. 170). By projecting this identity, Frost has performed as both a writer and a reader. To Holland, then, what constitutes performance is the process whereby individual readers experience narratives in consonance with their own identity themes. What must emerge from cognitive psychology, as I discuss in chapter 2, is a characterization of the mental representations that allow such identity themes to emerge in the ongoing experience of narratives.

Stanley Fish offers as a general credo, "Interpretation is not the art of construing but the art of constructing. Interpreters do not decode poems; they make them" (1980, p. 327). In his analyses of literary works, Fish frequently provides moment-by-moment accounts of the cognitive activities readers must perform, in language familiar to cognitive psychologists. What is unfamiliar, however, is his suggestion that part of the meaning recovered from the experience of the text is conditioned on meta-cognitive awareness of exactly those moment-by-moment processes. Consider his analysis of four lines from Milton's *Paradise Lost:*

> Satan, now first inflam'd with rage came down,
> The Tempter ere th' Accuser of man-kind,
> To wreck on innocent frail man his loss
> Of that first Battle, and his flight to Hell. (IV, 9–12)

Fish suggests that readers incorrectly believe at first that "his" in line 11 refers to "innocent frail man" and thus imagine that the passage refers to the loss of Eden. As readers progress through line 12, however, they must perform a reanalysis to understand that Milton is referring to Satan's loss of heaven:

> It is that loss of which Adam and Eve are innocent, and the issue of the Fall is not being raised at all. But of course it has been raised, if only in the reader's mind. . . . The understanding that the reader must give up is one that is particularly attractive to him because it asserts the innocence of his first parents, which is, by extension, his innocence too. By first encouraging that understanding and then correcting it, Milton . . . makes the reader aware of his tendency, inherited from those same parents, to reach for interpretations that are, in the basic theological sense, self-serving. (p. 4)

Fish offers a number of similar examples suggesting that the means by which both poetry and prose passages prompt the ultimate recovery of meaning partially constitutes that ultimate meaning. With respect to the metaphor of performance, the claim is that readers' observations of their own performances contribute to the experience of narratives.

Together, these three critics expand our notion of the types of acts readers might perform in the experience of narratives. Much of literary criticism, of course, has been concerned with the activities of readers who have acquired expertise in specialized interpretive strategies. In this book I am concerned almost exclusively with the reading done by those who are relatively innocent of such matters. (As Bruner comments, "It requires the most expensive education to shake a reader's faith in the incarnateness of meaning in a novel or poem" [1986, p. 155].) We can nonetheless use the insights of literary theory to explore the full potential of even ordinary visits to narrative worlds.

The Plan of the Book

Although I use the metaphor of being transported as a device for organizing the topics in this book, the metaphor itself does not constitute a theory of the experience of narratives. Rather, it brings into focus a number of issues that warrant theoretical treatment.

In chapters 2 and 3, I review and reframe psychological research to provide a broader account of issues of performance. Chapter 2 is concerned with inferences, and chapter 3 with noninferential responses to narratives.

In chapter 4, I consider the way language is experienced in narratives, contending that the controversy surrounding narrative versus ordinary language has been founded on too narrow a conception of the repertory of everyday language activities.

In chapter 5, I discuss some of the consequences of the on-going experience of narratives for access to aspects of the real world left behind.

And in chapter 6, I treat the effects of narrative experiences on thought and behavior in the real world, with particular attention to the special problems occasioned by visits to fictional worlds.

Inferential Aspects
of Performance

CHAPTER TWO

In the same essay in which they defined the "Affective Fallacy," Wimsatt and Beardsley (1954) expressed disdain for efforts to study literature in the laboratory. They suggested, "A distinction can be made between those who have testified what poetry does to themselves and those who have coolly investigated what it does to others. The most resolute researches of the latter have led them into the dreary and antiseptic laboratory, to testing with Fechner the effects of triangles and rectangles, to inquiring what colors are suggested by a line of Keats, or to measuring the motor discharges attendant upon reading it" (p. 31). In the decades since Wimsatt and Beardsley stated their objections, researchers have made progress toward developing an experimental psychology of reader responses that is not so easily assailed. In some sense, we can take the strongest form of Wimsatt and Beardsley's position (to be fair, they were mostly concerned with emotional responses) to be a blanket null hypothesis underlying the bulk of research on the experience of narratives: theories in this domain seek to banish fears of "impressionism" and "relativism" (p. 21) by predicting and documenting impressive regularities in reader performance. To be sure, there are responses to narrative worlds that are unique to each reader—each reader gives a unique performance—but, even there, theories of processes and representations can specify how such individual differences arise.

In this chapter, I consider at length one of the products of readers' performances, the familiar category of *inferences*. As I illustrate, readers are routinely called upon to use their logical faculties to bridge gaps of various sizes in texts. I review the research on inferencing with an eye toward the performance metaphor. At the end of the chapter, I give special attention to the subtleties of inferring the causal structure of narrative worlds.

In chapter 3, I describe a second category of readers' products, which I call *participatory responses—p-responses,* for short (Allbritton and Gerrig, 1991). This term covers all noninferential responses in the performance of narratives. At a performance of *Othello,* for example, audience members might entertain the proposition "I wish someone would expose Iago." Although such thoughts cannot be characterized as inferences, in chapter 3 I demonstrate that they make systematic contributions to the experience of narratives. I introduce p-responses here as a way of revealing an important part of my context for the discussion of inferences.

Much of the research I describe in this chapter applies equally well to the experience of the real world as to the experience of narrative worlds. We continually draw inferences and exhibit participatory responses in everyday life. In some respects, our real world is as much constructed as any narrative world (see Goodman, 1978). For exactly that reason, researchers have often turned to narrative comprehension as a microcosm in which to study the processes and memory representations that guide our existence. In some cases, therefore, narrative comprehension has been a given, and the processes and representations have been the object of scrutiny; in other cases these roles have been reversed. Although most of my discussion is organized around issues of narrative comprehension, I am expressly not claiming that any of the psychological apparatus is special purpose.

Inferences

Consider the opening paragraph of Don DeLillo's novel *Libra:*

> This was the year he rode the subway to the ends of the city, two hundred miles of track. He liked to stand at the front of the first car, hands flat against the glass. The train smashed through the dark. People stood on the local platforms staring nowhere, a look they'd been practicing for years. He kind of wondered, speeding past, who they really were. His body fluttered in the fastest stretches. They went so fast sometimes he thought they were on the edge of no-control. The noise was pitched to a level of pain he absorbed as a personal test. Another crazy-ass curve. There was so much iron in the sound of those curves he could almost taste it, like a toy you put in your mouth when you are little. (p. 3)

DeLillo's evocation of this mystery man's experience of the subway is so elegant that we're scarcely aware of how hard we have worked to share in the experience. If we could imagine excising all personal knowledge of subways, however, the passage quickly would lose its integrity. DeLillo relies on his readers to know about the design of subway cars ("hands flat against the glass"), the intricacies of schedules ("local platforms"), the vast roar of the tunnels ("a level of pain"), and so on. DeLillo also sets us hard at work wondering who "he" is. (In this book about John F. Kennedy's assassination, the boy riding the subway turns out to be Lee Harvey Oswald.) I chose this paragraph as a first illustration of the way knowledge outside the text is often critical to the adequate construction of a narrative world because it served as the stimulus for an experiment of nature. A friend of mine who had also read DeLillo's book couldn't understand why I was so enthusiastic about this opening subway scene. He revealed with a touch of pride that he'd never been on a subway. Because he had no standard represented in memory, he had no way of knowing how deftly DeLillo had individuated Oswald's experience of the subway. We must presume that DeLillo knowingly accepted the risk of bewildering the subway-innocents among his readership. (This experiment-of-nature now has a within-subjects design. Having finally ridden the subway in New York, my friend accedes to DeLillo's artistry.)

This paragraph from *Libra* provides solid evidence that readers must contribute to their own experiences of narrative worlds. The conclusion is a general one: whenever we attend a movie, watch television, or read a newspaper, we are actively supplementing the "text." The same rule holds true even when we are viewing paintings (Walton, 1990). Although we cannot see her lower torso, we are quite willing to infer that Mona Lisa has legs. To put this another way, we would be genuinely surprised to discover that she does *not* have legs. In fact, when asked to reproduce scenes from memory, subjects show a systematic bias toward expanding the boundaries of photographs to include details that were inferable but not depicted (Intraub, Bender, and Mangels, 1992; Intraub and Richardson, 1989). Thus, even when we interact with what seems to be a complete representation, we are hard at work filling in around the edges.

Our interactions with representational works of art also provide an excellent domain in which to develop what might be the central question of research on inferencing: Which inferences do we regularly make? This question presupposes that the inferences we "regularly" make are sampled from some larger set. Interactions with paintings can convince us that this is true. Consider Walton's (1990) observation: "One can *finish* reading a novel, but there is no such thing as completing either the task of examining a painting or that of visually investigating the real world" (p. 307). To the extent that we can never finish a painting, we can also never limit the range of potential inferences that could be generated by viewers given to continuing contemplation. Nonetheless, at any given moment only some finite subset of the possible inferences can be active in a viewer's mind (Rieger, 1975). We would like to be able to give some account of exactly how that subset is constituted. In Walton's terminology, we would like to know which *fictional truths* an artwork is likely to generate for the majority of viewers over a period of time. We would also like to capture generalities about the fictional truths that will be generated more idiosyncratically.

I can illustrate the presumed continuum of likely inferences with respect to DeLillo's subway scene. Some inferences are essential to immediate understanding. If, for example, we are unable to access general knowledge about subways, we probably can't make sense of "the first car" (see Clark and Haviland, 1977). Some inferences may not be essential but are likely to enrich our experience of the narrative. We might infer that the "he" of this passage enjoys the feeling of being endangered. Some inferences may be grounded in solid reasoning but be very unlikely to occur to the reader as part of the on-going experience of the text. As I observed in chapter 1, "he" is extremely likely to have a liver, but there's no particular need to call this to mind (and, perhaps, good reason not to) while constructing a narrative world around this text. Cognitive psychologists have attempted to replace such intuitions with explicit theories that motivate constraints on the range of inferences that readers "regularly" compute.

The Minimalist Hypothesis

The philosophy behind the *minimalist hypothesis* is that readers draw some limited range of inferences *automatically,* as a consequence of reading a text. McKoon and Ratcliff (1992) explain:

"Automatic inferences are those that are encoded in the absence of special goals or strategies on the part of the reader, and they are constructed in the first few hundred milliseconds of processing. They therefore merit attention because they form the basic representation of a text from which other, more purposeful, inferences are constructed" (p. 441). Few theorists would deny that a category of such automatic inferences exists. What individuates McKoon and Ratcliff's hypothesis is their high standards for accepting classes of inferences into this privileged category. Although they acknowledge that further research might add to the list, they argue that available evidence suggests that only "two classes of inferences, those based on easily available information and those required for local coherence, are encoded during reading, unless a reader adopts special goals or strategies" (p. 441). There are two components to McKoon and Ratcliff's defense of their position. First, they cite evidence that supports the inclusion of these two classes in the category of automatic inferences. Second, they provide evidence that other types of inferences should be excluded. In considering their views, I begin with the nonprivileged inferences, as a way of showing how the minimalist hypothesis came into being.

Much early research on the use of memory structures in narrative comprehension was motivated by rational analyses of knowledge readers would have to access to come to a coherent understanding of a passage—the same logic I followed in my analysis of DeLillo's subway passage. Because the passage is radically incomplete, I asserted with relative confidence that its phenomenological coherence was parasitic, dependent on information we already have stored in memory: unproblematic comprehension served as an "existence proof" for the ready availability of this knowledge to comprehension processes. The term *schema* is most often used to refer to these organized clusters of information in memory (see Bartlett, 1932; Brewer and Naka-mura, 1984; Rumelhart, 1980; Rumelhart and Ortony, 1977). Early research was intended to demonstrate more formally the structure of schemas and their use in narrative comprehension. One program examined the use of *scripts* in memory for simple stories. A script is a memory structure that specifies a stereotypical sequence of actions that people carry out in familiar situations (Abelson, 1981; Schank and Abelson, 1977). Individuals largely agree on the likely course of events when they visit a restaurant, attend a lecture, go to a grocery store, or see a doctor (Bower, Black, and Turner, 1979; Graesser, Gordon, and Sawyer, 1979). This is, once again, something authors count on. In *Casino Royale,* for example, Ian Fleming advanced his plot by having his hero, James Bond, and a female character named Vesper Lynd engage in conversation over a lengthy meal (pp. 56–67). Once Fleming invoked the restaurant script, he had only to allude to it from time to time to suggest complex activity occurring as a background to the static conversation (Gerrig and Allbritton, 1990):

Bond beckoned to the sommelier.

The maître d'hôtel bowed.

She took a sip of vodka.

The caviar was heaped on to their plates, and they ate for a time in silence.

The maître d'hôtel supervised the serving of the second course.

Fleming was able to enrich this scene greatly by engaging readers' recollections of the progress of an elegant meal. The use of a script, however, clouds memories for the actual details of the text. Bower and his colleagues (1979) demonstrated that readers were often unable to discriminate between statements that they actually had read and those that were only consistent with the appropriate script. When asked to identify which of a series of sentences had actually appeared in a script-based story, readers often falsely identified script-appropriate but newly created sentences as "old." Given this result, it is fortunate that Fleming was not counting on his readers to remember the specific details of Bond and Vesper's meal. Under other circumstances, of course, Fleming could make use of memory blurring precisely to catch his readers off guard. This "script" effect, which has been replicated with other types of schemas (see Brewer and Nakamura, 1984), can be straightforwardly transformed into an aesthetic strategy.

Although such research demonstrates that memory structures are active in the experience of narrative worlds, it provides limited constraints for moment-by-moment models of the inferencing process. Imagine, for example, that several minutes after finishing the chapter, readers of *Casino Royale* accepted the invented addition "Bond and Vesper slowly ate their second courses" as a sentence from Fleming's original scene. We could not be certain whether the readers generated the inference that Bond and Vesper would eat the second course, once it was served, as a part of the original experience of the text or whether they found the statement to be consistent with their recollection of the gist of the text when the assessment of their memories was made. To reduce this uncertainty, researchers have devised a number of techniques for determining the precise time-course with which inferences are drawn. Sharkey and Mitchell (1985) used a lexical decision task to demonstrate that the activation of scripted knowledge could facilitate the identification of words related to the script. In this task, subjects are asked to judge strings of letters as words (for example, butter) or nonwords (burret) of standard English (or some other appropriate language). After reading a brief story such as "The children's birthday party was going quite well. They all set round the table prepared to sing" (p. 258), Sharkey and Mitchell's subjects were able to correctly label *candles* as a legitimate word more swiftly than they could label a letter string like *rabbits,* which is otherwise of equal length and equally frequent in English. This result demonstrates the increased availability of scripted concepts in the moment-by-moment experience of the text.

The minimalist hypothesis began to emerge, however, as researchers came to identify a range of circumstances in which inferences seemed likely but readers failed to generate them. McKoon and Ratcliff (1992) review a number of cases that fit this pattern. I use, as a first example, the nongeneration of *instrumental inferences.* Consider, once again, this sentence from *Casino Royale:* "The caviar was heaped on to their plates, and they ate for a time in silence." It is impossible to create a concrete image of this scene without imagining what instruments Vesper and Bond used to eat the caviar. The hypothesis that readers draw instrumental inferences in circumstances like this one conforms to common sense—but this intuition does not hold up to empirical scrutiny. In one series of studies, Dosher and Corbett (1982) presented subjects with sentence contexts such as "The architect stabbed the man," which they determined reliably prompted readers to think of a particular instrument (in this case, "knife") when they were requested to do so. Dosher and Corbett used a Stroop interference task to determine whether, in fact, readers generated these instrumental inferences in the normal course of reading. In a Stroop task, subjects are responsible for naming the color of the ink in which a word is printed. In his original research, Stroop (1935) discovered that subjects had great difficulty naming the color (for example, blue) when the string of letters printed in that color formed the word for some other color (for example, red). On the whole, the more active in memory a word is, the harder it is for subjects to name the ink color. Thus, if subjects automatically activated "knife" when they read "The architect stabbed the man," they should have found it harder to name the color of ink in which it was printed relative to an appropriate control. Dosher and Corbett, however, found no evidence for such interference. The only circumstances in which their readers generated the highly probable instruments was when they were explicitly instructed to do so. As a general rule, then, readers acquire information—say, about James Bond eating his caviar—without automatically imagining the instrument involved (see also Garrod, O'Brien, Morris, and Rayner, 1990; Lucas, Tanenhaus, and Carlson, 1990; O'Brien, Shank, Myers, and Rayner, 1988).

Another class of inferences that we might nominate a priori as essential based on rational analysis would be those relating to characters' overarching goals for carrying out certain actions. McKoon and Ratcliff (1992), however, present compelling evidence that readers probably imagine Bond eating his caviar without simultaneously keeping in mind his greater reasons for sharing the meal with Vesper Lynd. As I review later, a variety of researchers have suggested that analysis of causality is essential to the experience of narratives. McKoon and Ratcliff have demonstrated, even so, that global goals are not automatically kept active for the duration of even brief texts. Consider this story:

> The crowd's cheers alerted the onlookers to the president's arrival. The assassin wanted to kill the president. He reached for his high-powered rifle. He lifted the gun to his shoulder to peer through its scope. The scope fell off as he lifted the rifle. He lay prone to draw a sight without the scope. The searing sun blinded his eyes. (McKoon and Ratcliff, 1992, p. 447)

We are introduced early on to the assassin's goal: he wishes to kill the president. By the end of the passage, he has not yet succeeded. Our expectation, therefore, might be that the goal would still be active as part of the reader's on-going experience of the text. McKoon and Ratcliff tested this intuition by presenting a word that instantiated the goal, in this case *kill,* and asking their subjects to judge whether or not that word had appeared in the immediately preceding text (a task that had successfully revealed processing differences in prior research). For comparison, McKoon and Ratcliff wrote control texts in which the protagonists discharged their goals (for example, "The assassin hit the president with the first shot from his rifle"). Satisfaction of the goal, in fact, had no effect on reader performance. Readers took an equal amount of time to verify the presence of global goal words like *kill,* whatever the status of the character's program. Again, the general conclusion is that readers are not automatically keeping a character's goals active in the moment-by-moment experience of a narrative world.

This series of results offers support for a model of narrative comprehension labeled minimalist: to the extent that researchers have demonstrated a range of inferences that readers fail to generate automatically—despite their pretheoretical allure—the classes of inferences properly attributed to this category do seem quite minimal.

This review of nonprivileged inferences was intended, in part, to give a sense of the care with which classes of inferences have been accepted into the minimal fold. While leaving open the possibility that future research will expand the category of privileged inferences, McKoon and Ratcliff (1992) argue that available data support the inclusion only of inferences "based on easily available information and those required for local coherence" (p. 441). We can look back to research on instrumental inferences to see, first of all, what it means for information to be easily available. McKoon and Ratcliff (1981) wrote brief stories in which an instrument was mentioned in the first of five sentences. Consider this story:

Bobby got a saw, hammer, screwdriver, and square from
his toolbox. He had already selected an oak tree as the site
for the birdhouse. He had drawn a detailed blueprint and
measured carefully. He marked the boards and cut them
out. (p. 674)

For some subjects the story's concluding sentence was "Then
Bobby pounded the boards together with nails." For others it
was "Then Bobby stuck the boards together with glue." Immediately following this final sentence, a test word—in this case
"hammer"—appeared on the computer screen, and the subjects
were required to decide whether that word had appeared somewhere in the story. McKoon and Ratcliff found that readers made
this judgment much more swiftly when the final sentence mentioned "pounding with nails" rather than "sticking with glue."
Dosher and Corbett's (1982) results suggest that it could not
have been that final sentence alone that made "hammer" accessible. Rather, the prior mention in the story made the instrument
easily available. In fact, McKoon and Ratcliff went on to show
that such "easy availability" accrues only to highly probable
instruments. When "hammer" was replaced by "mallet" in the
first sentence, responses to "mallet" were not facilitated when
subjects were asked to judge it as present or absent from the
story. Furthermore, when the instrument was rendered unavail-
able, as when the toolbox was said to include "a hammer which
had been broken earlier that week," no association was formed
between "hammer" and "boards." These results reinforce the
impression, based on Dosher and Corbett's work, that instrumental inferences are made only under highly favorable circumstances. Although the term "easily available" is inherently vague,
these experimental results suggest the substance underlying the
claim that these inferences are privileged.

Inferences of the second class are those that must be constructed to ensure local coherence. Consider this excerpt from

Julian Barnes's *A History of the World in 10–1/2 Chapters*. Lawrence Beesley, who survived the sinking of the *Titanic,* is watching the movie based on that event being filmed:

> Beesley was—not surprisingly—intrigued by the reborn and once-again-teetering *Titanic.* In particular, he was keen to be among the extras who despairingly crowded the rail as the ship went down—keen, you could say, to undergo in fiction an alternative version of history. The film's director was equally determined that this consultant who lacked the necessary card from the actors' union should not appear on celluloid. (pp. 174–75)

To bring coherence to this series of sentences, the reader must come to believe that "this consultant" refers to Beesley. Researchers have demonstrated in a variety of ways that such references are automatically resolved in the course of comprehension. Dell, McKoon, and Ratcliff (1983; see also O'Brien, Duffy, and Myers, 1986), for example, presented subjects with stories that began with sentences like "A burglar surveyed the garage set back from the street" and ended with either "The criminal slipped away from the streetlamp" or "The cat slipped away from the streetlight." When asked to judge whether "burglar" had appeared in the story, subjects were much swifter to give the correct answer when "the criminal" had been mentioned in the final sentence. Readers, thus, searched their text representations to reinstate "burglar" in response to the anaphoric mention of "the criminal." O'Brien, Plewes, and Albrecht (1990) demonstrated that this search process sometimes reinstates inappropriate antecedents. In their experiments, subjects read long passages that included two possible referents for a final anaphor. One story described two birds encountered by the character Jane on a trip to her grandparents' house, an owl in a nest near her bedroom window and a hawk flying over a field. The owl was mentioned early in the text, the hawk late. In the final sentence of the story, Jane's brother asked her either "what had built a nest by her window" or "what she'd seen flying over the field" (p. 248). If the antecedent that appeared late in the text (for example, hawk) had been sufficiently elaborated, it was reinstated even when the appropriate antecedent was the one that had appeared early in the text (for example, owl). (The measure, in this case, was time to pronounce out loud a visual presentation of the antecedent word.) This result, however, was obtained only when the two antecedents belonged to the same category. If the text mentioned an owl and a toy kite, "kite" was not reinstated under circumstances in which "hawk" would have been.

Gibbs (1990) extended the automatic reinstatement of anaphoric antecedents to nonliteral language. In his studies, the original concept was reinstated through either a metaphorical or a metonymic reference. A story might mention that "There was one boxer that Stu hated." At the end of the story, a character might remark, "The creampuff didn't even show up." Parallel to the earlier experiments, Gibbs required his subjects to indicate whether *boxer* had appeared in the story. He found that, although literal reinstantiations (such as "The fighter didn't even show up") worked best of all, subjects still made their judgments more swiftly with either metaphorical or metonymic referring phrases compared to an appropriate baseline (such as "The referee didn't even show up"). These experiments reinforce the idea that some sophisticated processing takes place in the name of local coherence: minimal inferencing is not trivial inferencing.

The representations constructed as a result of minimal inferencing, in fact, provide a critical scaffold for further recovery of meaning. They are minimal only by comparison to the vast range of possibilities. Even so, this body of research suggests that much of the richness of the experience of narrative worlds arises through processes that are not obligatory but, rather, are under the strategic control of the reader. This conclusion brings renewed vigor to the performance metaphor: having defined a core of automatic processes common to all readers, we can see, once again, how much latitude there is for individual readers to give a variety of performances to the same narrative.

Individual Performances

In much research on narrative comprehension, individual performances have been induced through overt experimental manipulations. Consider experiments by Owens, Bower, and Black (1979) that demonstrated a "soap opera" effect in story recall. All the participants read multiepisode stories that, on the whole, were quite bland. One excerpt read:

> Nancy arrived at the cocktail party. She looked around the room to see who was there. She went to talk to her professor. She felt she had to talk to him but was a little nervous about just what to say. A group of people started to play charades. Nancy went over and had some refreshments. The hors d'oeuvres were good but she wasn't interested in talking to the rest of the people at the party. After a while she decided she'd had enough and left the party. (p. 186)

What made the text more interesting for half the subjects was an introduction that provided extra framing for the story:

> Nancy woke up feeling sick again and she wondered if she really were pregnant. How would she tell the professor she had been seeing? And the money was another problem. (p. 185)

The presence or absence of this introduction had a sizable effect on readers' memories for the core episodes of the text. When asked to recall the story or to recognize statements from it, readers who had read the extra introductory material were much more likely to produce or recognize ideas related to Nancy's pregnancy. Owens, Bower, and Black suggested that the introductory material allowed readers to access a schema for "an unwanted pregnancy" and organize the information in accordance with that structure. Armed with knowledge of Nancy's motives, different readers adapted the text to fit their different expectations. This research illustrates a general principle: knowledge differences profoundly affect the interpretation of narratives.

A second research tradition has documented the wide-ranging impact of knowledge differences by contrasting the interpretive performances of readers who arrive at the laboratory possessing information of differing utility. In their experiments, Voss and his colleagues have examined the performance of subjects who have either low or high knowledge of baseball, a domain chosen because of its richly structured goals and actions. On the whole, these experiments have demonstrated that the rich get richer: "Knowledge in a given domain . . . facilitates the acquisition of new domain-related information" (Chiesi, Spilich, and Voss, 1979, p. 270). For example, after hearing a tape-recorded account of part of a baseball game, high-knowledge subjects recalled more information overall than low-knowledge subjects, which suggests that the knowledge structures they accessed to understand the narrative were also important to the retention of the information (Spilich, Vesonder, Chiesi, and Voss, 1979). Furthermore, high-knowledge subjects were likely to remember details that were relevant to the outcome of the game, such as how particular runners advanced. Low-knowledge subjects were more likely to act as if they were recalling unrelated facts and remembered better only unimportant details such as names of players. A second general principle can be derived from this research: enhanced knowledge enables readers to direct their attention toward the more informative aspects of narratives.

Fincher-Kiefer, Post, Greene, and Voss (1988) note, further, that high-knowledge subjects appear to be more motivated to perform well when they read texts related to their domain of interest. Individual performances of narratives, thus, can be distinguished by virtue of knowledge-driven alterations of focus. What often matters as much as a reader's possession of appropriate information, however, is whether that information becomes available at the appropriate time. By giving the special introductory material *after* presenting a core episode from the materials of Owens et al., I intended to provide a demonstration of this claim. When the introduction is read after the story excerpt, there is no way to change, retrospectively, the moment-by-moment experience of that excerpt. It is necessary to reread the party scene to see how thoroughly the knowledge that Nancy believes she might be pregnant changes the interpretation of sentences like "She felt she had to talk to [her professor] but was a little nervous about just what to say." The experiment presupposed that both groups of subjects (that is, those who did and did not receive the extra introduction) had a schema for unexpected pregnancy. Only the group that received the introduction understood its relevance.

This intuition has been captured more formally in the laboratory (see Bransford and McCarrell, 1977; Dooling and Lachman, 1971; Stern, Dahlgren, and Gaffney, 1991). Bransford and Johnson (1972), for example, presented readers with a paragraph of about fifteen sentences that began:

The procedure is actually quite simple. First you arrange things into different groups. Of course one pile may be sufficient depending on how much there is to do.

It helps in understanding even the beginning of this paragraph to know that the topic is washing clothes. In the experiment, subjects were given this information either before they heard the paragraph read to them, after it was read, or not at all. Self-ratings of the extent to which the subjects could comprehend the paragraph and scores for their recall of the "idea units" in the paragraph both revealed that an advantage accrued only to subjects who received the topic information before hearing the paragraph. From this research, we can derive a third principle: the mere possession of knowledge is not sufficient to ensure that it will be accessed in appropriate instances. If some of Bransford and Johnson's subjects in the "no topic" or "topic after" conditions had themselves stumbled onto the idea that the paragraph was about washing clothes, they could have caught up in performance to the "topic before" subjects. The experiment, of course, was rigged to minimize that possibility.

In nonexperimental circumstances, by contrast, we need to look to differences in the way information is represented to explain why readers do or do not access appropriate knowledge. For this point, I will state the principle first: the knowledge must be represented in a fashion that is accessible to comprehension processes. Consider, once again, McKoon and Ratcliff's (1981) result that "hammer" becomes available upon mention of a "board being pounded together with nails," but not "mallet." Their explanation was that actions produce activation only of highly associated instruments. The association between "hammer" and "pounded" is, of course, formed through readers' experiences of situations in which the concepts have been paired. Different readers will have different strength associations (and some readers, reared under atypical circumstances, may even have a stronger association to mallet). In principle, we could devise an independent measure of this association for any individual that would enable us to predict with great accuracy the likelihood that he or she would reactivate "hammer" in the presence of the "pounded" sentence. (This formulation presupposes a threshold for reactivation. Alternatively, we could imagine that the amount of reactivation varies as a function of the strength of the association but that very low levels of reactivation fail to exert an appreciable influence on comprehension processes.)

In principle we could extend the logic of this test to all areas of memory, with the general goal of understanding what it means for information to be represented in "a fashion that is accessible to comprehension processes." Nested within this goal is a critical distinction between inferences that are constructed as part of the moment-by-moment experience of the narrative world and those that are constructed from outside the narrative world. The "inside" category is anchored by the types of privileged, automatic inferences I have already discussed. The "outside" category requires, perhaps, an evocation of consciousness: we might, that is, label as outside inferences those that require conscious problem-solving behavior with respect to the narrative. The rest of the inferences within the narrative world should include the set that is strategic (that is, nonautomatic) but not brought about (even so) by conscious planning. What I am arguing for is a distinction between applying knowledge (through effortful planning) and experiencing knowledge (through ordinary comprehension processes). I have no evidence, of course, to defend the existence of such an absolute demarcation: I am appealing once more to the metaphor of being transported, which presupposes a well-defined boundary. Even so, we can use the idea of a boundary to drive our inquiry into the types of representations that can be directly available to comprehension processes.

Consider a classic instance of an inference derived through problem solving. Here, Freud (1900/1965) applies his evolving theory of childhood sexuality to Shakespeare's *Hamlet:*

> What is it, then, that inhibits [Hamlet] in fulfilling the task set him by his father's ghost? . . . Hamlet is able to do any-

thing—except take vengeance on the man who did away with his father and took the father's place with his mother, the man who shows him the repressed wishes of his own childhood realized. Thus the loathing which should drive him on to revenge is replaced in him by self-reproaches, by scruples of conscience, which remind him that he himself is literally no better than the sinner whom he is to punish. Here I have translated into conscious terms what was bound to remain unconscious in Hamlet's mind; and if anyone is inclined to call him a hysteric, I can only accept the fact as one that is implied by my interpretation. (p. 299)

In brief, from the evidence available in Shakespeare's play, Freud inferred that Hamlet suffered from an unresolved Oedipus complex. Freud, as its originator, had to support this case through the effortful application of his theory. Many readers in present times, however, are in a situation akin to the subjects' in the experiments by Owens et al. (1979): the critical framing information precedes the experience of the narrative. Even then, we can be fairly certain that some readers will have insufficient familiarity with Freud's theory to draw the appropriate inferences inside the world of the text. Although Freud's hint might focus their attention on certain aspects of the text, they will have to work out the implications in an explicit fashion. What remains uncertain is whether other readers will have their experience transformed without conscious effort. Can access to a schema for an unresolved Oedipus complex alter the way these readers bring coherence to the text? I chose the example of Freud because it originated as a "discovery." The empirical question is whether such richly structured theories can become appropriately represented so as to function effortlessly in comprehension. To frame the point in a somewhat different fashion, we can ask, Are all knowledge differences relevant to the experience of narrative worlds?

In discussing individual performances, the conclusion that knowledge differences matter comes quite easily. What we know much less about is what types of representations are required for knowledge to become effortlessly incorporated into the moment-by-moment experience of a narrative. In the next section, I consider the class of inferences about causality that researchers have often suggested readers make within the narrative world (although they would not put it that way).

The Assessment of Causality

Several traditions of research on narrative worlds have converged on the single conclusion that the perception of causality is critical: experimentation has shown that comprehension is guided by the search for causal relations and that those causal relations, once recovered, provide much of the global coherence of memory representations. Trabasso and his colleagues (Trabasso and Sperry, 1985; Trabasso and van den Broek, 1985; Trabasso, van den Broek, and Suh, 1989; van den Broek, 1988; see also O'Brien and Myers, 1987) have suggested that the ultimate product of understanding is a *causal network* that represents the relationships between the causes and the consequences of events in a story. Readers discover causal links as they proceed through a text; in particular, they derive a main *causal chain* for the story, which preserves the sequence of causally important events that serves as the backbone for the story. Consider this brief excerpt from Ian Fleming's story "For Your Eyes Only," in which James Bond has been charged with avenging a pair of murders by bringing about the deaths of those responsible:

> The [gun] shuddered against [Bond's] shoulder and the right-hand man fell slowly forward on his face. Now the other man was running for the lake, his gun still firing from the hip in short bursts. Bond fired and missed and fired again. The man's legs buckled, but his momentum

still carried him forward. He crashed into the water. The clenched finger went on firing the gun aimlessly up toward the blue sky until the water throttled the mechanism. (p. 71)

Much of the coherence in this paragraph arises because the reader is able to undertake an analysis of Bond's goals, his targets' goals, and how these goals interact to cause the described series of actions. Much of the information is directly related to the story's core causal sequence and, therefore, ought to be represented in the causal chain. Other information (that "the other man" was firing his gun "from the hip in short bursts") constitutes a *dead end* from the standpoint of causal analysis (Schank, 1975). Trabasso and his colleagues have constructed causal network representations for several short texts. They have demonstrated that the importance and memorability of the clauses in these texts can be predicted by the causal connectedness of each clause as well as by whether it lies along the main causal chain. Readers judge dead-end information to be of lower importance and recall it poorly by comparison to causally critical events.

When reading an excerpt like Fleming's, we must make these discriminations on the fly. Fletcher and his colleagues (Bloom, Fletcher, van den Broek, Reitz, and Shapiro, 1990; Fletcher and Bloom, 1988; Fletcher, Hummel, and Marsolek, 1990) have suggested that readers build causal networks by strategically deploying the resources of working memory: "The causal structure of a narrative controls the allocation of attention as it is read" (Fletcher, Hummel, and Marsolek, 1990, p. 239). The model suggests that readers use a *current-state selection strategy* to use the scarce resources of working memory to best advantage. According to this strategy, readers identify "the most recent clause with causal antecedents—but no consequences—in the preceding text. All propositions that contribute to the causal role of this clause remain in short-term memory as the following sentence is read" (p. 233). (Note that Fletcher and his colleagues use the term "short-term memory." I prefer "working memory" because it does not imply that information kept specially active for the short term is held in some separable memory store [see, for example, Crowder, 1982].) The intuition behind this strategy is that any clause that has not yet yielded causal consequences is likely to do so as the text continues and, thus, readers would be well advised to keep it active. Based on this strategy, the theory differentiates circumstances in which the formation of causal links should be facilitated, because all the necessary propositions are active in working memory, from those in which the reader will have to consult long-term memory to establish causal links. Fletcher and his colleagues have successfully predicted some rather subtle differences in performance. Consider this text (Fletcher, Hummel, and Marsolek, 1990):

> Kate was having some friends over for her boyfriend's birthday and wanted to serve birthday cake. She took out the ingredients she had bought and began to make a chocolate cake. As she was mixing the batter, her sister came home and told Kate the oven was broken. (p. 234)

Fletcher et al. labeled the third sentence the "critical sentence." For some subjects, the story continued with a sentence that provided an antecedent to the critical sentence:

> Her sister had tried to use the oven earlier but discovered that it would not heat up.

If readers use the current-state selection strategy, the appearance of an antecedent sentence should cause the critical sentence to remain active in working memory. For other subjects, the story continued with a sentence that provided a consequence:

> Since she had the cake batter all ready she thought she would use the neighbor's oven.

In this case, the current-state selection strategy suggests that the critical sentence should be ousted from working memory. If this is so, readers should find it difficult to understand any subsequent sentence that still needs to make causal reference to the critical sentence. That was exactly the type of "continuation sentence" that Fletcher et al. next presented to both groups of subjects:

> From the parlor, Kate's mother heard voices in the kitchen.

In accordance with the predictions from the current-state selection strategy, subjects took reliably longer to read the continuation sentence when a consequence sentence had intervened than when an antecedent sentence had intervened. This result provides a compelling demonstration of the strategic underpinnings of causal analysis in the moment-by-moment experience of narrative worlds.

Of concern, however, is whether the models developed for readers' application of causal analysis in these simple narratives will generalize to the more causally complex narrative worlds that enrich—and constitute—our real lives. In most of the research on causality within the narrative understanding tradition, the antecedents and consequences of actions are well defined. Causality has typically been assessed by reference to a straightforward formula:

> To judge whether a causal relationship exists between two events, the criterion of necessity in the circumstances is used (Mackie, 1980). Necessity is tested by the use of a counterfactual argument of the form: If not A then not B. That is, an event A is said to be necessary to event B if it is the case that had A not occurred then, in the circumstances, B would not have occurred. (Trabasso and Sperry, 1985, p. 598)

The problem with assessing causality in complex narratives can be located precisely with respect to this formula: there are often a range of mutually exclusive possible antecedents for events, any of which we are able to recast as necessary, in accordance with our predilections. Consider this excerpt from Richard Russo's novel *The Risk Pool:*

> By the time Eileen was finished bringing [a great deal of food to a small table], it was possible for me to knock something off her end of the table by nudging something at my end by slender centimeters. To make matters worse, we passed things, setting off chain reactions. Lifting the platter of roast pork would upset the bowl of green beans, which someone would try to save, his elbow sending the big bottle of Thousand Island dressing to the floor. In this way, the person who appeared to have made the mess seldom actually *caused* it, but was rather trying to prevent another calamity altogether, the threat of which he alone perceived. (p. 146, original emphasis)

Here, the narrator, Ned Hall, testifies to the ready availability of two contrasting causal analyses of this situation. The one he prefers is his own analysis, in which the situation of the overcrowded table in itself brings about calamities. Hall acknowledges, however, that it seems as if (that is, it looks to others as if) these calamities were caused by particular individuals. We can see immediately how overt evidence could support either causal analysis. What we would like to know is which, if either, of them would emerge in moment-by-moment processing.

The expectation of multiple causal analyses increases dramatically when we enter narrative worlds in which the assessment of causality may be driven by elaborate theories. For an instructive example, I turn to John Updike's memoir, *Self-Consciousness.* Throughout the book, Updike invokes conventional wisdom about the experiences of only children to explain some details of his emotional and professional life:

Lacking brothers and sisters, I was shy and clumsy in the give and take and push and pull of human interchange. That slight roughness, that certainty of contact we ask for from others, was hard for me to administer; I either fled, or was cruel. (p. 12)

My debits [as a novelist] include many varieties of ignorance, including an only child's tentativeness in the human grapple. (p. 109)

We assume that only children are spoiled and pampered; but they also are made to share adult perspectives. Possibly the household that nurtured me was a distracted and needy one—in severe Depression shock—which asked me to grow up too early. . . . (p. 256)

Consider, now, the very different conclusions drawn by researchers who have compared the actual social behavior of only children to that of children with siblings (Snow, Jacklin, and Maccoby, 1981):

The present findings suggest that the popular opinion that only children are maladjusted, self-centered, and unlikable . . . is unfounded, at least in the early years. On the basis of popular opinion, parents may have exaggerated fears that the social development of only children suffers as a result of the lack of sibling interaction. Instead it may be that parents of later borns should be made more sensitive to the potential social difficulties faced by the child of this ordinal position. (p. 594)

Fablo and Polit (1986) reviewed 115 studies comparing only children to children in other circumstances and concluded, "In achievement, intelligence, and character, only borns excelled beyond their peers with siblings, especially those with many or older siblings" (p. 185). Although we might want to salvage

Updike's allusion to conventional wisdom by imagining general changes in the life stories of only children since the 1930s, when Updike grew up, Fablo and Polit's review includes research as early as the 1920s reporting only children to be advantaged with respect to children with siblings.

Knowledge of the researchers' version of the only child could prompt us to perform at least two causal reanalyses of Updike's life:

1. We might be inclined to wonder why his life, in fact, appears to conform to conventional wisdom's only child: if most only children are socially *advantaged,* why was Updike's experience nonaverage? Snow, Jacklin, and Maccoby (1981) suggest that advantages accrue to only children because of greater amounts of parent-child interaction. We might wonder about specific behaviors of Updike's parents (as Updike himself does to a limited extent) that counteracted the typical effects of more-frequent contact.

2. We could, alternatively, imagine that Updike is simply wrong in attributing aspects of his adult behavior to his mistaken notion of the inevitable consequences of being an only child. We might wonder what other aspects of his formative experiences could better explain the details of his life. We might believe that Updike's invocation of conventional wisdom's only child is causing (or allowing) him to overlook forces in his life that were much more salient in their impact. In this latter case, we would feel perfectly comfortable in applying a more sophisticated psychological perspective to Updike's life than was readily available to him (a tradition that dates back, at least, to Freud's (1910/1964) psychobiography of Leonardo da Vinci).

My intention, of course, is not to decide among versions of Updike's life but, rather, to show how it is that the same narrative can straightforwardly license different causal analyses. I am not concerned with true causality as much as with the way such causal theories may or may not be able to function during comprehension. This is the same juncture I reached in my discussion of Freud's account of Hamlet. The question, again, is whether, or what sorts of, causal theories can function within the narrative world.

Departures from Impartiality in Causal Assessment

Social psychological research has turned up a number of circumstances in which causal judgments depart from strictly logical standards of impartiality. I develop three examples that have particular relevance to the experience of narrative worlds: temporal order in perceived causality, the fundamental attribution error, and perspective and causal analysis. (For convenience, I refer collectively to current and future tokens of the type of processing models described in this section as *causal network models*.)

Causal assessments are often very sensitive to the order in which information is presented. Consider this scenario from Miller and Gunasegaram (1990):

> Imagine two individuals (Jones and Cooper) who are offered the following very attractive proposition. Each individual is asked to toss a coin. If the two coins come up the same (both heads or both tails), each individual wins $1000. However, if the two coins do not come up the same, neither individual wins anything. Jones goes first and tosses a head; Cooper goes next and tosses a tail. Thus the outcome is that neither individual wins anything. (p. 1111)

Miller and Gunasegaram asked subjects in an experiment to answer two questions: (1) Who will experience more guilt: Jones or Cooper? and (2) Who will blame whom more for their failure to win $1000? Both questions, thus, were directed toward evaluating the reader's assessment of causality. Eighty-six percent of the subjects believed that Cooper would experience more guilt; 92 percent believed that Jones would blame him more. Nonetheless, it should be clear that Jones and Cooper were equally responsible for the outcome—which is to say that neither of them was responsible since coin tosses are chance events. We can see here the difference between logical and psychological assessments of causality. What we want to ensure is that causal network models are most likely to follow psychological rules of causality. In this case, were we to create a text based on Miller and Gunasegaram's scenario, we would be surprised if readers failed to construct a causal network that assigned blame to the character in Cooper's role. And, in fact, it appears that the Fletcher et al. model would not have to be altered to capture this intuition. If Jones's toss is taken as part of the circumstances, as a given that precedes Cooper's toss, then blame should be uniquely attributed to Cooper's action. I start with this example because I wish to project optimism with respect to the possibility of accommodating causal network models to the details of genuine causal analysis.

In the excerpt I cited from *The Risk Pool,* Ned Hall suggested that accidents at the overcrowded dinner table were caused by situational factors, although he believed the other participants at the dinners were attributing causality to individual actors. Hall has observed one of the most intensively studied ambiguities in causal analysis. Much of that research has provided evidence for what Ross (1977) called the *fundamental attribution error* (FAE, for short): when performing causal analysis of behavior, observers evince a strong tendency to make dispositional rather than situational attributions. If we were able to distinguish the true causes of events, we would accurately point in some cases to dispositional factors, internal to individuals, and at other times to situational factors, external to individuals. Some characters in novels, for example, become murderers because they enjoy the sport; others, such as James Bond, murder because they are compelled to do so by their social role. To make accurate assessments of causality would require readers to consider carefully both situational and dispositional factors in each instance. The FAE suggests, however, that readers regularly depart from such impartial weighing of the evidence. In particular, readers (and again, I intend the term broadly) typically attribute causality to characters, not to situations.

Social psychological demonstrations of the FAE have most often focused on circumstances in which attributing causality to dispositions rather to situations is, in fact, an error. Ross, Amabile, and Steinmetz (1977) constructed a laboratory analog to a general-knowledge quiz game. Participants were randomly assigned to one of two roles: half became questioners and were instructed to create questions sufficiently esoteric to stump the other half, who became contestants. If the questioners perform this task reasonably well, the contestants will be made to look rather uninformed: relative advantages and disadvantages are unambiguously conferred by the situation. Even so, when asked to rate the general knowledge of the questioner and the contestant, observers, although well aware that the roles were assigned randomly, rated the questioners as far superior to the contestants. When asked to make these same ratings, the questioners put themselves and the contestants at the same level; they were not misled by participation in this exercise. The contestants, however, were likely to rate themselves as considerably lower in general knowledge than the questioners.

Under the circumstances of this study, it is hard to deny that the dispositional attributions constitute errors: observers and contestants should not have attributed the contestants' poor performances to anything but the heavily rigged situation. We see, therefore, that the FAE can appear even under transparent circumstances (for discussions of factors influencing the prevalence of the FAE, see Miller and Lawson, 1989; Tetlock, 1985; Wright and Wells, 1985). Even so, if we are most interested in the consequences of the FAE for causal analysis in narrative worlds, we can focus uncontroversially on the tendency it encodes (see Funder, 1987). How, then, could the readers' bias toward making dispositional attributions affect the course of narrative understanding?

For an answer, we might start by looking for circumstances in which the "type" of causality an author might incorporate into a work diverges from the "type" of causality the reader might be trying to extract (see Gerrig and Allbritton, 1990). This potential might be realized, for instance, when a modern reader tackles Tolstoy's *War and Peace*. Tolstoy used his novel partially as an opportunity to display his theory of history on a broad canvas (for discussions, see Chiaromonte, 1985; Morson, 1987). He argued against a version of history in which great events are caused by individual actors:

> In historical events (where the actions of men form the subject of observation) the most primitive approximation to present itself was the will of the gods, and later the will of those who stand in the historical foreground—the heroes of history. But one has only to penetrate to the essence of any historical event, that is, to the activity of the mass of men who take part in it, to be convinced that the will of the historic hero does not control the actions of the mass but is itself controlled. (p. 1178)

War and Peace is peppered with reminders that the reader should not imagine the characters (historical or fictional) to have caused the events described in any deep sense of causality. *War and Peace* thus provides a great naturalistic setting in which we can observe how readers' predilections with respect to causal analysis may play out in a world that is consciously designed not to support those predilections.

If, in fact, we were to query the causal structures readers construct through experience of *War and Peace,* Tolstoy would probably be disappointed. The research I have reviewed suggests that causal connections are made locally in the immediate processing of texts (this is a conclusion of both the minimalist hypothesis and the current-state selection strategy), so it is unlikely that the grand themes of Tolstoy's causal theory would be encoded directly into a causal network, unless, of course, the themes were explicitly stated as antecedents or consequences in the text. This does not mean that at the end of *War and Peace* readers might not thoroughly agree with Tolstoy's theory: readers' explicit theories of causality could fail to conform with the "theory" of causality that is an emergent property of moment-by-moment processing.

Against this background, it is an empirical question whether readers' bias toward dispositional attributions functions only as a type of explicit commentary on causality or whether the bias might actually function to deform causal networks under construction, by, for example, marshaling attentional resources independent of processes like the current-state selection strategy. To anchor these two possibilities, I present a somewhat more modest example than *War and Peace.* Consider this brief (invented) text:

> An evil agent of SMERSH rigged a bomb so that it would explode when James Bond opened the door to his hotel room. This made the door harder to open than it normally would be. Just minutes before Bond returned to his room, a chambermaid opened the door so that she could turn Bond's bed down for the night. The chambermaid was killed instantly by the force of the explosion.

If we asked James Bond who was the cause of the chambermaid's death, he would probably identify the SMERSH agent. Even so, were we to construct a causal network for this brief anecdote (along the lines of existing theories), it would certainly include the chambermaid's actions as part of the central causal chain, as a direct antecedent to the explosion, because, in fact, her actions *did* cause the bomb to explode. In particular, I would expect by virtue of the current-state selection strategy that the chambermaid's action (opening the door) and its consequence (the explosion) would be bound closely together in memory. My suspicion, however, is that readers in an experiment would find it easier to agree with a statement that "The SMERSH agent caused the explosion" than to agree with "The chambermaid caused the explosion." In this example, I have, of course, improved my case (at least in this thought experiment) by having the target of the dispositional attribution be correlated with the target for moral disapprobation. The chambermaid—who caused the explosion only in the sense that her actions in this preexisting situation unintentionally produced a certain effect—is blameless on moral grounds. Let me suggest a scenario that uncouples morality and attributional biases:

> James Bond rigged a bomb so that it would explode whenever anyone opened the door to his hotel room. He had been forced to do so by an evil agent of SMERSH. SMERSH's leaders wanted to discredit Bond in the eyes of his superiors. At around ten o'clock, a chambermaid opened the door so that she could turn Bond's bed down for the night. The chambermaid was killed instantly by the force of the explosion.

My guess, in this case, is that readers would find it easier to agree that "James Bond caused the explosion" than to agree that "The SMERSH agent caused the explosion" or "The chambermaid caused the explosion," even though Bond did not bring about the explosion of his own free will.

I have offered these examples because I believe they focus on how attributional biases may exert an influence on moment-by-moment causal analysis. If my intuitions are correct, causal network theories would have to be amended to allow salient causal connections between statements that may have otherwise failed to be brought together in working memory. I am suggesting that the dispositional bias may function as a strategy alongside, for example, the current-state selection strategy. If true, we may have discovered yet another way to constrain the category of minimal inferences.

One of the most striking results to emerge from the Ross, Amabile, and Steinmetz (1977) experiment was that the questioners' ratings of their own and the contestants' general knowledge were virtually unaffected by participation in the quiz show. Across a range of circumstances, in fact, observers tend to make more dispositional attributions than do actors (see Jones and Nisbett, 1971; Watson, 1982). (It is exactly this disparity between actors and observers that Ned Hall noted at the crowded dinner table.) Yet, if observers and actors are made to take each other's perspectives, the pattern of attribution shifts. Storms (1973), for example, made two videotapes of the same interaction between two people, one from the perspective of a participant and a second from the perspective of an observer. As in other research, observers tended to make more dispositional attributions for the participants' actions than they did for themselves. However, when the participants and observers were shown the videotapes that switched their perspectives, the observers' attributions were less dispositional than the participants'. In some very literal sense, therefore, perspective on the interaction had a considerable effect on causal assessment.

The effect of perspective extends to attributions about remembered actions. Frank and Gilovich (1989) asked the participants in their experiments to make causal attributions about their behaviors during a brief conversation. Some subjects recalled the conversational scene from their own perspective as an actor; others recalled it from an observer's perspective, imagining seeing themselves as part of the scene. Frank and Gilovich found that the attributions of participants who recalled from an observer's perspective were reliably more dispositional.

We can speculate, once again, about the consequences these results might have for the moment-by-moment assessment of causality. Authors, filmmakers, and artists have almost unlimited freedom to manipulate the perspective from which readers and viewers experience the events that transpire in narratives. They can present an event purely from a character's perspective or so as to include the character within the scene. In some cases, they can penetrate directly into the thoughts of one or many characters to provide explicit causal perspectives on events. Research results suggest that some of these shifts in perspective will alter the types of causal structures readers construct.

Consider another version of the rigged-door scenario that manipulates visual perspective:

> An evil agent of SMERSH had rigged a bomb so that it would explode when James Bond opened the door to his hotel room. This made the door harder to open than it normally would be. The agent lingered in the hallway to observe the fruits of his efforts. After several minutes of waiting, he saw a chambermaid turn into the hallway and approach Bond's door. She gradually came closer and closer, pausing to look at the number on each room before stopping finally in front of Bond's door. He saw her fumble momentarily with the keys, and then push open the door. She was killed instantly by the force of the explosion.

Imagine, one more time, that readers were asked to judge the truth of the statements "The SMERSH agent caused the explosion" and "The chambermaid caused the explosion." My expectation would be that, by virtue of the change in visual perspective, readers would be more likely in this case to attribute the cause to the chambermaid. The actual words I have used to change perspective are, of course, quite different from the earlier scenario. Even so, all the antecedents and consequences remain unchanged. The only important difference is that we are experiencing the events from the SMERSH agent's perspective, and from this perspective the chambermaid caused the explosion.

It is important to note that not all manipulations of perspective will have an effect on causal attributions. Fiske, Taylor, Etcoff, and Laufer (1979) showed that imagining a story from the visual perspectives of different characters will not necessarily alter causal attributions, even if one of the characters is an actor and another is an observer. They suggest that "salience effects on attribution are confined to real-life rather than imaginary scenes" (p. 369). I am disinclined to dissociate the experience of narrative worlds from real life. Rather, I suggest that Fiske et al. failed to find perspective effects because they manipulated perspective from outside the narrative world. Their subjects were specifically instructed to try to take the visual role of one or another of the characters in the story. Authors, however, can straightforwardly cause readers to take a particular perspective within the narrative world, as I did with my third recasting of the rigged-door scenario. I suspect that such manipulations of perspective within the experience of the narrative will lead to performance differences most critical to theories of the process of causal analysis.

Manipulations of perspective might also provide fertile ground for studying individual differences in causal analysis. Lee-Sammons and Whitney (1991) have supplied evidence in that direction in an attempt to reconcile disparate reports of the effects of perspective on memory for texts. In the original demonstration, Anderson and Pichert (1978) asked subjects to read a passage describing the "fine old home" of a wealthy family from the perspective of either a potential homebuyer or a potential burglar. The story contained facts that were more relevant to one or the other perspective: homebuyers should be more interested in leaky roofs and burglars in coin collections (Pichert and Anderson, 1977). When asked to recall the texts, subjects' responses tended to be dominated by their perspective: "burglars" recalled more burglar facts; "homebuyers" recalled more homebuyer facts. Anderson and Pichert required their subjects to recall the text a second time, however, but switched the perspectives. Subjects were now able to retrieve information—appropriate to the switched perspective—that they had failed to report on first recall. Because these data suggest that information relevant to both perspectives was committed to memory, Anderson and Pichert argued that the perspectives were largely wielding their influence at the time subjects recalled the information rather than at the time they encoded the text. This interpretation was challenged by Baillet and Keenan (1986), who altered the paradigm to include both lengthier texts and a longer period between reading and recall. Under these modified conditions, they demonstrated that subjects could not produce previously unrecalled information when they were asked to shift perspective. Baillet and Keenan argued, contrary to Anderson and Pichert, that perspective largely affects the original encoding of narrative information.

To reconcile these points of view, Lee-Sammons and Whitney (1991) explored individual differences in perspective effects as a function of comprehension ability. To define groups of differing ability, they obtained measures of *working memory span* (WMS). For this measure, pioneered by Daneman and Carpenter (1980), subjects are asked to try to hold in memory the final words of sets of sentences, the number of which are systematically increased. Daneman and Carpenter demonstrated that reading and comprehension ability is highly correlated with this measure. For their experiments, Lee-Sammons and Whitney constructed groups of low-, medium-, and high-span readers. The procedures in their two experiments replicated the earlier research. What they found was that only high-span individuals were able to recall new information following a switch in perspective. Recall by low-span readers, by contrast, was almost entirely dominated by encoding perspective. Lee-Sammons and Whitney concluded that "the extensive use of an encoding perspective by some subjects appears to be a kind of compensatory process in which a strategy is adopted that allows for more-effective use of working memory capacity" (p. 1080).

This conclusion lends credence to the suggestion that manipulations of perspective could be used to examine individual differences in causal analysis. We saw earlier that the current-state selection strategy (Fletcher, Hummel, and Marsolek, 1990) represents a strong claim about the way working-memory capacity is allocated during narrative comprehension. To refine this position, we could obtain measures of WMS and look for a relationship between reading ability and adherence to this strategy. Lee-Sammons and Whitney's research suggests that we might find an inverse relationship: readers with a large WMS should have less cause to adhere to the current-state selection strategy. Furthermore, we could use shifts in perspective to study the uniqueness of causal analyses. If readers' recall for causally relevant information shifted following a change in recall perspective, we would be somewhat more skeptical about the encoding claims made by theorists of causal analysis.

Although I have avoided reflexive invocation of the performance metaphor in this chapter, I return to it now as a way of bringing together the research I have reviewed. My first goal was to specify what is common to the performances that all readers give. I reviewed evidence for the minimalist hypothesis as a way of suggesting that the range of inferences undertaken automatically is limited. Against that background, we could start to examine some of the ways individual performances differ. Unsurprisingly, a significant factor was what sorts of things different readers know. I concluded, however, that we must also understand how knowledge comes to be represented so that it can have an effect within the narrative world. In the final section, I reviewed evidence that one of the activities readers perform most regularly is causal analysis. I tried to illustrate how research on causal analysis under more-general circumstances could inform theory-building within the domain of narrative understanding. My general approach has been to exploit analogs to real-life aspects of performance—in the sense that we perform our own real lives—when we look to the experience of narrative worlds.

Participatory Responses

The performance metaphor presupposes that each reader will experience a slightly different version of a particular narrative world. We saw in chapter 2, however, that it is possible to generalize about the types of inferences readers will regularly draw. In this chapter, I lay out similar generalizations for the noninferential participatory responses that readers generate while experiencing narrative worlds. Consider this description of a sequence from a 1946 film called *The Verdict* (Gow, 1968):

> The doorknob sequence of *The Verdict* begins when Mrs. Benson (Rosalind Ivan), a landlady very much on edge because a murder has been committed in her house and the killer is still at large, informs one of her lodgers, Victor Emmric (Peter Lorre), who has come home rather late at night, that he would do well to follow her example and wear a whistle on a string around his neck in case somebody breaks into his bedroom. Victor, who might for all we know at this point of the

story be the murderer himself, remarks that once your throat is cut you cannot blow a whistle. . . .

[Somewhat later], we are confronted by the first doorknob, the one on the inside of Victor's bedroom door. Victor seems to be sleeping when our attention is drawn to the doorknob (or, to be precise, door handle, for it is rather an elegant thing in itself). Beneath it, Victor's key, with a chain dangling from it, remains in the keyhole where he left it, but as we watch it is pushed out by somebody on the other side of the door. (pp. 14–15)

It is hard to imagine seeing this sequence without struggling to inhibit the impulse to shout, "Watch out!" This is an excellent example of a participatory response. David Allbritton and I (Allbritton and Gerrig, 1991) coined this phrase with the performance metaphor very much in mind. We wanted a term to refer to noninferential responses that would also include within it the notion that these responses arise as a consequence of the readers' active participation. Some viewers of *The Verdict* might never, in fact, have the least inclination to warn Victor Emmric of the approaching danger because, for whatever reasons, they choose not to participate in the appropriate way.

I intend this example to make it clear that p-responses and inferences are intimately entangled. Viewers of *The Verdict* would not feel any compulsion to shout "Watch out!" if they were not able to generate the expectation, based on past experiences of such situations, that Emmric was in danger. Gow (1968), in fact, argued that the slowly turning doorknob alone conventionally gives rise to inferences of impending doom: filmmakers know this and use the device to elicit a predictable response. If the film goes on to show that our fears were unwarranted, we may emit the p-response of relief. Or we may emit a p-response of anger at the director for manipulating us so successfully. Because these responses do not fill gaps in the text, they do not fit the classic definition for inferences. Although the responses rely on the products of inferential processing, they constitute a different category of experience. The temporal dependence of p-responding and inferencing can also be reversed. Often, p-responses will provide the impetus for inferencing. Imagine that we wish Emmric to survive whatever danger is lurking behind the door—the impulse to shout "Watch out!" presupposes that this is true. Once we have realized that we cannot, in fact, warn him, we might turn our attention to trying to infer what elements of the situation will allow him to rebuff the danger. The presence of the p-response "I hope he pulls through" would, thus, cause us to focus our attention in a particular way. Were we acting under the agency of a different p-response (for example, "I dislike this character, and I hope he's dispatched swiftly and painfully"), we might undertake very different trains of inferences. I suggest that this attention-directing function emerges because so many p-responses encode highly emotional content. A real-life cry of "Watch out!" will often cause a startle or fear response that will immediately change our attentional stance (see Ortony, Clore, and Collins, 1988). It is this real-life retuning of attention that we also bring to the experience of narrative worlds.

Although I have been trying to demonstrate that there is a motivated distinction between inferences and p-responses, my central concern is not to create a strict taxonomy, for at least two reasons:

1. There are cases in which the propositions readers may generate could be equally inferences or p-responses. Consider the proposition "Vesper Lynd means to do James Bond some harm"—although the book fails to provide direct evidence (at least early on) to support this inference. Perhaps this response is purely a p-response, in the sense that it is a gut response to "something about" Vesper Lynd. Or perhaps this response is an inference

based concretely on evidence that is too diffuse in the text to come into the consciousness of the readers (that is, the readers can't explicitly defend their inferences). Note the parallel here to real-life circumstances in which we find ourselves trying to analyze or defend gut reactions. As a second, similar example, imagine a circumstance in which a proposition such as "James Bond can't die!" comes to mind. Such a thought might represent a preference engendered by the text or an inference based on long experience with Bond, or both.

2. It's not particularly important to settle cases like these unless we want to make strong claims about, for example, processing differences that covary with category membership. My second point is that we have no reason to believe in any such correlations. In defining the content of p-responses as noninferential, I do not wish to imply that the types of processes that give rise to p-responses differ from the types that give rise to inferences. My discussion of p-responses in the next sections should make it evident that p-responses are quite a heterogeneous class. I couldn't even attempt to make processing or representational claims for every type of p-response. In particular, p-responses will suffer the same split between those made within and without the narrative world that I discussed for inferences in chapter 2. Some p-responses will feel as though they arise in the normal course of processing; others will emerge through more phenomenologically effortful problem-solving activities. Unfortunately, there are no data available to anoint categories of obligatory versus strategic p-responses.

My discussion of three types of p-responses is intended to show that we can bring the same sort of rigor to the characterization of p-responses as we did for inferences. I will also show that an analysis of certain types of p-responses is critical to adequate cognitive psychological models of narrative understanding because p-responses have exactly the sorts of consequences that have been the objects of these models. Finally, I have chosen these three particular types of p-responses to give some sense of the diversity within the category. The first section considers p-responses that consist of readers' expressions of hopes or preferences. The second examines the way suspense presupposes reader participation. The third examines the process by which readers replot the events of a narrative both within and without the narrative world.

Hopes and Preferences

Consider this claim about the inevitable behavior of experiencers of narrative worlds (Denby, 1991): "Narrative art forms like novels and movies are governed by certain mysterious but implacable laws, and one of them is that when people are in danger of being caught—even if they are doing something awful—we root for them to get away. Our identification overcomes our scruples" (p. 32). I cite this claim because it bears witness to the regularity with which we actively express our hopes or preferences in the experience of narrative worlds. My review of the evidence on causal analysis in chapter 2 highlighted the great attention readers devote to goals and outcomes. Each time a character arrives at a situation in which a goal may or may not be met, we have an opportunity to express a preference. When the goals of different characters conflict, we might express our preferences even more vociferously (if the voice inside our head can be taken to modulate its volume).

David Allbritton and I (Allbritton and Gerrig, 1991) sought to demonstrate that the mental expression of hopes and preferences could directly affect the representation of textual information. Our intuitions were shaped by the experience of narrative worlds in which outcomes did not follow our preferences. Recall the scene from Doctorow's *Billy Bathgate* described in chapter 1. Bo Weinberg, we believe, is about to be killed by Dutch Schultz, but Bo makes a strong case for being spared. "I protected you, I saved your life a dozen times, I did your work and did it like a professional," he says to Schultz (p. 15). Although the scene is morally complex (since Weinberg is himself an exultant murderer), we come to hope that Schultz will spare him. Our preferences are not honored; Schultz does not relent. Allbritton and I theorized that the very act of entertaining preferences such as "I hope Weinberg is set free" could concretely affect readers' ability to recall what actually transpired.

We developed our experimental hypothesis by applying Kahneman and Miller's (1986) *norm theory* to situations of narrative comprehension. Arguing that exceptional events are more likely than normal events to evoke thoughts about counterfactual alternatives, Kahneman and Miller stated, "An abnormal event is one that has highly available alternatives whether retrieved or constructed; a normal event mainly evokes representations that resemble it" (p. 137). Consider this brief scenario, which explains the circumstances surrounding Mr. Jones's car accident (Kahneman and Tversky, 1982):

> On the day of the accident, Mr. Jones left the office earlier than usual, to attend to some household chores at his wife's request. He drove home along his regular route. Mr. Jones occasionally chose to drive along the shore, to enjoy the view on exceptionally clear days, but that day was just average. (p. 204)

One group of subjects read this scenario, which made it clear that the time at which Jones left his office was exceptional. Others read a scenario in which Jones's normal route was altered. Kahneman and Tversky asked both groups of subjects to imagine the sorts of thoughts that might follow from the accident:

As commonly happens in such situations, the Jones family and their friends often thought and often said, "If only . . . ", during the days that followed the accident. How did they continue this thought? Please write one or more likely completions.

Kahneman and Tversky found that whenever their subjects mentioned the time or the route, 83 percent of the time they "if only"-ed the exceptional event in the direction of normality. When readers call to mind counterfactual alternatives, they are most likely to do so in response to exceptional events.

In our experiments, Allbritton and I extended this logic to normal and exceptional preferences about the outcomes of events. We suggested, in particular, that different types of preferences, which we called *positive* and *negative,* would lead to predictably different patterns of p-responding as a function of their ordinariness. To define positive and negative preferences, we invoked a priori reader responses. To begin, we identified as *negative outcomes* a range of events—including, for example, a successful killing—as outcomes that most readers would, with a high probability, not prefer. Without a special story context, we presumed that most readers would prefer a priori positive events—such as the preservation of life—which we identified as *positive outcomes.* In the context of a particular narrative, however, readers can be made to prefer either kind of outcome. Readers might have found it perfectly acceptable, for example, if someone had burst upon the scene to kill Dutch Schultz so that Bo Weinberg could be spared. In our terms, a *positive preference* represented a situation in which, through the course of understanding a narrative, a reader formed a preference for a positive outcome. A *negative preference* indicated a hope for a negative outcome, such as a successful murder.

The critical assumption underlying our research was that in real-life situations positive preferences are the norm, and negative preferences the exception. Given this assumption, norm theory allows us to predict that positive and negative preferences will give rise to different patterns of p-responses. Because they are exceptional, we would expect negative preferences to have a greater tendency to evoke representations of counterfactual alternatives to the outcome of a story. Just as exceptional events elicit a greater number of propositions representing alternative events, Allbritton and I hypothesized that exceptional preferences would elicit a greater range of propositions representing instantiations of alternative versions of the outcomes. This broader range of propositions could then interfere with readers' ability to correctly identify the actual outcomes.

Consider a scenario in which readers were made to have preferences about the success of a bomb squad in preventing an explosion in a scientific laboratory. In the story, we used two sentences to create a positive preference:

> The scientists at the lab had nearly perfected an AIDS vaccine. It was the only hope for stopping the deadly epidemic.

Under these circumstances, we would expect readers with normal social values to generate a small set of p-responses, including "I hope the bomb squad is successful." We also used a pair of sentences to create a negative preference:

> Libyan scientists at the lab had nearly perfected a deadly chemical weapon. Qadafi planned to supply the lethal brew to international terrorists.

After reading these lines, we would expect readers to emit the p-response "I hope the bomb squad fails," but also, in keeping with norm theory, we would expect that this atypical negative preference would prompt the readers to think about alternatives, "Will the explosion kill innocent people?" "Could the explosion spread the chemical weapon?" and so on. Our primary hypothesis was that by considering a wider range of alternative scenarios, our subjects would have greater difficulty confirming actual outcomes while experiencing a negative preference versus a positive preference.

In our experiments, each story began with a statement of a positive or negative outcome. We chose to put the outcomes first in order to test the effects of p-responses on information that was known to readers before those responses were generated (see Gerrig, 1989b). Although this text structure may seem somewhat out of the ordinary, exposition often follows the statement of outcomes in both literary texts (Sternberg, 1978) and real-life storytelling. Labov (1972) noted that narratives often begin with an "abstract" that summarizes an entire story. Our stories were designed so that they permitted outcomes that, a priori, were clearly positive (for example, someone winning a race, passing a test, or getting accepted into college) or clearly negative (a bomb exploding, someone running out of gas, or a head of state being assassinated). Within each story, however, we inserted lines that, in the fashion I illustrated earlier, created preferences for or against the a priori polarity of these outcomes. Here is a full version of the bomb squad story, which begins with a negative outcome but creates a positive preference:

> Suddenly, an explosion rocked the building. The bomb had
> been discovered at the beginning of the morning shift. If it
> were not defused, three years work would be destroyed. The
> scientists at the lab had nearly perfected an AIDS vaccine. It was
> the only hope for stopping the deadly epidemic. As the bomb
> continued to tick, explosives experts began working on it.
> They finally managed to locate the detonator. Removing it
> would either defuse the bomb, or set it off if done incorrectly.
> Slowly, they began to remove the detonator. (p. 618)

Readers encountered stories that contained all four possible combinations of positive and negative outcomes and positive and negative preferences (the four versions of each story were read by equal numbers of subjects). Pilot testing confirmed that the story segments intended to create positive and negative preferences had that intended effect (for details, see Allbritton and Gerrig, 1991).

In our first experiment, the participants were required to read thirty-two stories with this structure. After reading a full set of stories, the subjects spent five minutes on an unrelated activity, writing a description of a friend. Following this intervening task, the subjects were required to verify the outcomes of the stories, and we recorded their reaction times to do so. For each subject, half of the verification sentences matched the outcome stated in the version of the story they had read (for the above example, "The bomb exploded") and half of the outcomes were mismatched ("The bomb was disarmed").

Our most important prediction was that readers' p-responses would cause verification times to be particularly long under circumstances in which we had created a preference for the negative outcome. This expectation was confirmed. Negative preferences led to reliably increased verification times for both true and false statements of the actual outcomes. Thus, if readers had been made to hope that the bomb would explode, they found it particularly difficult to verify whether it did or did not explode. Note that the excerpts of the stories that created the positive and negative preferences did nothing to change the probabilities of the outcomes. The differential effect of the negative versus positive preferences must be attributed to responses they engendered in the readers.

In our second experiment, Allbritton and I sought to demonstrate an effect of p-responses under less favorable circumstances. Rather than ask our subjects to verify the outcomes of the stories after a period of delay, we required them to verify the outcomes directly after completing each story. This procedure puts p-responses to a stricter test. Under these circumstances, for example, readers were being asked about the identity of outcomes that they had seen only a brief time before. Generally, only six to eight lines of text intervened between the first-sentence statement of the outcome and the verification sentence. We would expect, thus, that the actual representation of the outcome information would be more strongly activated in memory than it would be in the case of a delay. The propositions engendered by negative preferences might be less able to interfere with strongly activated information about the actual outcome. Furthermore, the participants in our study could have easily adopted the strategy of ignoring all the story information except the statements of the outcomes. After completing five practice stories, and certainly by early in the experiment, it would have become evident that the verification sentences all made reference to the stories' outcomes. We feared that readers would simply ignore everything in the middle.

Our sense, given this array of concerns, was that the enduring appearance of an effect of negative preference would provide strong support for the robustness of p-responses. In this second experiment, negative preferences, in fact, produced verification times about 237 milliseconds longer than those in circumstances of positive preferences. This difference was somewhat more modest than in experiment 1 (that difference was 319 milliseconds), but was still reliable. That the preference effect was evidenced even under reasonably unfavorable conditions supports the major conclusion we drew from our initial experiment: participatory responses can engender salient competition for the actual content of narratives even, in this case, under adverse conditions.

In a final experiment, we demonstrated that the p-responses evoked by the negative preferences had a specific effect on our subjects' ability to verify the outcomes of the stories. We wanted to ensure that the negative preferences were not just acting in some global fashion. It could be that by virtue of the negative preferences readers would construct an overall larger memory structure that would interfere with the verification of all facts from the stories (see Lewis and Anderson, 1976). To eliminate this alternative hypothesis, we returned to the delayed test methodology of experiment 1 and asked our readers to confirm or disconfirm statements about non-outcome information. In the bomb squad story, for example, subjects were expected to respond either "true" to "The bomb was found in the morning" or "false" to "The bomb was found in the evening." Our predictions about the effect of negative preferences in the first two experiments were based on the belief that readers had generated p-responses that would specifically compete with outcome information. In this final experiment, we believed that the manipulation of preference would have no effect on our subjects' ability to recognize non-outcome information.

We found, in fact, that our readers verified the non-outcome information somewhat more quickly, by about 153 milliseconds, in situations of negative preference—a result that argues strongly for the specificity of p-responses. This conclusion is bolstered by the near equivalence of our subjects' performance in verifying the two types of information. The overall error rate from experiment 3 (16.4 percent) was quite close to the error rate in experiment 1 (15.6 percent). We cannot, therefore, attribute the difference in the effect of preference in the two experiments to the overall lower memorability of non-outcome information. Rather, we believe that the p-responses brought about by the negative preferences are p-responses exactly about outcomes.

Allbritton and I concluded that this series of experiments served as a sort of "existence proof" for a certain class of highly predictable p-responses. That readers have responses to narratives is uncontroversial. What we have demonstrated, however, is that at least one class of these responses had measurable consequences for the memory representations constructed in the course of experiencing a narrative world. Our conclusions, of course, are still highly inferential: we have no direct evidence about the form or content of the actual p-responses. Our one certainty, however, is that our creation of unusual preferences altered our readers' experiences of the stories. Theories of narrative understanding must incorporate the products of those preferences.

Suspense

Typically, readers are thought to experience suspense when they lack knowledge about the outcomes of events that have reasonably important consequences. Ortony, Clore, and Collins (1988) suggest that suspense involves "a Hope emotion and a Fear emotion coupled with a cognitive state of uncertainty" (p. 131). To anchor what is "reasonably important," they offer the example of the weather: "A person might be uncertain about whether it is going to rain, but, except in unusual circumstances, is not likely to be in suspense waiting to find out". Within this straightforward definition, we can immediately see why p-responses must play a role in the experience of suspense. Uncertainty can take its toll only if readers allow themselves to consider a range of possibilities. Hope and fear are operative only when the reader begins to have preferences about the desirability of subsets of those possibilities.

Consider a situation in which Arkady Renko, the central character of Martin Cruz Smith's novel *Polar Star,* finds himself. Arkady is investigating a suspicious death on a Soviet fishing vessel. He has been attacked by unknown men and thrown into a sack. At first, he reassures himself that they don't mean to kill him right away, because he can imagine an action they haven't taken:

> They could have just thrown him down the fishhold [the compartment in which the catch is stored]; his body

wouldn't have been found for days. So perhaps being hit, gagged and sacked was a good sign. (p. 152)

We quickly learn that Arkady has been overconfident. He *is* thrown into the fishhold, where the temperature is $-40°C$. Now, to whatever extent readers care about Arkady's fate, they should start to explore the possibilities for his escape. All the mentally expressed propositions that begin "Maybe he could..." are p-responses. To be sure, readers will rely on information stored in memory to generate these possibilities— so aspects of the generation of the p-responses are inferential— but the propositions themselves are not inferences. Furthermore, different readers will undertake this problem-solving activity to different extents. Smith, like many successful authors of suspenseful works, mimics the process of problem solving. He heightens the tension by specifying and then eliminating potential means for escape:

> [Arkady] stopped himself as he reached for the wheel of the door, because bare skin would adhere to the metal. He covered the wheel with the sack and then put his weight into it, but it wouldn't budge. The men outside must be holding it shut, and there was no chance he was going to overpower three or more of them. He shouted. Around the cold store were ten centimeters of fiberglass wool insulation; even the inside of the door was padded. No one was going to hear him unless he walked right by. (pp. 152–53)

As the scene continues, the reader is made to generate a series of p-responses of increasing desperation. Arkady is finally rescued because he—unknowingly—is laughing hysterically. (And I, for one, emitted a p-response of disappointment at the deus ex machina resolution to the crisis.) With this example in hand, I now sketch a p-response account of the creation and maintenance of suspense.

The experience of suspense should occur when a reader (1) lacks knowledge about (2) some sufficiently important target outcome. Feelings of suspense will be heightened to the extent that (3) the target outcome maps out a challenging problem space and (4) the author is able to sustain participatory responses over a period of delay.

1. The reader lacks knowledge. I noted earlier that the experience of suspense typically requires that some important information not be known to the reader. A more accurate statement of this requirement is somewhat more complex: readers must participate in a narrative world in such fashion that the knowledge critical to sustaining suspense is not immediately accessible. This added complexity is necessary because readers often experience suspense even when they know what will happen, a circumstance that I have called *anomalous suspense* (Gerrig, 1989a, 1989b). Walton (1978b) exemplified this phenomenon in its purest form:

> Suspense may remain a crucial element in our response to a work almost no matter how familiar we are with it. One may "worry" just as intensely about Tom and Becky while rereading *The Adventures of Tom Sawyer,* despite one's knowledge of the outcome, as would a person reading it for the first time. A child listening to *Jack and the Beanstalk* for the umpteenth time, long after she has memorized it word for word, may feel much the same excitement when the giant discovers Jack and goes after him, the same gripping suspense, that she felt when she first heard the story. (p. 26)

Walton suggested that each time readers reexperience a narrative, they are engaging in new games of make-believe: within these games they do not know the outcomes, and so suspense is preserved. In chapter 5 I develop an account of anomalous suspense that shares in spirit Walton's view of making a strict demarcation between information that is held within and without the narrative world. (There I also attempt to bring greater precision to theoretical terms like "immediately accessible.") Here, I bring up anomalous suspense simply to illustrate how fundamentally the experience of suspense relies on reader participation. Even if we know exactly what will take place (Jack will survive his trip up the beanstalk) and how (by chopping down the beanstalk, thus killing the giant), once we undertake a performance of the narrative world, this information somehow becomes inaccessible. For current purposes, therefore, I begin with the assumption that whatever information has prompted the experience of suspense is absent within the narrative world.

2. *Some sufficiently important target outcome.* I share the intuition of Ortony et al. (1988) that weather conditions are unlikely to encourage suspense "except in unusual circumstances." What authors do, of course, is create unusual circumstances. We can easily imagine plot contrivances that would leave characters— and the reader along with them—desperately scanning the sky. A theory of suspense must explain how certain outcomes become sufficiently important in local contexts. (Note that I use outcome here as a convenient shorthand expression. Readers can also feel suspense with respect to the means through which an outcome comes about, the individual whose actions bring about an outcome, and so on.) To a large extent, a theory of suspense must include within it a theory of empathy: Under what circumstances do we care sufficiently about other people to engage in active thought about their fates?

Developmental research carried out by Jose and Brewer (1984) provided strong evidence for a link between empathy and the experience of suspense. These researchers wrote short stories for second, fourth, and sixth graders that included suspenseful elements. In one story, for example, the outcome in question was whether a spider would bite the main character, Mike:

When the spider reached the edge of the bed it slowly stepped onto the blanket. One furry leg at a time it silently walked across the blanket. Mike was just about asleep. (p. 922)

Two of Jose and Brewer's manipulations related to the characteristics of the main character. For some of the children, the main character in the story matched their own gender (for example, for some girls in the study, "Mike" would have been replaced by a girl's name). Also, the sections of the text that preceded the suspenseful episode established the main character as either a good child or a bad child. After reading the stories (or, for the second graders, hearing the stories), the children provided ratings on a number of dimensions. They were asked to judge how similar they were to the main character, how much they liked that character, and how much they worried about the character when he or she was in danger. Jose and Brewer found that the children considered themselves to be most similar to and also liked best good characters and characters of their own gender. The children also felt more suspense (that is, worried most) about the good characters. Jose and Brewer went further to perform an analysis that revealed a causal pathway connecting these findings: closer identification with the characters specifically prompted greater feelings of suspense.

Jose and Brewer suggested that this link arises because close character identification encourages the reader to share the experiences of the character. To this explanation I would add that close identification also encourages the reader to work more actively to imagine how the characters might be able to extricate themselves from the threatening situation. If the character is bad, we might p-respond, "I hope the spider bites him." If the character is good, we might respond, "Maybe he could roll away from the spider," "Maybe he'll roll on top of the spider and kill it," "Maybe his cousin will save him," and so on. My suggestion, therefore, is that identification promotes an investment of resources toward p-responding.

Jose and Brewer's study illustrates how distant a goal a general theory of "sufficient importance" must necessarily be. In their stories, evaluations of suspense were affected even when changes were made only with respect to the way the characters were constituted. This result suggests that whatever general statements we might want to make about "important outcomes" would have to be appropriately relativized to the identities of the characters and the readers. Jose and Brewer have demonstrated, nonetheless, that some generalizations can be drawn. My prediction is that we can find others, and that in each case we shall discover that the situations triggering strong feelings of suspense are exactly those in which the reader is most motivated to take on the explicit role of problem solver.

3. A challenging problem space. Classic analyses of problem solving (see, for example, Newell and Simon, 1972) conceptualize the process of finding a solution as an activity akin to searching a space. The solver's initial situation is called the *initial state*. The *goal state* is the desired solution. To get there, the solver moves through *intermediate states,* which are defined by the particular characteristics of the problem domain. My suggestion is that the experience of suspense is very much like the experience of navigating a problem space. If we return to Arkady's icy predicament, we can see that each element of the analogy is well defined. For an initial state, we have Arkady trapped in the fishhold. The goal state (which we adopt by virtue of appropriate identification) is for Arkady to get out. The intermediate states are, in this case, whatever we can imagine might enable him to do so. This example also makes evident the flaws in the analogy. First, readers can't actually perform the operations that they imagine might bring about a solution to the problem. Second, the solution is in many, if not most, cases specifically intended to be inaccessible. Even so, readers apparently take great pleasure in the imaginary experience of problem solving.

We can understand some of the salient features of the experience of suspense by means of the analogy to problem solving. We can predict, for example, that the intensity of feelings of suspense will covary with the availability of obvious solutions. In some literal sense, readers should be less worried if a character's fate depends on familiarity with simple arithmetic rather than with the equations of combinations and permutations. Suspense with respect to some familiar real-world problem—how will a character get back into a car when the keys are locked inside?—might also fail to generate much concern. To make the reader really feel suspense, the author must sufficiently constrain the space of possible solutions so that the situation appears beyond hope. In my analysis of Arkady's dilemma, I suggested that Smith adopted the strategy of successively narrowing the range of possible solutions so that the reader became more and more convinced that the goal state was unattainable. As each solution is eliminated, the perception of suspense is heightened.

On the whole, we can employ the analogy to problem solving to see why writers are often so successful at evoking and sustaining suspense. Authors often implicitly avail themselves of a common block to problem solving, termed *functional fixedness*. In an early demonstration of this phenomenon, Duncker (1945) challenged his subjects to mount a candle on a door when the only materials at hand were the candle itself, a box of tacks, and a book of matches. The appropriate solution is to empty the tacks out of the box to use it as a support for the candle. Many subjects, however, failed to find this solution, apparently because they were focused on the box's function as a container. Similarly, authors often focus our understanding in a way that obscures the solution to a problem. Following Edgar Allan Poe's lead from "The Purloined Letter," mystery authors have often teased their readers by leading them to overlook critical evidence in plain view. We could even imagine a suspenseful tale based on Duncker's problem: Will the hero be able to find a way to attach the candle to the door? Note that Smith also relies on a form of functional fixedness to make Arkady's situation seem even more desperate. He encourages the reader to focus on Arkady's own conscious actions as the only possible sources of escape. In fact, the eventual solution—the deus ex machina resolution—comes from outside this realm of possibilities. Although, as I admitted, I was disappointed in this case, often when the author reveals the solution, the reader gets to indulge in pleasurable self-recrimination: Why didn't I think of that?

Note that the analogy between the experience of suspense and problem solving is maintained even when the situation presented by a narrative is not one in which a character must explicitly find a solution to a problem. Consider a case in which we wonder whether a character, Trudy, will live or die. We then have a problem space defined by the opposing goal states, Trudy lives and Trudy dies. The reader can imagine what operations within the narrative world could lead to either of these goal states—"Perhaps," the reader might think, "the villain's gun will misfire"; "Perhaps there is no antidote to the poison Trudy has imbibed"—and arrive at a solution that may or may not be borne out by further revelations of the text. Any situation that incorporates uncertainty can be reframed as a problem to be solved.

Furthermore, the experience of suspense does not require that the reader play problem solver through identification with a character. Consider this excerpt from John Kennedy Toole's novel *A Confederacy of Dunces*:

It was all a matter of storage. From almost one to three every afternoon George was stuck with the packages. One

afternoon he had gone to a movie, but even there in the
dark watching a double bill of two nudist colony films he
wasn't comfortable. He was afraid to put the packages
down on an adjoining seat, especially in a theater like that
one. (p. 269)

For the next two pages, the narrative is taken up with George's
attempts to keep his packages safe. Readers could hardly navigate
this passage without starting to speculate about what they might
contain: clearly George knows already, so this problem-solving
activity is carried out purely for the readers' enjoyment. Note
that some readers might fail to emit any p-responses—the activity is nonobligatory—but Toole structures the tale in such a
way that readers are, in fact, overwhelmingly drawn to search
the solution space. (On page 300 we learn that the packages
contain pornographic photographs.)

My discussion so far has almost certainly overemphasized the
well-formedness of readers' attempts at problem solving. In fact,
these types of p-responses will most likely not, under ordinary
circumstances, come into consciousness in an explicit way. Most
instances of this class of p-responses will emerge alongside the
moment-by-moment experience of the narrative. They can be
completely well formed only if the reader shifts attention fully
away from the narrative—a practice that will be impractical if
the narrative itself cannot be momentarily arrested (as will be
the case for plays, conversational stories, and so on). Even when
the narrative is in printed form, the reader may not want to delay
access to the desired knowledge by deliberately shifting attention
to the activity of p-responding. Nonetheless, I suspect that most
readers could catch themselves imagining at least ill-formed operations ("Perhaps he could . . . ") or offering themselves sketchy
proofs ("I'm sure she won't die because . . . ") as part of the
experience of a narrative. Furthermore, as I have suggested repeatedly, skillful authors facilitate the experience of suspense by

modeling aspects of the problem-solving process. To the extent that they make readers feel as if they have created important dilemmas for which even some subtle solutions have been eliminated—and to the extent that they have invalidated steps in a proof toward a desired outcome—authors can ensure that their works will be considered particularly suspenseful.

4. Suspense survives a period of delay. Authors often avail themselves of one other technique for increasing feelings of suspense: they impose a sometimes painful delay between the moment at which the suspense is initiated and the moment at which truth is revealed. Literary analyses of suspense have often focused on the mechanisms of delay as a window on an author's craft. These analyses have preceded from the widely shared assumption that "one of the criteria for judging the effective creation of suspense is the duration between promise and fulfillment: the longer disclosure is deferred, the greater the suspense" (Batty, 1987, p. 62; see also Monti-Pouagare, 1988; Porter, 1983; Sternberg, 1978). Against this background, it is the author's task (that is, the author's pleasure) to make readers wait as long as possible without exiting the narrative world in disgust or dismay (which may take the form of flipping pages, for example). The successes and failures of authors of varying skill have been the subject of literary analysis.

Monti-Pouagare (1988) compares two dramatic renderings of the Oedipus myth, by Sophocles and by Dryden and Lee. He observes that the writers start at a disadvantage with respect to suspense because Oedipus's tale is so well known. Perhaps as a consequence, both plays display active—and contrasting—attempts to increase suspense through delay. Monti-Pouagare deems Sophocles' technique less successful in that Sophocles "causes delay by having a character linger on secondary issues instead of getting to the point" (p. 7). In one instance, in the prologue, Oedipus asks Creon what message he brings from the oracle of Apollo—and Creon simply fails to get to the answer in a timely fashion. Monti-Pouagare suggested that the artificiality of this technique is likely to undermine feelings of suspense. Dryden and Lee, by comparison, bring about the critical delays by incorporating elements of a subplot into the main flow of action. In act 2, for example, Teiresias arrives with information about who killed Laius. "He says, however, that the god is like a fury in his breast, tearing him apart. Therefore, he asks his daughter, Manto, to sing a song asking Apollo to be mild" (pp. 7–8). Directly after the song, Teiresias reveals his information. Monti-Pouagare argues that this technique for suspense succeeds because the delay grows naturally out of other themes at work in the play.

The contrast between these two techniques is between the types of response the reader or playgoer is encouraged to emit. If, as I have suggested, readers must participate in the experience of suspense, Sophocles' technique for delaying revelation is likely to fail largely because frustration—a sense that the author is not playing by the rules—is antithetical to participation. If the author's technique causes readers to opt out of the narrative world, suspense cannot be sustained. Dryden and Lee, by contrast, create a richer solution space in which readers can play out problem-solving aspects of suspense. Of course, suspense is not the only goal the authors have in telling Oedipus's story. What is most important about Monti-Pouagare's observations is that they demonstrate how solidly suspense relies not only on formal properties of a narrative (for example, the number of lines of dialogue that intervene between the initiation and undoing of suspense) but on the responses the narrative evokes. Although it seems relatively straightforward to initiate suspense—any duffer can invent a good guy, a bad guy, and a loaded gun—it clearly takes reasonable skill to sustain suspense—particularly if we accept Sophocles as an example of a brilliant poet who nonetheless failed at suspense.

What emerges, I hope, from this account of reader participation in suspense is that from the perspectives of both readers' cognitions and their emotions, suspense is a lot of work. If we care about the fates of characters and if knowledge of those fates is willfully being denied us, we may feel frustration or even anger. Worse still, strong feelings of suspense require that readers themselves have tried and failed to find their own answers to the problems of those fates—part of the frustration of suspense comes from a failure to be clever enough problem solvers to settle the dilemmas at hand. It is, therefore, somewhat paradoxical that readers thoroughly enjoy well-executed narratives of suspense.

Brewer and his colleagues (Brewer and Lichtenstein, 1981, 1982; Brewer and Ohtsuka, 1988a, 1988b) have proposed a *structural-affect theory* to explain the strong link between suspense and readers' reports of their enjoyment of stories. They draw on the work of Berlyne (1971) to show how suspense structures are ideal for inducing patterns of response that are biologically privileged to give pleasure. Brewer and Lichtenstein (1982) explain that "Berlyne attempted to use constructs from motivational and physiological psychology to produce a general theory of pleasure. He postulated that enjoyment is produced by moderate increases in arousal ('arousal boost') or by a temporary sharp rise in general arousal followed by reduction of the arousal ('arousal jag'), and if both processes operate together enjoyment is produced by both the rise and the subsequent drop in arousal ('arousal-boost-jag')" (p. 480). Brewer and his colleagues have suggested that suspenseful stories produce exactly this pattern of arousal boost and jag, which leads to great enjoyment by readers.

To demonstrate the link experimentally, Brewer and Lichtenstein (1981) wrote short narratives that could be rearranged either to be suspenseful or not. The base narrative for "The Trip Home," for example, described "a man driving home from work, coping with several minor mechanical obstacles" (p. 368). The suspense version contained, in addition, an "initiating event": "a bomb with a 10-min timer was activated in the car as the driver got in" (p. 368). There were three narratives used in the experiment. Some subjects read the base version of these narratives, some the suspense version. (Brewer and Lichtenstein also included other versions to test a broader range of hypotheses than those specifically relating to suspense.) After reading each of the four segments into which the narratives were divided, the subjects rated how much suspense they were experiencing. At the end of each narrative, the subjects rated (among other things) how well they had liked each story. Not surprisingly, the subjects were reliably more worried about the events to come while reading suspense versions of the narratives. When suspense was resolved at the end of the fourth segment of the stories, these ratings converged. There was also a strong relationship between the experience of suspense and liking. On a seven-point scale, subjects gave, on average, ratings that were two points higher for the suspense versions of the narratives. Brewer and Ohtsuka (1988a, 1988b) have replicated the association between suspense and liking for naturally occurring stories of both American and Hungarian origin.

Brewer and his colleagues also demonstrated that subjects rate narratives incorporating suspense as being more "story-like." Brewer and Lichtenstein (1981) asked subjects to indicate "the extent to which the passage was, or was not, a 'story' " (p. 369) on a seven-point scale. Subjects' ratings were nearly 2.5 points higher, on average, for the suspense than for the base versions of the three narratives. This result provides an important corrective to theories of narrative comprehension dominated by purely structural concerns, such as story grammars or story schemas. This class of theories (for a review, see Mandler, 1984) often tried to capture generalities about the experience of narratives based solely on the canonical order of information in texts. What Brewer and Lichtenstein have shown is that texts containing the right information in the right sequence—the base versions of their narratives—are nonetheless not considered by readers to be particularly story-like. The ratings, in fact, averaged less than three on the seven-point scale, the point that the experimenters defined as "barely a story." Brewer and his colleagues (see also Jose, 1988) make a strong case for including reader responses in theories of the experience of narratives. The p-response analysis of suspense very much shares the spirit of their work.

Replotting

P-responses to outcomes do not cease once suspense has been alleviated. Rather, once readers are made privy to particular outcomes, they mentally begin to comment on them, often engaging in an activity I call *replotting*. It is easiest to observe these replottings when an outcome has been particularly negative. In Larry McMurtry's novel *Some Can Whistle* unexpected violence has erupted, ending the lives of several characters. The narrator, Danny Deck, muses:

> Muddy Box and I spent three years endlessly trying to reverse the clock with our minds—to get back beyond the moment T.R. danced out of the house and drove off to her death. Hundreds of times, privately and together, we reenacted her last half hour at Los Dolores, trying to rearrange events so that she didn't leave, and therefore didn't die.
> (pp. 341–42)

Here, readers can join with Deck in wishing that events could be altered both within the narrative world (we can agree with Deck that the characters might have acted differently and averted the tragedy) and without the narrative world (we can wish that the author had simply written a different novel). I intend *re-plotting* to cover the full range of p-responses in which readers consider alternatives to the real events, with whatever motivation.

Just as there is a type of anomalous suspense that survives within the narrative world despite real-world knowledge, narratives can also induce a phenomenon that goes beyond ordinary replotting, which I call *anomalous replotting* (Gerrig, 1989a). Under ordinary circumstances, readers replot only after they have become aware of an outcome. In anomalous replotting, knowledge of the outcome precedes the experience of the narrative. Consider Philip Roth's report on his experience of the assassination of Martin Luther King, Jr., from his autobiography, *The Facts:*

> In April 1968 I was virtually the only customer eating an
> early dinner at Ballato's Restaurant on Houston Street
> when the news came over the radio that Martin Luther
> King had been shot. . . . I went to the phone and called May
> [his girlfriend], who was working late at the Quaker Cen-
> ter. We agreed to meet back at her apartment, where we
> later sat up on the bed together and watched again and
> again the TV footage from Memphis, which never stopped
> being terrible or true no matter how many times it was
> played. (p. 146)

Roth asserts that the "footage . . . never stopped being . . . true no matter how many times it was played." At the risk of reading too much into his words, I suggest that each time the footage was played, he allowed himself to construct a narrative world in which the story would have a different ending. This hope-driven activity led repeatedly to terrible disappointment, because the original story never stopped being true. What makes this replotting anomalous is that Roth knew full well that King had been shot even as he tried to imagine otherwise. Without this foreknowledge, he would have been unlikely to have emitted whatever p-responses he did. In watching the footage, Roth might very well have formulated the imperative "Don't go out on the balcony!"—which would be incoherent without knowledge of the consequences. Although the time-course might be different, the experiences of anomalous and ordinary replotting are likely to be rather similar. In both cases, readers imaginarily amend a narrative's outcome. (I return to anomalous replotting in chapter 5.)

My discussion of the variety of p-responses has emphasized the ways in which their occurrence has an impact on the experience of the narrative. This is true with respect to both phenomenology and cognitive psychology. P-responses can often function to direct readers' involvement in a narrative world. Consider a study in which subjects imagined how they would feel if they experienced near-positive and near-negative outcomes. Johnson (1986) invented neutral stories in which a college undergraduate named Chris went through a number of daily events. In one augmented version of the story Chris came very close to a glamorous, positive outcome:

> Chris learned that his family had just won a grand prize in the sweepstakes, but later discovered that the letter informing them of the prize was fraudulent and had been disclaimed by sweepstakes officials. To compensate for the inconvenience, however, sweepstakes officials sent the family $25.00 and a certificate for a free dinner at a local Mexican restaurant. (pp. 54–55)

In another version, Chris narrowly escaped a tragic, negative outcome:

> Chris was stricken with a critical illness, from which his doctors believed that full recovery was doubtful. Two days

later, however, he was "resting comfortably in his hospital bed," recovering fully from what was finally diagnosed as food poisoning. He was informed that he had "escaped death by a hair." (p. 55)

Johnson asked his subjects (each of whom read one version of the story) to imagine themselves in these situations and to rate how lucky, happy, and satisfied they would feel. On all three dimensions, subjects who assumed Chris's role gave higher ratings after near-negative outcomes than after near-positive outcomes, with ratings for the neutral stories falling in between.

To explain these results, Johnson invoked the *simulation heuristic* of Kahneman and Tversky (1982), who suggested that "there appear to be many situations in which questions about events are answered by an operation that resembles the running of a simulation model" (p. 201). Johnson explained the results of his experiment by arguing that subjects are comparing what actually happened to a simulation of what might have happened: near outcomes acquire their affective power through easy comparison to what might have been. Although Chris lived, we can easily imagine that he might have died; although his family failed to win the sweepstakes, we can easily suppose that it was otherwise. The simulation of an alternative outcome in the presence of knowledge of the actual outcome is exactly what I have labeled replotting. Replotting, thus, is often a specific, directed use of readers' power to carry out simulations. The emotional power of many narratives will arise from readers' abilities to situate the outcomes an author describes with respect to a range of imaginable alternatives. If the reader fails to p-respond appropriately, the narrative world will be left emotionally dulled.

Replotting often becomes a public activity when motivated by aesthetic considerations. Critical analyses of works of fiction regularly include suggestions for what else the author might have done to improve the aesthetic impact of the work. In table 3.1 I have culled examples of replotting from a collection of Pauline Kael's (1985) movie reviews for the *New Yorker*. In each case, Kael articulates how changes of plot—big and small—would have resulted in more-successful films. She always has some precise notion of what might have been done to bring the movies into line with her aesthetic preferences. Overall, Kael's recommendations for reworking span a broad range of the elements of moviemaking, including choice of actors and director, the volume of musical scoring, and the camera perspectives used to capture scenes.

What is most striking, perhaps, is how certain Kael is of her changes—but this is a presumptuousness she shares with amateur replotters. Readers all seem to have strong intuitions about what might have been done to improve their experience of a narrative. We could, in fact, collect replottings as a way of deriving readers' implicit theories of aesthetics. This measure could provide converging evidence for developmental changes in story-liking. Consider Jose and Brewer's (1984) finding that age and character "goodness" interacted in affecting children's liking for story outcomes: Second graders preferred positive outcomes to negative outcomes irrespective of whether a character (the subject of the outcome) was good or bad. Sixth graders preferred positive outcomes for good characters but negative outcomes for bad characters. By adulthood we have often been taught to savor the pleasure obtained when, by contrast, bad things happen to good characters. Thus, we might desperately hope (via anomalous replotting) that Othello would see through Iago's deceptions in time to save Desdemona, but were our hopes granted, we would probably judge Shakespeare's work to be much less successful as an aesthetic experience. Many of Kael's replottings reveal just such a dissociation of what makes a viewer happy versus what succeeds as a work of art. My general suggestion is that examination of replottings can lay bare theories of aesthetic

TABLE 3.1
Some Replottings by Pauline Kael

1. *Superman III:* [Richard] Pryor as a computer genius doesn't ring any bells; I wondered why the moviemakers hadn't tried the ploy of using Pryor to wise up Superman, or as the demoralized Superman's tempter—that way he wouldn't have had to be so limp, and he and Superman could have had more scenes together. (p. 11)

2. *The Survivors:* And the plot, for symmetry, could use considerably more of the third key character—Jerry Reed's bullying thug; we need to know more of what's going on inside his handsome hard head. Reed . . . has a fine maniacal presence here, and his performance is so promising that I regretted that there wasn't more for him to do. (p. 18)

3. *The Right Stuff:* I wish that Kaufman had followed through on the disturbing, awkward quality of this incident, which grips us at a different emotional level from the other scenes. I realize I'm asking for a different kind of movie, but if he'd taken a different approach to the Gus and Betty Grissom episode he might have opened up some of the implications of the phrase "the right stuff" that have bothered me ever since Tom Wolfe's book came out. (pp. 66–67)

4. *Heart Like a Wheel:* These heaping hairdos keep appearing on her, like a blight, and since we never go into her dressing room or see her primping or instructing the women at the beauty parlor, we have no way of knowing what weird notions of femininity they serve. . . . Wouldn't it give the film's Shirley Muldowney more dimensions if we could see that unlike college-educated professional women who ask to be accepted for what they are, Shirley the hot-rod champ is still trying to pass as a classy belle? And *does* she pass? Does she get pleasure from it? Or does it add to her feeling of loneliness and isolation? (p. 82)

5. *Scarface:* We miss out on the frightening exhilaration of Tony's winning his crown; there's no satisfaction for Tony or for the audience. We don't even get any of the gangster conspiracies that we might enjoy. The middle of the movie is missing. We get the aftermaths but not the capers. (pp. 103–04)

TABLE 3.1 (continued)
Some Replottings by Pauline Kael

6. *The Purple Rose of Cairo:* Woody Allen's full vision here could take a less tidy, airier finish—he needed to pull something magical out of his hat. . . . Woody Allen puts a strain on his light, paradoxical story about escapism when he gives it a desolate, "realistic" ending. (p. 340)

7. *Lost in America:* But the movie needs another turnaround, because although the ending is right for David, it isn't right for Linda. . . . By talking her into quitting her job, David has unloosed something in her that Brooks and his co-writer don't quite know what to do with. (pp. 345–46)

pleasure: readers understand that artistic endeavors involve choices, and sometimes we wholeheartedly believe that artists have made the wrong ones.

My emphasis in this chapter has been on the active ways readers contribute to the experience of narrative worlds. Although many of the participatory responses emerge in symbiotic relationships with inferences, they do not in any direct sense serve to bridge gaps in a text. Rather, p-responses often function to enrich emotional and aesthetic aspects of a narrative world: by p-responding, readers draw themselves solidly into the narrative world. P-responses, on the whole, are quite heterogeneous. Some arise outside of conscious awareness, while others occur when readers explicitly focus their attention on dilemmas of the text. Some arise within the moment-by-moment experience of the narrative, while others are made upon reflection from outside the narrative world. I have tried to illustrate why p-responses are critical to theories of narrative experience.

Language Use in
Narrative Worlds

CHAPTER FOUR

In "The Logical Status of Fictional Discourse," John Searle observed, "It is after all an odd, peculiar, and amazing fact about human language that it allows the possibility of fiction at all. Yet we all have no difficulty in recognizing and understanding works of fiction." He concludes with a question: "How is such a thing possible?" (1975, p. 325). In this chapter, I lay out the circumstances of language use that brought Searle to this query, and I attempt to provide an answer. I suggest that Searle and other theorists have largely misdiagnosed the problem by focusing almost exclusively on fiction rather than on narrative in general, and on the activities of authors rather than on the activities of both authors and readers. My goal is to make the use of language in narrative worlds seem at once more ordinary and more special.

Note that in this chapter I have in mind almost exclusively narrative worlds that are experienced through interactions with texts. In this instance, therefore, I intend the terms *reader* and *text* to be interpreted narrowly. Part of my strategy, in fact, is to draw upon other circumstances in which people experience narratives to work toward an account of narrative texts.

Fictional Utterances and Infelicity

Searle made the claim that fictional uses of language are "odd, peculiar, and amazing" against the background of a theory of language use first set forth by John Austin in his classic work, *How to Do Things with Words* (1962). Austin's central insight was that in ordinary circumstances, speakers are carrying out several acts each time they produce an utterance: they are making a series of movements with their jaws and tongues, they are emitting a series of words with particular referents, and they are "making statements, asking questions, issuing commands, giving reports, greeting, and warning" (Searle, 1971, p. 39). Austin's scholarly descendants have turned particular attention to the last of these acts, which Austin had named the *illocutionary act*. Searle (1969, 1971), in particular, attempted to lay out sets of *felicity conditions* that constitute the rules for appropriate performance of illocutionary acts. Fictional utterances appear to pose a particular problem with respect to such conditions.

To fill out this argument I offer, as Searle did, one brief excerpt from a front-page *New York Times* article by Michael Wines and a second from a novel at hand, John Kennedy Toole's *A Confederacy of Dunces*. The excerpt from the *Times* is nonfictional:

> Tokyo, Thursday, Jan. 9—President Bush fell suddenly ill and collapsed at a state dinner being given for him Wednesday night at the home of the Japanese Prime Minister. This morning, his spokesman said the President was "up and about" and making phone calls.

Toole's passage introduces us to a fictional creature:

In the shadow under the green visor of [his] cap Ignatius J. Reilly's supercilious blue and yellow eyes looked down upon the other people waiting under the clock at the D. H. Holmes department store, studying the crowd of people for signs of bad taste in dress. Several of the outfits, Ignatius noticed, were new enough to be considered offenses against taste and decency. Possession of anything new or expensive only reflected a person's lack of theology and geometry; it could even cast doubts upon one's soul. (p. 13)

What acts have Wines and Toole undertaken by performing their varied utterances? On the surface both excerpts seem to consist of assertions. According to Searle's system, however, speakers must adhere to the following set of rules to make a felicitous assertion (1975, p. 322):

1. The essential rule: the maker of an assertion commits himself to the truth of the expressed proposition.

2. The preparatory rule: the speaker must be in a position to provide evidence or reasons for the truth of the expressed proposition.

3. The expressed proposition must not be obviously true to both the speaker and the hearer in the context of the utterance.

4. The sincerity rule: the speaker commits himself to a belief in the truth of the expressed proposition.

Wines's utterances adhere to all these rules—or at least we suppose that to be the case. Subsequent information might prompt him to amend some of the details of his article, but we believe that at the time he wrote it, Wines intended his assertions to be felicitous. Toole's utterances, by contrast, follow none of these rules. He has not, in any sense, committed himself to the truth of the events he describes in *A Confederacy of Dunces*. He could probably not provide evidence for any of the propositions that are expressed. The difficulty, then, is that Wines's and Toole's utterances look about the same, but an analysis of felicity strongly suggests that these two writers could not be carrying out the same acts of assertion.

Searle's analysis, in fact, presupposes that there are no surface distinctions that would instantly reveal Toole's utterances to be different in kind from ordinary language. This presupposition contradicts a long history, reviewed by Pratt (1977), of literary theorists' accepting as given that poetic language forms a system different from ordinary language—a tradition of belief that Pratt refers to as the "Poetic Language Fallacy." The undoing of this fallacy has relied on a comparison of actual utterances as well as quasi-experimental data (for example, Culler, 1980; Fish, 1980; Pratt, 1977).

Fish (1980) describes an exercise he has repeatedly carried out in the classroom. In its first instantiation, he showed his students a vertical list of names on a blackboard and asked them to explicate its meaning as a token of the type of religious poem they had been studying (p. 322):

Jacobs-Rosenbaum

Levin

Thorne

Hayes

Ohman (?)

The students performed brilliantly—although the names were only a list left over from an earlier class. Fish concludes: "It is not that the presence of poetic qualities compels a certain kind of attention but that the paying of a certain kind of attention results in the emergence of poetic qualities" (p. 326). The "look" of the language, therefore, cannot differentiate factual and fictional assertions. The *New York Times* passage could easily be embedded in a novel. Toole's passage, with all its delightful excess, could appear as part of an ornate, nonfictional article of the "New Journalism."

Searle's focus, consequently, is not on the utterances themselves but on what the authors intended by performing those utterances. Wines, we believe, intended to perform felicitous assertions. According to Searle's main theoretical innovation, Toole intends only to *pretend* to do so. The pretense here is not intended as a form of deception. On Searle's reading, "To pretend to do something is to engage in a performance which is *as if* one were doing or being the thing and is without any intent to deceive" (p. 324, original emphasis). This buffering through pretense allows authors of fictions to remain morally pure: their violations of the rules of felicitous assertions are entirely on public view.

It is at this juncture that Searle wonders how fiction is possible. What allows language to function under ordinary circumstances, he says, is the sets of rules, such as those for felicitous assertions, that have the effect of "correlating words (or sentences) to the world"—that "establish connections between language and reality" (p. 326). Fictional competence is "odd, peculiar, and amazing" exactly because readers are able to suspend these connections: "The pretended illocutions which constitute a work of fiction are made possible by the existence of a set of conventions which suspend the normal operation of the rules relating illocutionary acts and the world" (p. 326). This, unfortunately, is where Searle more or less stops. Although his analysis strongly implicates the activities of the *reader* as the ones that make fiction possible, Searle has nothing more to say about those activities.

The absence of the reader in Searle's theory forces him to nonsolutions of some prominent problems. For example, he argues that "a work of fiction need not consist entirely of, and in general will not consist entirely of, fictional discourse" (p. 332). He comes to this conclusion because of utterances like Tolstoy's celebrated opening to *Anna Karenina*, "Happy families are all happy in the same way, unhappy families unhappy in their separate, different ways." Here, according to Searle, Tolstoy is not engaging in pretense. This "is a genuine assertion" (p. 332). But how is the reader to know? Consider, again, part of the passage from *A Confederacy of Dunces:*

> Possession of anything new or expensive only reflected a person's lack of theology and geometry; it could even cast doubts upon one's soul.

Is this utterance a pretend or a serious assertion? Because it is attributed to the thoughts of Ignatius J. Reilly, who emerges quickly as an idiosyncratic, if not unreliable, narrator (see Booth, 1983), we are perhaps inclined to believe it to be pretense. But this is the sort of reasoning the *reader* must undertake in the absence of knowledge of the author's intentions: defining the experience of fiction by reference to the often-opaque activities of authors does not move us a long way toward explicating how such experiences are possible. By closely examining the activities of readers, as I do in this chapter, I hope to develop a more adequate theory of the narrative experience of language.

What emerges strongly is my belief that theorists have almost always gotten off to the wrong start by taking the fictional aspects of fiction to be of primary importance. By focusing on a taxonomy that divides fiction and nonfiction from the start, these theorists have generally been forced to invent special mental activities performed only by the authors and readers of fictions. I suggest, instead, that with respect to the cognitive activities of readers, the experience of narratives is largely unaffected by their announced correspondence with reality.

Hearers' Roles in Conversation

Accounts of how readers experience narrative language have often proved murky, largely because theorists have failed to consider the varied roles language users adopt in everyday conversation. My position is an extension of Clark and Carlson's (1982) theory for everyday language use, which is based on the straightforward observation that standard treatments of speech acts systematically fail to acknowledge that utterances are often made in the presence of more than one individual. Recall one of Searle's constitutive rules for felicitous assertions: "The expressed proposition must not be obviously true to both the speaker and the hearer in the context of the utterance" (1975, p. 322). What Searle means is not *hearer* but *addressee:* many conversational participants might hear an utterance, but speakers have been infelicitous only if they knew that the particular listeners to whom they addressed the utterance already possessed the information. Clark and Carlson use an excerpt from *Othello* to fill out this point (p. 332):

> *Othello, to Desdemona, in front of Iago and Roderigo:* Come, Desdemona. (1.3.299)

This request is addressed to Desdemona, but Iago and Roderigo are clearly intended to hear it as well. Clark and Carlson's theory spells out exactly what acts Othello has performed with respect to his three hearers. By way of preview, I suggest that much of our experience of language in narratives consists of assuming the same role given to Iago and Roderigo in this speech situation.

What, then, are the illocutionary acts Othello has performed when he says, "Come, Desdemona"? By any standard account (for example, Searle, 1969), Othello has made a felicitous request of Desdemona. He has not, on the other hand, made any request of Iago or Roderigo, nor do they believe that he has done so. But, clearly, his words have had some effect on them. Specifically, by uttering "Come, Desdemona," Othello has *informed* Iago and Roderigo (and Desdemona as well) that he has made a request of Desdemona. "Informed" is the key. Clark and Carlson argue that under these circumstances the speaker is performing an *informative illocutionary act* toward all the participants. In this example we see the basis for two of Clark and Carlson's most important hypotheses (p. 333):

> *The Participant Hypothesis.* Certain illocutionary acts are directed at hearers in their roles as addressees, and others are directed at hearers in their roles as participants.

> *The Informative Hypothesis.* The fundamental kind of participant-directed illocutionary act is one by which the speaker jointly informs all the participants fully of the illocutionary act that he is simultaneously performing toward the addressee or addressees.

According to these hypotheses, when Othello performs his utterance, he has designated Desdemona as his addressee, and Iago, Roderigo, and Desdemona as participants. All three are jointly informed of the request he has made of Desdemona, even though the request is made only of her.

Clark and Carlson muster a variety of evidence to support their *informative analysis*. In an ordinary conversations with three or more participants, each utterance might ordinarily be directed toward one particular addressee, but each participant, as Clark and Carlson put it, "is responsible at all times for keeping track of what is being said, and for enabling everyone else to keep track of what is being said" (p. 334). To make this more concrete, imagine that we are participating in a real-life conversation that includes the following material (an excerpt from Eudora Welty's short story "Petrified Man"):

> "Reach in my purse and git me a cigarette with no powder in it if you kin, Mrs. Fletcher, honey," said Leota to her

ten o'clock shampoo-and-set customer. "I don't like no perfumed cigarettes." (p. 32)

Although Leota's request is unambiguously directed toward Mrs. Fletcher, we would not be surprised in real life if Mrs. Fletcher were to pass the request along to us by mentioning, for example, that she, too, couldn't quite get to the purse. Mrs. Fletcher would assume that we had been informed of Leota's request, although we were not the intended addressee.

As a second example, consider a situation described in *New York* magazine (Walls, 1992, p. 8):

Larry Kramer's protest against neighbor Ed Koch has been silenced—sort of.

Kramer, who wrote *The Normal Heart,* was a vocal critic of the Koch administration, accusing city officials of ignoring the AIDS crisis. When the former mayor moved into the building where Kramer lives, on lower Fifth Avenue, Kramer yelled at him in the lobby. The building's management warned the activist to leave Koch alone, saying he might be evicted.

"Sometimes I run into Koch in the lobby when I'm walking my dog, Molly," says Kramer. "Then I address all my comments to *her.*" Those comments, loud enough for Koch to hear, are along the lines of "There's the man who murdered all of Daddy's friends."

For this situation, Clark and Carlson (1982) suggested that the speaker is making only a "pretense of speaking linearly when the primary illocutionary act is lateral and indirect" (p. 337). This primary illocutionary act is the genuine informative, directed in this case at Ed Koch, who would surely not be baffled by the pretense of Molly's participation.

The conclusion I'm moving toward is this: as language users, we have vast experience in both informing others with language that is not specifically addressed to them and in being informed by language that is not specifically addressed to us. To develop this position, I have to bring into consideration speakers' intentions. The examples so far have presupposed that the speakers have intended all the hearers to be informed by their utterances (that is, the informative illocutionary act was felicitous for all hearers). In many cases, however, there will be hearers whom the speaker would explicitly like to exclude or toward whom the speaker has no intentions. Clark and Carlson term hearers who are intentionally included *side-participants*. Those who are excluded on purpose or by accident they call *overhearers, who* may be either *known* or *unknown*. Consider the experience of Ned Hall, a known overhearer, from Richard Russo's *The Risk Pool:*

> When "Will" left, at around ten in the evening, I was supposed to believe that he was gone for good, never mind that the back stairs groaned under his considerable bulk when he returned a short hour later. I wasn't supposed to know that the signal for his return was the lowering, then raising, then lowering again of her bedroom shade, though this maneuver was nearly as noisy as the stairs.
>
> Theirs was about the dumbest signal ever, and not just because it reduced the life expectancy of window shades (she [Ned's mother, Jenny] went through three during my high school years), but because it required such extraordinary vigilance on the part of the person awaiting the signal. (pp. 280–81)

In this case, Ned is a known overhearer because his mother knows that he is bound to be listening, and he is clearly intended not to be informed by his mother's signal—the whole purpose of the elaborate nonlinguistic signal is to exclude him. Just as clearly, he has not been excluded. This is often the case with real-life conversationalists who may design their utterances with the unsuccessful intention of excluding some known members of an audience (see Clark and Schaefer, 1987). Whatever the level of success, however, under these circumstances the speaker (or, in Jenny Hall's case, the signaler) consciously differentiates participants from overhearers.

This differentiation is attempted by virtue of the information that speakers take to be *mutually known* to the various hearers. Consider a situation in which Ann and Barbara have previously agreed that they will leave a party whenever Chris arrives:

Ann to Barbara, in front of Donna: 'Oh look, Chris is here.'

Barbara, but not Donna, will understand that Ann intends to communicate more than the simple observation. Formally, some proposition *p* is *mutually known,* or in *common ground,* when a speaker (S) and a hearer (H) can assure themselves of an infinite number of recursive statements that begin "S knows that *p*,": "H knows that *p*," "S knows that H knows that *p*," "H knows that S knows that *p*," and so on. In practice, however, speakers and hearers rely on certain heuristics—and an assumption of rationality—to assess what is in common ground (see Clark and Marshall, 1981). Speakers take as evidence that *p* is in common ground, for example, if *p* is presumed to be known by all members of a well-defined community (*community membership*), if *p* is directly present in the environment (*physical copresence*), or if *p* has been supplied in preceding conversation (*linguistic copresence*). Speakers intend their utterances to be understood with respect to their rational expectations of common ground. Jenny Hall, for example, had confidence in her signal by virtue of a correct belief that she and her son Ned did not mutually know its import. Although Ned was able to interpret the signal in the absence of mutual knowledge—this is the risk inherent in attempted exclusion—Jenny did not intend that to be so.

Ned, in any case, was aware that his mother intended him not to understand. When speakers are successful, hearers will not ordinarily be aware that they are overhearers rather than side-participants. When Ann says, "Oh look, Chris is here," Donna will not be aware that the utterance has been designed specifically to exclude her from one of its implications. Arguably, Donna is both a side-participant and an overhearer with respect to this utterance because she is intended to understand the assertion and informative (that is, "Chris is here") but not the indirect speech act ("It's time for us to go"). To be sure, there will be circumstances in which overhearers explicitly know that they have been cast in that role. Sometimes speakers purposely use language that makes reference to common ground (Clark and Carlson, 1982, p. 345):

> *Ann, to Barbara, on crowded bus:* Do you remember that thing about you-know-who that we were talking about last week? Well, it happened.

In this case, an overhearer could make only a vague guess at the meaning underlying the utterances. Under circumstances more like Donna's, however, the hearer will never know if and when she is intended by the speaker to be a side-participant or an overhearer. This observation leads to a hypothesis about hearers' default processing stance:

> Although speakers differentiate side-participants and over-hearers by virtue of their intentions, hearers ordinarily process utterances as if they are side-participants.

This hypothesis, which I will call the *side-participant stance,* can be recognized as a corollary to Grice's (1975) suggestion that speakers and hearers adhere to an expectation of cooperative behavior in their conversational interactions. Grice formulated the *cooperative principle* as an admonishment to the speaker: "make your conversational contribution such as is required, at the stage at which it occurs, by the accepted purpose or direction of the talk exchange in which you are engaged" (p. 45). Hearers, he suggested, derive meanings against the assumption that speakers are behaving in this fashion. My suggestion is that a side-participant stance is a further consequence of faith in the cooperative principle. The alternative to this hypothesis would be something like an *overhearer stance:*

> In multiparty conversations, nonaddressees at all times act as if speakers are trying to withhold some aspects of their meaning from some hearers.

If hearers in fact adopted such a stance, each conversational utterance would require hearers who were interested in uncovering the speakers' true meanings to undertake extended problem solving. An overhearer stance would thus constitute a dramatic discontinuity in hearer behavior from two- to three- (or more) party conversations because the mental activities of the nonaddressee would so differ from those of the addressee. (Although addressees might suspect speakers of being obscure in two-party conversations, the suspicion could not arise from structural uncertainties about common ground.) The problem-solving activities themselves would be impractical both because conversations proceed quite rapidly and because any utterance could take on an infinite number of meanings with an appropriate arrangement of common ground (just as "Chris is here" can come to mean "It's time for us to go"). None of this argues against hearers' adopting volitionally a more suspicious stance toward particular speakers. (General adherence to the cooperative principle, in fact, makes it quite easy for speakers to be deceptive.) What I am suggesting, rather, is that under ordinary circumstances it is most parsimonious for hearers to behave as if they are bona fide side-participants.

I have been focusing almost entirely on overhearers who are known to speakers. Clark and Carlson also observe that some overhearers will be unknown—in at least two senses. In some cases, speakers produce utterances without knowing that an extra hearer is lurking around the corner. In other cases, the unknown overhearers are in plain view, but the speaker is not acquainted with these individuals. Speakers may design their utterances so as to prohibit or permit understanding by such overhearers.

An Informative Analysis of Narrative Utterances

I have assembled all the elements necessary to lay out a hypothesis of the experience of language in narrative worlds, which I refer to as the *informative analysis:*

> Authors and readers most often behave as if readers are side-participants; in that role, authors intend readers to be genuinely informed by narrative utterances.

A central claim of this informative analysis is that authors intend their informative acts to be genuine. At the same time, depending on whether the utterance is intended as fiction or nonfiction, a narrative assertion (and so on) may not have its ordinary illocutionary force. I have reviewed Searle's (1975) arguments to demonstrate this point, but other theorists have reached the same conclusion either independently or in echo of Searle (see, for example, Beardsley, 1981; Brown and Steinman, 1978; Eaton, 1973; Genette, 1990; Lewis, 1978; MacDonald, 1954; Ohmann, 1971, 1973). Although the details vary, all of these theories presuppose that authors do not sincerely perform most of the speech acts that appear in narrative works. I will continue to adhere closely to Searle's account because it has proved to be the most salient and has most often served as a lightning rod for disapproval (for a review, see Mandelker, 1987). What I am most interested in demonstrating, in any case, is how the class of theories of which Searle's is the prototype fits within the informative framework.

Consider how the informative analysis illuminates an issue that has arisen in the application of speech-act theory to poetry. Theorists have repeatedly made the observation that lines of poetry are nominally directed toward nonsensical addressees (see Beardsley, 1981; Eaton, 1973; Sirridge, 1987). Keats, for example, addressed a star:

Bright star! would I were steadfast as thou art! (p. 198)

Milton, time:

Fly, envious Time, till thou run out thy race (pp. 105–06)

and Shakespeare, the sun:

Why didst thou promise such a beauteous day? (p. 74)

In response to this phenomenon, theorists have been inclined to create special mental acts dedicated to the experience of poetry, and perhaps prose fiction. I suggest, instead, that we need only consider the conversational practice that I exemplified earlier with reference to Larry Kramer and his dog, Molly. Kramer made the pretense of addressing Molly with the real intention of informing Ed Koch. Koch, though not the addressee, was an intended side-participant. Just so, Keats, Milton, and Shakespeare can pretend to address a star, time, or the sun while genuinely informing the readers of their sentiments. This analysis of poetic circumstances, therefore, falls back on what is familiar and natural for readers. Poets can, therefore, confidently pretend to address the sun and stars.

Even when narrative utterances do not give their pretense away by virtue of their announced addressees, the informative analysis provides an account of readers' experiences. Consider the scene from *Othello* in which Iago assures Othello he will provide proof that Cassio has cuckolded Othello:

For I will make him tell the tale anew,
Where, how, how oft, how long ago and when
He hath and is again to cope your wife. (4.1.84–86)

As each of the theorists in Searle's tradition would agree, Iago has in no sense made this promise to the reader. Even so, the reader has been informed—genuinely—that a promise has been made. It is not Iago, however, who has performed this informative act (although we might credit him with some other informative act with respect to Othello). Rather, by virtue of his having caused Iago to utter these words, Shakespeare has informed his readers. Although the promise itself may be only an act of pretense, Shakespeare's informative act is sincere. This is exactly why readers need not learn any new "rules" (in Searle's sense) to experience language in narrative worlds: the informatives are well formed, and readers can treat them as such.

Thus far, this account may appear naive in lumping all narrative utterances into an undifferentiated category—a complaint that has been leveled against other speech-act analyses of fiction. Consider Pavel's (1981) scolding reminder (see also Hancher, 1977):

> To show that the Cartesian image of a well-individuated speaker in full control of his voice does not fit literary fiction, it may be enough to remind the speech act theorist of the complexity and elusiveness of the originating voice in literary discourse. The writer as an individual, the authorial voice, the implied author, the narrator, reliable or not, the voices of the characters, distinct from one another or more or less mixed together, make spurious any attempt to comment on fiction as if it had one well-individuated originator. (pp. 170–71)

The chief reason I find Pavel's criticism undaunting is that I feel confident we could find speakers participating in exactly this same range of functions in everyday conversation, both in earnest and in pretense (see Pratt, 1977, 1981). Speakers regularly mingle other voices with their own when they use direct quotation in conversation (Clark and Gerrig, 1990). Hearers must, therefore, be accustomed to apportioning responsibility to different originators within the same conversational turn. All that is required, in general, for the informative analysis to go through is for readers to have had appropriate experience as side-participants. As long as authors' informatives are sincere, they can indulge in virtually unlimited varieties of pretense.

The main assumption I have been making with respect to authors is that, on the whole, they wish their intentions to be recoverable. My claim, in essence, is that authors intend to produce a range of effects—not all of which are linguistic meanings—and that they believe all these intentions are accessible in the completed narrative work. The critical term in this equation is "believe." In everyday speech situations, we believe that addressees will recover our intentions correctly for at least two reasons: first, we are able to design our utterances (and other nonlinguistic communicative acts) by continuing reference to the common ground we share with the members of our audience; second, we are able to receive feedback from those members about our relative intelligibility. To a large extent, authors are cut off from these corrective processes. Some authors may obtain feedback from a few critics while a work is in progress. Once the narrative has been put into some permanent form, however, authors are barred from amending their work to enhance recovery of their intentions (unless, of course, they issue a corrected edition of a work). What authors must do, therefore, is write with some set of *intended participants* in mind and with an implicit model of what their readers must know to experience a narrative fully. Under those circumstances, the common ground to which authors make reference consists of assumptions about what the intended participants ought to know as members of particular communities supplemented by the shared experience of the on-going narrative. Consider this series of excerpts from Michael Cunningham's novel *A Home at the End of the World:*

> One of [the teenagers], an Eddie Haskell for all his leather and hair, tells her she is looking good. She is willing to hear it. (p. 31)

> "Jonathan and I are bickering . . . and you just sit here like Dagwood Bumstead." (p. 272)

> "What are you all of a sudden, some sort of Nancy Drew of the psyche?" (p. 272)

> I sometimes thought of myself as Snow White living among the dwarfs. (p. 280)

> "I'm afraid I'm turning into Morticia Addams, with my husband's ashes on the mantelpiece." (p. 287)

Each excerpt makes reference to a character from popular culture. When the novel was published, in 1990, Cunningham expected his intended participants to be able to interpret each of these references successfully (or, at least, there is nothing internal to the novel that suggests this was not Cunningham's goal). By choosing these references as a vehicle for some of his intentions, Cunningham consciously delimited the untutored audience for his work. Should this novel endure as a classic, it is perfectly possible that understanding of these lines will require special scholarly knowledge.

There are several claims I do not wish to make. For example, I don't mean to imply that any individual reader would be able to recover all of an author's intended meanings. Almost certainly, authors cannot write in such a fashion that all their intentions will remain forever transparent to all readers. This is a natural consequence of the lack of feedback between reader and author. Similarly, I don't mean to imply that the author intends only unambiguous linguistic meanings encoded in the words of a text. To suit their aesthetic goals, authors may purposely leave certain issues of meaning unclear. Eaton (1983) suggested that the enduring critical controversy surrounding the "meaning" of Henry James's *The Turn of the Screw* arises as a result of James's intention to demonstrate the great range of interpretations that can be licensed by even one speech act. Eaton proposes that *The Turn of the Screw* is partially about "the capacity of language that allows for such ingenuity" (pp. 341–42): to strive for a unique meaning would be to fail to experience the novel in the way James intended.

In addition, I do not mean to suggest that readers should always defer to the author's intentions as the ultimate arbiter of a narrative's value. (I do not mean to commit what has been called the "Intentional Fallacy" [Wimsatt and Beardsley, 1954b].) Although it might be of some genuine literary interest to discover an author's true intentions in a narrative, in practice readers can be counted on to detect only those meanings that can be recovered directly from the text. Finally, I do not wish to imply that the entire experience of a text is circumscribed by language. As I illustrated in chapters 2 and 3, authors may intend to induce participation in a number of ways that are encouraged by the text but not encoded within it.

With all these restrictions in place, what remains intact is the rather straightforward suggestion that authors write with some loosely formulated notion of who ought to be able to derive full value from their narratives. This group of intended participants can be differentiated from a larger group that shades off into overhearers. Consider this excerpt from a *Newsweek* article about Toni Morrison's novel *Beloved* (Clemons, 1987, p. 75):

Morrison tries to clear up a misunderstanding. She has been quoted as saying she writes for a black audience. Does this mean that whites can't adequately respond to "Beloved"? "I meant something else," she says. "When I write, I don't try to translate for white readers. I imagine Sethe [a main character in the novel] in the room. If I read to her what I've written, will she say I'm telling the truth? Dostoevski wrote for a Russian audience, but we're able to read him. If I'm specific, and I don't overexplain, then anybody can overhear me."

In this quotation, Morrison may be using "overhear" partially in its technical sense. To the extent that certain members of her potential audience fail to share appropriate common ground, they will be left to guess at Morrison's true intentions. Her analogy to Dostoevski is apt: some aspects of his narratives fail to resonate with modern audiences; others succeed quite wonderfully. At times the readers are side-participants; at times they are overhearers. As I argued earlier, this is exactly our experience of day-to-day conversation. Our status as participant or overhearer is often determined by speakers, outside our conscious awareness. When reading Dostoevski, however, and perhaps when reading Morrison, readers may sometimes become aware that they do not share appropriate knowledge to experience particular passages fully. The author's expectations of community membership have been undone: what makes readers participants or overhearers is some local or global match or mismatch between what the author expected the intended participants to know and what specific readers actually know.

In works of nonfiction and in the essays that introduce works of fiction, authors often warn their audience about the way failure to belong to a particular community may color the interpretation of particular language or events. Consider the conclusion to

Schama's (1989) description of mass displays of fraternity during the French Revolution:

> It is difficult, in the twentieth century, to sympathize with these mass demonstrations of fraternal togetherness. We have seen too much orchestrated banner waving—great fields of arms harvested in ecstatic solidarity—heard too much chanting in unison to avoid either cynicism or suspicion. But however jejune the experience, there is no question that it was intensely felt by participants as a way of turning inner fears into outward elation, of covering the dismaying sense of recklessness stirred by revolutionary newness with a great cloak of solidarity. (pp. 503–04)

Schama is explicitly admonishing modern readers to imagine themselves as members of a different community and instructing them on how their interpretations would change as a function of that change in identity. Even so, Schama's historical allusions and choice of vocabulary very much situate his intended participants late in the twentieth century.

My evocation of community membership in some ways matches the construct of an *interpretive community* as advanced in literary theory (see, for example, Fish, 1980, 1989). This construct emerged, in part, to explain how it is that communities of readers can settle on similar interpretations of literary works. The difficulty, as critics in the reader-response tradition have noted, is that texts themselves are radically ambiguous (see essays in Suleiman and Crosman, 1980; Tompkins, 1980b). Although this observation is most often motivated independently for works of fiction, it is the problem of ordinary conversation writ large. Recall Ann's utterance, "Oh look, Chris is here," which meant something different to Barbara ("It's time for us to go") than to Donna. With appropriate arrangement of common ground, this one undistinguished utterance could communicate an infinite number of intentions. Literary works, of course, contain a sizable number of utterances, each of which permits a formally infinite number of interpretations—even before we begin to count up the greater range of interpretive activities indulged in by students of literature.

As this radical ambiguity became an article of faith among critics, they sought ways to explain how it is that interpretation is nonetheless constrained. A recurring solution has been to refer to the sort of common ground that has figured prominently in my argument. In ordinary conversation, addressees and side-participants typically come to a unique understanding of an utterance—out of the infinite possibilities—because of the constraints imposed by common ground. The meanings of literary texts are winnowed down (though rarely to a unique solution) because interpretive communities bring particular common ground to the experience of narratives. Interpretive communities often, of course, bring special competence to their task (see Culler, 1980a, 1980b). Common ground includes specific knowledge about what readers should do with texts: how readers *should* read. As this body of shared assumptions changes, interpretations will change as well. The determination of what constitutes the correct reading of a narrative "will not be made once and for all by a neutral mechanism of adjudication, but will be made and remade again whenever the interests and tacitly understood goals of one interpretive community replace or dislodge the interests and goals of another" (Fish, 1980, p. 16). I have used *community membership* to stand for the more general discontinuities of knowledge that explain less goal-directed changes in interpretation.

Authors also manipulate the logical status of reader roles by parceling out information within a narrative text: they build common ground by virtue of linguistic copresence. Under ordinary circumstances, authors have complete control over what readers are allowed to know and at what times (prior knowledge only can come from outside the narrative world). Authors, that is, pick and choose the instances at which readers will knowingly or unknowingly be side-participants or overhearers. Consider this interchange, also from Cunningham's *A Home at the End of the World*. The "I" here is a character named Clare:

> "Sure you don't want some wine?" Bobby asked. I shook my head.
> "I'm going on the wagon for a little while," I said. "Maybe she could bring me a club soda or something."
> (p. 220)

At first readers must take Clare's claim that she's going on the wagon at face value. Shortly (roughly half a page later), however, she makes a mental confession:

> I was over two months' pregnant. I hadn't told anyone. I wasn't sure what I wanted to do about it.

With this information in hand, readers can reinterpret Clare's original utterance to see that it gave a mistaken impression of her motivation. Just briefly, then, Cunningham cast the readers in the role of overhearers. The original utterance, "I'm going on the wagon for a little while," was designed so that part of its intended import was obscured for lack of common ground. Only with Clare's further revelation could readers know that they had initially been placed in the position of an overhearer.

Under other circumstances, readers will understand at once that speakers have excluded them from some aspects of meaning. When, in fact, speakers (and thus authors) design utterances that provide "less than full disclosure with the tacit cooperation of the participants" (Clark and Carlson, 1982, p. 365), these speech acts are called *partial informatives*. Recall the suspense situations I illustrated in chapter 3. When readers of *A Confederacy of Dunces* learn that "from almost one to three every afternoon George was stuck with the packages" (p. 269), John Kennedy Toole is treating them not as if they were overhearers but, rather, as if they had agreed to cooperate in being partially informed. In real life, of course, we can demand full disclosure. When we read, to cooperate largely means not skipping ahead to see how the suspense is resolved.

From time to time, authors create situations that almost literally cast readers in the role of overhearers. Consider an excerpt from another of Eudora Welty's short stories, "Why I Live at the P.O.":

> Just then something perfectly horrible occurred to me. "Mama," I says, "can that child talk?" I simply had to whisper! "Mama, I wonder if that child can be—you know—in any way? Do you realize," I says, "that she hasn't spoken one single, solitary word to a human being up to this minute? This is the way she looks," I says, and I looked like this. (pp. 98–99)

The experience of this passage is like overhearing a conversation with one's back turned. We have no hope of knowing what it meant for the speaker to look "like this." Welty could not have been unaware that readers would not be able to come to a precise understanding. Even so, this example could be analyzed either as a partial informative directed toward a participant or as an utterance designed to exclude an overhearer. I cite it to emphasize, once again, how quickly a reader's logical identity shifts in the experience of a narrative. All is well until "and I looked like this." At that point, readers are forced to give up their side-participant stance and, if they so choose, to speculate about exactly how the child might look.

My discussion thus far has focused on the way authors make assumptions about common ground to design their utterances. I do not mean to suggest, even so, that authors are not at a great disadvantage with respect to speakers in ordinary conversation. As I observed earlier, an important reason that authors can only *believe* that they have successfully communicated their intentions is that they are unable to obtain any moment-by-moment feedback from their addressees. In ordinary conversation, speakers and addressees are mutually responsible for making sure that each utterance has been understood (see Clark and Schaefer, 1989; Clark and Wilkes-Gibbs, 1986; Schober and Clark, 1989). The buildup of meaning is collaborative: speakers proffer utterances, and addressees must tacitly or explicitly provide confirmation that they have understood the utterances. (Side-participants are also expected to ask for clarification or signal acceptance through their silence.)

This process of collaboration has been studied most often under circumstances in which speakers must refer to novel objects (see Clark and Wilkes-Gibbs, 1986; Krauss and Glucksberg, 1969, 1977; Krauss and Weinheimer, 1964, 1966, 1967; Schober and Clark, 1989). In the following excerpt, for example, the director (D) is trying to give a description that will enable the matcher (M) to identify one of a group of tangram figures (Schober and Clark, 1989, pp. 216–17; asterisks indicate overlapping speech in adjacent turns; periods indicate a brief pause):

D: Then number 12 . is (laughs) looks like a, a dancer or something really weird. Um . and, has a square head . and um, there's like, there's uh- the kinda this um .

M: Which way is the head tilted?

D: The head is . eh- towards the left, and then th- an arm could be like up towards the right?

M: Mm-hm.

D: *And . It's- *

M: *an . a big* fat leg? *You know that one?*

D: *Yeah, a big* fat leg.

M: and a little leg.

D: Right.

M: Okay.

D: Okay?

M: Yeah.

This is the conversation on the first trial. By the sixth and last trial of the experiment, the director needs little effort to refer to this same figure (p. 217):

D: Um, 12 . the dancer with the big fat leg?

M: Okay.

What is critical in Schober and Clark's experiment, however, is that the individual trying to identify the figures actually participated in the negotiation to establish the referring phrase. Schober and Clark included a group of subjects who were overhearers: they heard all the exchanges of the directors and matchers without being able to participate themselves. Although they heard every word spoken, these subjects were much less successful at identifying the figures, implying strongly that the particular collaboration that occurs between speakers and addressees is critical to successful communication.

Schober and Clark's experiments, therefore, suggest that because collaboration between authors and readers is impossible, authors risk not being understood. Even so, I have argued that authors conceptualize their readers as intended participants, not (under most circumstances) as overhearers. What makes understanding particularly difficult for conversational overhearers is that the speaker expends no effort to ensure that the world is being described from a shared perspective. The task of the author, by contrast, is to create that shared perspective. Furthermore, readers are able to review parts of a text that may figure heavily in the way an author establishes meaning. The result often is examples of language use that strongly mimic collaborative products. Consider this series of excerpts from Toni Morrison's novel *Tar Baby* (see Gerrig and Banaji, 1991):

> Fog came to that place in wisps sometimes, like the hair of maiden aunts. Hair so thin and pale it went unnoticed until masses of it gathered around the house and threw back one's own reflection from the windows. The sixty-four bulbs in the dining room chandelier were no more than a rhinestone clip in the hair of the maiden aunts. (p. 62)

> Jadine and Margaret touched their cheeks and temples to dry the places the maiden aunts were kissing. (p. 62)

> The maiden aunts smiled and tossed their maiden aunt hair. (p. 65)

> The maiden aunts, huddled in the corners of the room were smiling in their sleep. (p. 77)

> . . . and now a scream so loud and full of terror it woke the maiden aunts from their sleep in the corners of the room. (p. 78)

Morrison introduces "maiden aunts" with a full description that echoes the earliest turns of the tangram task. The later uses, again in parallel, refer with truncated ease. In no sense have readers negotiated with Morrison in creating this image. But because it depends on linguistic copresence, her language feels like the product of real-life collaboration.

It may be that certain authors—Morrison chief among them—create a sense of intimacy with their readers specifically by modeling the experience of collaboration. Cohen (1979; see also Gibbs and Gerrig, 1989) argued that the use of metaphor presupposes and reinforces a sense of intimacy between speakers and addressees. Because the correct interpretation of a novel metaphor often requires access to specially shared knowledge, each use of a metaphor, according to Cohen, constitutes a kind of "concealed invitation." The hearer must expend "a special effort to accept the invitation," and "this transaction constitutes the acknowledgement of a community" (p. 6). The speaker and (intended) hearers are bound by the shared experience of the image. Although Cohen suggested that the way metaphors function to promote intimacy is unique, Raymond Gibbs and I (Gerrig and Gibbs, 1988; see also Gerrig and Banaji, 1991) have argued that the cultivation of intimacy extends to broader instances of creative language. In table 4.1 I have provided several examples of innovative uses of language (see also Clark, 1983; Clark and Clark, 1979) from fictional and nonfictional works. I do not intend the observation that authors use creative language to be surprising. In everyday conversation, however, intended participants would have the responsibility of confirming that these nonconventional phrases could be understood. With respect to fictional and nonfictional texts, I suggest that the use of such innovations mimics the act of collaboration and draws the readers more strongly into the intimate environs of the narrative world. This is one of the strongest effects authors can achieve by treating readers as side-participants.

I have claimed thus far that authors more often than not conceptualize readers as side-participants. By "more often than not," I mean that authors are, in fact, capable of inventing other roles in which to cast their readers. Often, for example, readers are briefly transformed into overhearers to suit aesthetic purposes. Even so, I wish to make the parallel claim that readers habitually take a side-participant stance with respect to the experience of narratives. Unlike authors, however, who may deliberately consider the ways they are manipulating their audience, I suggest that readers take up the posture of side-participant without conscious deliberation. In discussing Clark and Carlson's (1982) analysis of hearer roles, I extended their observations to conclude

TABLE 4.1
Innovative Language from Fiction and Nonfiction

1. *Manhattan '45,* Jan Morris
[The slums of New York were] bursting most of all with people, especially in hot weather, when [some would be] hilariously hosing themselves, if young enough, from the corner fire hydrant—hardly a book of photographs of Manhattan in the 1940s is complete without its statutory **hydrant children.** (pp. 163–64)

2. *A Bad Man Is Easy to Find,* M. J. Verlaine
They usually met for a fast one, while Cary was on his break and Peter between the office and the city night: the new-wave dandy and the cop in his blues **greasy-spooning** in the West Fifties amid a storm of prostitutes and browsers, tourists and trash, residents and professional intruders. (p. 142)

3. *You'll Never Eat Lunch in This Town Again,* Julia Phillips
Excited, I **Mario Andretti** to the Marina. (p. 366)
She thought about community responsibility, and should she call the cops, and then she **Kitty Genovesed** the situation. (p. 599)

4. *A Confederacy of Dunces,* John Kennedy Toole
She was wearing her short pink topper and the small red hat that tilted over one eye so that she looked like a refugee starlet from the *Golddiggers* film series. Her brown wedgies squeaked with **discount price defiance,** as she walked **redly** and **pinkly** along the broken brick sidewalk. (p. 88)

5. *The Origin of Consciousness in the Breakdown of the Bicameral Mind,* Julian Jaynes
These notions are impossible unless the before and after of time are **metaphored** into a spatial succession. (p. 280)
We are learned in self-doubt, scholars of our very failures, geniuses at excuses and **tomorrowing** our resolves. (p. 403)

6. *Midnight's Children,* Salman Rushdie
And, moving across to Versailles Villa, here is Mrs. Dubash with her shrine to the god Ganesh, stuck in the corner of an apartment of such supernatural untidiness that, in our house, the word "dubash"

TABLE 4.1 (continued)
Innovative Language from Fiction and Nonfiction

became a verb meaning "to make a mess"..."Oh, Saleem you've **dubashed** your room again, you black man!" Mary would cry. (p. 151)

7. *Citizens,* Simon Schama
This local renown made Maillard a trusted figure among the women—as Lafayette was no longer, for there were several murmurs and some shouts that if the general refused their demands, he too should be strong up on the *lanterne.* Maillard cut down the unfortunate Abbe Lefevre, who had been strung up, ready for **lanternization,** on account of his refusing the women guns, and promised to lead their march to Versailles. (p. 461)

8. *Beloved,* Toni Morrison
124 was spiteful. Full of a baby's venom. The women in the house knew it and so did the children. (p. 4)
But this was not a normal woman in a normal house. As soon as he stepped through the red light he knew that, compared to **124,** the rest of the world was bald. (p. 41)
[The number **124** is used throughout the novel to designate the house and its attendant spirits.]

that hearers have vast experience being informed by language that is officially directed at others—a superfluity of experience that enables readers to be so readily transported to narrative worlds.

Although researchers have rarely labeled it as such, much experimentation in psycholinguistics has been directed toward exposing the prodigious skills of side-participants. As Schober and Clark (1989) observed, theories of language use have most frequently been tested by having subjects experience texts for which they were not the intended addressees. In many of the experiments described earlier, subjects read what were in essence brief fictional texts and then reacted in a variety of ways. Although, as Schober and Clark argued, this methodological reality might undercut generalizations that can be made about the experiences of addressees, it provides a wealth of information about the cognitive processes of side-participants.

I will describe one experiment to demonstrate the skill of readers in processing language as side-participants. In this experiment, Gibbs (1986a) explored the time-course with which language users understand sarcastic indirect requests. Consider the following story:

> Tony's roommate always kept the windows open in the living room. He did this even if it was freezing out. Tony kept mentioning this to his roommate but to no avail. Once it was open and Tony wanted his roommate to shut it. Tony couldn't believe that his roommate wasn't cold. He said to him, "Sure is nice and warm in here." (p. 45)

Gibbs expected his subjects to interpret the final utterance to mean "Please close the window" (and, in fact, in the experiment they readily agreed with that paraphrase). In another story, the context yielded a literal interpretation of the same utterance:

> Martha went to her sister's house. It was freezing outside and Martha was glad to be inside. She said to her sister, "Your house is very cozy. Sure is nice and warm in here."

According to a prominent theory of understanding, which Gibbs dubbed the *standard pragmatic model* (see Grice, 1975, 1978; Searle, 1979), the sarcastic indirect request should be very hard to understand. This model presupposes that literal meanings are unfailingly computed first. It should, therefore, take longer to understand a sarcastic indirect request than a literal use of the same utterance. What Gibbs found, rather, was that subjects were reliably faster at understanding the sarcastic indirect requests. He used these data largely to discredit the standard pragmatic model (for reviews see Gibbs, 1984, 1989). I cite them here because I believe they give a strong sense of how efficiently readers process language as side-participants. Although the critical utterances were not addressed to the readers—they were directed to either the roommate or the sister—the readers were able to come to a swift and accurate interpretation of even sarcastic indirect requests. This is solid support for the assertion that readers are talented side-participants.

Side-Participation and Nonfictional Narratives

The side-participant analysis applies equally effectively to readers of nonfiction. Theorists frequently make special claims about fiction by contrast to nonfiction. This was Searle's (1975) method when he introduced the notion of pretense. What these theorists have regularly overlooked is that the felicity conditions for nonfictional assertions are often equally inconvenienced by the circumstances in which readers encounter them—because, as I stressed in chapter 1, a defining feature of the experience of virtually all narratives is that readers are transported away from the here and now. Rarely can the assertions made in nonfictional narratives be verified with respect to immediate experience. Recall the excerpt cited from the *New York Times:*

> Tokyo, Thursday, Jan. 9—President Bush fell suddenly ill and collapsed at a state dinner being given for him Wednesday night at the home of the Japanese Prime Minister. This morning, his spokesman said the President was "up and about" and making phone calls.

Following Searle, we were inclined to accept each of these sentences as felicitous utterances. On some strict reading of "truth," however, this excerpt stopped being true as of January 10, 1992.

The problem is that the deictic references to the particular times "Wednesday night" and "this morning" fail to refer correctly unless the reader takes the original circumstances of the utterances into account (for a similar analysis, see Bruce, 1981). Readers can suppose that in writing this article Wines designed these utterances to be read on January 9th. At a later date, readers must construct a narrative world in which they act *as if* they were reading the article on that date. Searle's original *New York Times* example also included a deictic expression (from an article by Eileen Shanahan, December 15, 1972):

> Washington, Dec. 14—A group of federal, state, and local government officials rejected today President Nixon's idea that the federal government provide the financial aid that would permit local governments to reduce property taxes.

The events from this article now constitute history, yet readers have no difficulty understanding the passage with its reference to "today," even though they must work (if they so choose) to fill in much of the context themselves. Specifically, the article presupposes knowledge that would no longer be readily available to average readers. The readers have gone from being bona fide side-participants to something less (that is, Shanahan presumably didn't design her utterances with an eye to history). But none of this feels exceptional to the readers: what we are seeing is that readers are able to construct narrative worlds for true events that fail to match current circumstances. Searle (1975) suggested that fictional discourse works because of the suspension of "the normal operation of rules relating illocutionary acts and the world" (p. 326). Clearly, some aspects of these rules must also be suspended to create an appropriate understanding of what George Bush did "this morning" or government officials did "today."

This unity between fiction and nonfiction applies to only one of the two ways fiction can be said to depart from the here and now. Fiction and nonfiction are not unified at the level of the nonapplicability of fictional assertions to the real world. I have been emphasizing, instead, the second type of departure, the one that is encoded in the side-participant stance: readers must be able to construct a context—different from the here and now—that enables them to understand the fictional text. The distinction boils down to knowing that no one named Sherlock Holmes really lived on Baker Street and yet also knowing that Holmes would not seriously utter, "I have never played the violin." Although authors of nonfiction may intend all characters genuinely to exist (unless they announce otherwise), readers of nonfiction must nonetheless almost always depart from the here and now to construct a context for comprehension.

I will try to establish the generality of this parallel by examining a nonfictional passage that has no explicit date. Consider the beginning of a firsthand account of the storming of the Winter Palace in St. Petersburg on November 7, 1917, written by the journalist John Reed (from Carey, 1987, p. 480):

> Like a black river, filling all the street, without song or cheer we poured through the Red Arch, where the man just ahead of me said in a low voice, "Look out, comrades! Don't trust them. They will fire, surely!" In the open we began to run, stooping low and bunching together, and jammed up suddenly behind the pedestal of the Alexander Column.

As with the newspaper articles, readers (presumably) believe that Reed's utterances were intended to be felicitous in the context in which they were uttered. Once again, however, readers must come to an understanding of these utterances in circumstances well removed from that context. Reed, like authors of fiction, is informing us about a world to which we have no immediate access. This is no less true because the world in question was, at one time, real. Some theorists have made too much of the fact that statements in nonfiction can be verified against the real world (see, for example, Adams, 1985). As Pratt (1977) pointed out, authors of nonfiction are not routinely available to defend their assertions while their works are being read. What this means, in particular, is that all the issues of common ground and noncollaboration that are active for fiction are equally pressing for nonfiction. Pratt, in fact, staked out an extreme case: "Without the slightest hint of infelicity, I can recount an anecdote I heard from someone else whose name I can't remember to an audience I don't know about events I didn't witness that happened somewhere I've never been" (p. 94). Here, the parallel between the experience of fiction and of nonfiction is compelling, and the one remaining difference—that someone at some time vouched for the authenticity of the nonfictional narrative—appears to matter much less. In each case, readers adopt the side-participant roles that authors intended for them.

My claim that readers ordinarily adopt a side-participant stance when they experience a narrative does not in any way limit the activities they might carry out. Literary critics, for example, often uncover themes or properties of a work that may not have been consciously intended by the author. Such was the case when Holland (1988) dissected the "brain of Robert Frost" or when Freud (1901/1965) exposed oedipal themes in *Hamlet*. Under these circumstances, I suggest that the readers have adopted a stance closer to that of the overhearer. That is, they act as if speakers (in this case, authors) are trying to camouflage some aspects of meaning. This perspective appears to capture nicely the philosophy underlying much literary analysis, both in the sense that authors might purposely conceal meanings, and also that meanings might be hidden from the authors themselves through the agency of unconscious forces. My position, therefore, is not that readers cannot or do not bring a range of analytic techniques to the experience of narratives—they can and do. Rather, I believe that everything but the side-participant stance is optional.

To close this section, let me revisit the idea I introduced in chapter 1, namely, that narratives project *narratees* or *mock readers*. I reviewed evidence that real readers are often self-evidently not the real addressees of the utterances of a narrative. Furthermore, narratives often contain hints as to the type of person meant to experience a work, and, as Gibson (1980) put it, "if we cannot assume [that set of attitudes and qualities which the language asks us to assume] we throw the book away" (p. 1). This framework obtains renewed vigor within the informative analysis. I have suggested throughout this chapter that authors encode their intentions with respect to assumptions about the knowledge—including "attitudes and qualities"—they expect to be in common ground for their intended side-participants. Exactly as Gibson suggested, narrative works often retain explicit clues about these assumptions. Readers have the opportunity to throw away any book in which they are not willing to participate.

A Comparison to Alternative Theories

To refine further the claim that readers most often function as side-participants, I will contrast it with earlier speech-act and anti-speech-act treatments of the author-reader relationship. What should emerge is that my particular speech-act analysis is anchored in aspects of language use that are solidly in effect outside the realm of narrative.

My suggestion that readers can be conceptualized as side-participants strongly presupposes that authors have specific intentions about the meanings they wish to share with those readers. I claim that the chief goal of reading is to recover the author's intended meanings in performing the utterances of a narrative. (I am using *reading* as the name of the activity readers perform before they begin to reorder their goals in response to particular critical theories.) In his seminal theory, Grice (1957, 1968) proposed that meaning is carried by *reflexive intentions:* to say that a speaker meant something by uttering *p* is to say that the speaker intended the utterance of *p* to produce an effect on the addressee by virtue of the addressee's recognition of that intention. Note that nothing in this formulation presupposes the perfect transmission of meaning. Speakers are surely capable of fashioning utterances for which addressees will fail to recognize the appropriate reflexive intention. Speakers may, in fact, aim to have their intentions be obscure. Even so, Grice's formulation captures speakers' and addressees' expectations about the type of behavior in which they are participating. Addressees (and thus side-participants and readers) are inevitably drawn toward the activity of attempting to recover speakers' (and authors') reflexive intentions.

Much of the distress in treating readers as the objects of an author's intentions along Gricean lines has arisen because utterances performed in narratives are often unambiguously *not* addressed to the reader. The most obvious cases are instances of dialogue in which the addressee is named within the narrative world. When Eudora Welty's Leota says, "Reach in my purse and git me a cigarette with no powder in it if you kin, Mrs. Fletcher, honey," she in no sense addresses the reader. Such utterances cannot, furthermore, be treated strictly as pretense because, as Adams (1985) observed, they "function normally" within the fictional world in the sense that characters who make promises are expected to keep those promises in accordance with normative felicity conditions and so on. Rather than accept the duality that fictional utterances are at once pretend and genuine, Adams argues, "The major convention that constitutes fictional discourse is an act performed by the writer, but it is not a speech act and it is not pretended: the writer attributes the words he writes to someone else. In novels this someone is usually called the narrator, and it has been long recognized that the narrator is not the writer but rather a fictional figure that performs the speech acts of the writer's text" (p. 12). Adams's position, unfortunately, fails to account for many of the effects authors achieve independent of their narrators. Booth (1974) presents cases in which an author indulges in irony at the narrator's expense:

> "You could hear a bomb drop," says the narrator of James Thurber's "You Could Look It Up" concerning a moment of complete silence. "Well, I'll own up that I enjoyed wearin' the soup and fish and minglin' amongst the high polloi and pretendin' we really was somebody," the narrator of Ring Lardner's "Gullible's Travels" says, early in the story. Taken by themselves the confusion of pins with bombs and the double error about *hoi polloi* might conceivably mean that Thurber and Lardner are themselves ignorant of standard expressions: not ironic, just ignorant. But in a context of other "incredible" errors, probabilities become certainties: Thurber and Lardner are communicating with us from behind their narrators' backs. (pp. 57–58)

If authors can communicate "from behind their narrators' backs," we won't get very far by attributing all the authors' intentions to the narrator. Booth's examples reinforce the conclusion that writers are performing genuine communicative acts. My suggestion is that those acts are informatives and that readers are the object of authors' intentions not as addressees but as sideparticipants.

This type of claim is still not uncontroversial. In fact, Walton (1983, 1990) has reached the conclusion that any evocation of intentional acts to analyze narrative language is misguided. He argues that "our primary interest in stories is not an interest in their role as vehicles of *persons'* storytelling. I see no reason not to say that the basic concept of a *story*—and the basic concept of *fiction*—attach to works rather than to human actions" (1983, p. 86). Two lines of argument lead Walton to this conclusion. First, he suggests that theories of the experience of fiction that make reference to speech acts (he takes Searle's [1975] pretense theory to be representative) cannot be extended to fiction outside the verbal domain. As he put it, "Renoir's painting, *Bathers,* and Jacques Lipchitz's sculpture, *Guitar Player,* are surely works of fiction. But I doubt very much that in creating them Renoir and Lipchitz were pretending to make assertions (or to perform other illocutionary acts)" (p. 82). Walton makes quite clear with this argument that it is of primary importance to him to give a unified account of the experience of *fiction.* Walton's taxonomy effects an unbridgeable divide between fiction and nonfiction. Unfortunately, as I will continue to argue, by letting fiction be his most important taxonomic distinction, Walton gathers together categories of experience that are supported by considerably different mental acts. Consider the strong contrast Walton himself (for example, 1990, pp. 293–304) makes between *descriptions* and *depictions.* Imagine a description of the scene in Meindert Hobbema's painting *The Water Mill with the Great Red Roof* versus the painting itself, which depicts that scene. Walton argues convincingly that the description does not prompt readers to imagine that they are actually viewing the scene, whereas the painting does. Any cognitive psychological theory would suggest, along the same lines, that information is acquired in different fashions from the description and the depiction. What Walton is denying, by trying to achieve theoretical unity at the level of fiction, is exactly those cognitive psychological differences. He thus provides strong arguments against his own taxonomy.

Let me press this point by considering the second type of evidence Walton adduces against speech-act theories. He begins by imagining a situation in which the naturally occurring cracks in a rock might by "pure coincidence" spell out the words "It is raining in Singapore (p. 85)." Walton argues that anyone reading these words and knowing that they occurred through natural forces would not believe that there was rain in Singapore. This analysis is in accord with speech-act theory, which insists upon a speaker who can provide evidence for an assertion. Walton, however, provides a second case to show why speech-act theory fails for fiction: "Contrast a naturally occurring 'story,' cracks in a rock, let us say, which spell out the words, 'Once upon a time . . . ,' and so on. The realization that the inscription was not made or used by a person to tell a story need not prevent us from reading and enjoying the story in much the way we would if it were told by someone. It may be entrancing, suspenseful, spellbinding; we may laugh and cry" (p. 86). To this hypothetical situation, I respond that it is the reader who chooses to treat the marks as fiction (see Currie, 1986; Lamarque, 1991). So far, I believe Walton would agree: he argued against eliminating the acts of the creator, not the acts of the reader, from consideration in a theory of fiction.

We part company, however, with respect to the contrast between "It is raining in Singapore" and "Once upon a time." Walton argues that the former is not a genuine assertion, but that the latter is a genuine story—but these are two very different levels of analysis. "It is raining in Singapore" could be taken as a very brief story, and "Once upon a time" as a sequence of infelicitous assertions (that is, of course, exactly Searle's [1975] suggestion). What sets the examples apart, even so, is that seemingly in the single-sentence case a reader would be able to take special care to remember that nothing about the use of the language ought to be taken as genuine; whereas in the story case, the reader would be overwhelmed by its story-ness and be unable to remain immune to its effects. If this is true, it is only because the story very much resembles all the stories the reader has encountered in the past, so the reader is compelled—automatically, unreflexively—to treat it in a similar fashion. What I am arguing, in essence, is that a reader, even of cracks on a rock, is not prepared to keep in mind while reading that the story is "unintended": knowledge of the unintendedness of the story cannot penetrate the moment-by-moment experience of the narrative world. To bring the knowledge of unintendedness to mind is to exit the narrative world. I am most certain of this claim because under ordinary circumstances readers will never have cause to question that each utterance is intended sincerely as an informative. In Walton's terms, I am suggesting that one of the unchangeable rules of the games of make-believe readers play with respect to texts—unchangeable because this rule is an inherent property of the cognitive processes that enable readers to play the games— is that side-participation is intended.

Other elements of Walton's theory come close to replicating details of the analysis of fictional utterances as informatives. One of the questions Walton (1978a, 1990) addressed is in what sense speakers can be taken to be speaking truthfully when they make an assertion such as "Tom Sawyer attended his own funeral." The difficulty with such an utterance, as has been recognized in a great variety of theoretical treatments (see Crittenden, 1991, for a review), is that Tom Sawyer did not exist in the real world so that (it seems that) an assertion to the effect that he attended his own funeral cannot be true in the real world—although it strikes most readers as a true statement (by contrast, for example, to "Tom Sawyer saved Desdemona from death by Othello's hand"). Walton's way out of this dilemma is to suggest that "it might be plausible to regard [the speaker] as *both* pretending to assert that Tom actually attended his own funeral and at the same time actually asserting that *fictionally* it is the case. . . . In pretending (seriously) to assert something one is likely to use the very same words one would choose if one were not just pretending" (1978a, p. 20). Although Walton is making this claim with respect to commentators, it parallels the informative analysis for authors. The utterances Mark Twain performed to make it true in the fiction that "Tom Sawyer attended his own funeral" are as accurately characterized as both pretend assertion and genuine informative as is any commentator's summary statement of those fictional circumstances.

One of the virtues of the informative analysis of narrative utterances, I believe, is that it makes a straightforward division between what is serious and nonserious about authors' utterances while avoiding any overtones of moral judgment. I am trying to avoid an ambiguity in the word *serious* that has plagued discussions of speech-act approaches to fiction since Austin (1962) made it the cornerstone of his original formulation. Austin defined uses of language in fiction as *nonserious:* "A performative utterance will, for example, be *in a peculiar way* hollow or void if said by an actor on the stage, or if introduced in a poem, or spoken in soliloquy.... Language in such circumstances is in special ways—intelligibly—used not seriously, but *parasitic* upon its normal use.... All this we are *excluding* from consideration" (p. 22). Commentators have all too often taken "nonserious" as an evaluation of the effect of the utterance rather than as a statement of the author's intentions (for a review, see Graff, 1981). This distinction, in fact, reproduces one of the oldest problems in the study of fiction: How can assertions within fictional worlds have consequences in the real world? How is it, that is, that nonserious utterances can have serious implications? Searle (1975) openly acknowledges that "serious (i.e., nonfictional) speech acts can be conveyed by fictional texts, even though the conveyed speech act is not represented in the text. Almost any important work of fiction conveys a 'message' or 'messages' which are conveyed *by* the text but are not *in* the text" (p. 332). But he also admits that "there is as yet no general theory of the mechanisms by which serious illocutionary intentions are conveyed by pretended illocutions" (p. 332). (I evaluate solutions to this problem in chapter 6. For now, I wish only to expose this "serious" ambiguity.)

Searle (1977) asserts in a later article that Austin intended no slight by labeling fictional language as nonserious or parasitic: he was not "claiming that there is something bad or anomalous or not 'ethical' about such discourse" (p. 205). Rather, the distinction between serious and nonserious discourse was an element of Austin's research strategy. He believed that an account of language use in circumstances of serious use must logically precede an application to nonserious discourse. Austin believed that, ultimately, such an application would be possible. Searle (1977) suggested that his essay "The Logical Status of Fictional Discourse" fulfilled that promissory note.

Searle's defense of Austin was occasioned by Jacques Derrida's (1977a) whirlwind rejection of the speech-act program. Derrida expresses a number of objections, but perhaps the most telling is the great difficulty in determining how to draw a boundary between serious and nonserious language (see Pavel, 1981, 1986, for similar concerns). The virtual conclusion of his second essay on the topic is this (1977b, p. 251):

I promised (very) sincerely to be serious. Have I kept my promise? Have I taken Sarl [*sic*] seriously? I do not know if I was supposed to. Should I have? Were they themselves serious in their speech acts? Shall I say that I am afraid they were? Would that mean that I do not take their seriousness very seriously?

Derrida has proved, both as a point of theory and in practice, that speakers, and authors, can be obscure as to their intentions. (Derrida is not always this immoderate; see Fish, 1989.) This demonstration, however, in no way undermines the claim that hearers, and readers, obligatorily strive to recover unique intentions. Within literary criticism, for example, it has often been controversial whether an author's intentions should matter in the determination of the meaning of a text. Derrida appears to argue strongly that they should not. Graff (1981) summarizes the general position and then exposes its great insularity: "Some critics of intentionalism have argued that it is irrelevant whether the meanings we apprehend in the text are intended by the author or not, but this view does not seem to me to square with the actual behavior of readers, who in fact worry a good deal about whether or not they are connecting with the author's purposes" (p. 149). Graff's intuition closely matches the psycholinguistic gestalt for theories of "actual behavior": Derrida might wish to reform the rules of "reading," but he cannot legislate cognitive processes out of existence.

What Derrida has offered can, in fact, be conceptualized as cognitive analogs to perceptual illusions. Most such perceptual illusions arise because our sensory or cognitive processes can be made to yield nonveridical inferences. These illusions help define the classes of perceptual experiences that have most preferentially influenced our evolution (see, for example, Rock, 1983). Although knowledge of these illusions can provide an important impetus to theory building, their existence fails to deconstruct the overall veridicality of moment-by-moment perception—and perceivers' "actual behavior" safely presupposes veridical perception. Derrida has demonstrated circumstances under which our cognitive processes may deliver nonveridical "intentions." We can, once again, use these examples as theoretical touchstones, but they undermine neither the probability nor the expectation of veridical recovery of meaning.

The informative analysis is intended, in any case, to recognize that authors are performing serious acts with every utterance (or, at least, readers take that to be the case). This aspect of the analysis speaks to another type of uneasiness that Austin's use of "nonserious" has provoked. By characterizing fictional utterances as nonserious, Austin appeared to suggest that such uses of language fall beyond the bounds of ordinary recovery of reflexive intentions. Readers are expressly not meant to recognize that authors intend fictional assertions to reflect accurately defensible truths about the world. Theorists have generally attempted to bring fictional utterances back into the ordinary language fold by motivating the existence of companion speechacts that silently accompany acts of pretense while providing a vehicle for reflexive intentions. (My invocation of informatives fits this schema.)

Currie (1985, 1990; see also McCormick, 1988) argued that "the author of fiction intends that the reader make-believe *P*, where *P* is the sentence or string of sentences he utters. And he intends that the reader shall come to make-believe *P* partly as a result of his recognition that the author intends him to do so" (1985, p. 387). Genette (1990) arrives at a similar conclusion by developing an analogy between fictional utterances and declarations: "Declarations are speech acts by which the utterer, by virtue of the power vested in him, brings about some change in the world" (p. 307). According to Genette, fictional utterances produce such changes. With respect to a story that begins "Once upon a time there was a little girl living with her mother near a forest," the author's speech act can be paraphrased as "I, author, hereby decided fictionally, by adapting both the words to the world and the world to the words and without fulfilling any sincerity condition (without believing it or asking you [that is, the reader] to believe it), that p (that a little girl, and so on)" (p. 63). The author declares that he or she wishes "to arouse in your [the reader's] mind the fictional story of a little girl, and so on" (p. 66). Currie and Genette, therefore, both suggest that readers must recognize an author's intentions to get them to perform certain mental acts. Those acts are serious by contrast to the pretend products of the acts. My main concern with these theories is the now-familiar one that they invoke special mental activities associated only with the experience of fiction. Both theories need a discontinuity between fiction and nonfiction to explain how fictional utterances have force, yet there is no apparent discontinuity in the cognitive processes. In the informative analysis, by contrast, the "serious" aspects of fictional utterances emerge by virtue of cognitive processes that are common to all instances—fictional and nonfictional—of side-participation.

Within the Informative Analysis

In this final section, I narrow my attention from the general theory of side-participation to more-specific phenomena of language use in narratives. In my description of the informative analysis, I made repeated reference to the way authors' intentions—and readers' recovery of those intentions—are filtered through allocations of knowledge. Here, I consider in more detail some of the effects authors can achieve by exploiting dissociations of knowledge. In part, I wish to show how specific topics of language use can be explicated within the more general theory of informative acts.

In crafting their stories, authors often present readers with complex arrangements of shared and unshared knowledge. Recall the situation in Michael Cunningham's *A Home at the End of the World* in which readers are let in on the secret that the character Clare is pregnant (which prompts a reinterpretation of her abstinence from liquor). The readers, in fact, are informed of Clare's state long before the characters in the novel are. For several pages, Clare suffers from morning sickness. Because she and her companions are sightseeing on a long drive east from Arizona, she at first suggests, "Maybe I'm allergic to national monuments," then passes it off as "just some little bug" (p. 246). In this case, Clare's utterances have extra import that is shared by the reader but denied to the other characters. In other circumstances, readers may come to understand that a character's words have a greater impact than even that character knows. In *Othello*, for example, the villain Iago skillfully manipulates contexts so that innocent utterances take on unintended meanings with tragic consequences. The audience watches as Iago advances his plot to make Othello believe that Desdemona has been unfaithful with Cassio. Each time Desdemona tries to arrange a reconciliation between Othello and Cassio by noting his virtues—"You'll never meet a more sufficient man" (3.4.95)—she unknowingly contributes to Iago's plot. The audience, however, understands exactly how she is hastening her own demise. When, toward the end of the play, she laments to Othello,

> Upon my knees, what doth your speech import?
> I understand a fury in your words,
> But not the words. (4.2.31–33)

the audience does understand Othello's words. To appreciate the intense irony of these scenes, readers must be able to monitor which characters are in possession of what knowledge at what times. Readers cannot simply interpret an utterance with respect to the information they have acquired but must also determine what effect the utterance would have on others with differing samples of knowledge. Dexterity at this task is another skill honed in conversation that readers bring to the experience of narratives. It is exactly the experience of designing utterances with respect to common ground—and, in doing so, defining addressees, side-participants, and overhearers—that allows readers to be prepared for the experience of narratives.

Authors have devised a variety of techniques for parceling out knowledge and may inform readers of particular information at a number of junctures within the experience of a narrative. Sometimes the title of a work will give away important information, as in the case of Jay Cantor's novel *The Death of Che Guevara*. No inhabitant of the fictional world can share the reader's great confidence that Guevara is heading toward his death within the time frame of the novel, so the work is deeply ironic. Within a book, it is often the major responsibility and privilege of the narrator to reveal to readers information that may or may not be shared with characters within the work (which is to say that authors often make narrators the agents of their informatives). As I noted earlier, however, with examples borrowed from Booth (1974), authors sometimes achieve irony at the expense of their narrators. Narrators, furthermore, are often deficient in a number of ways (see Booth, 1983) so that part of what a reader must come to know—part of the knowledge an author can choose to share—is in what ways the information acquired from the narrator should be kept at a distance. Readers are also responsible for sorting out what they ought to believe of the information acquired directly from the characters themselves and what portion of that information has been withheld from or shared with other characters.

Readers also are often made privy, in a variety of ways (see Cohn, 1978), to the thoughts and feelings of various characters. Because language users are typically not mind readers, readers have much less experience with this source of information in day-to-day conversation. Even so, authors are able to use characters' thoughts to establish dissociations between what the characters profess and what they truly believe. And so on: I do not intend this catalog to be complete. My aim in compiling even this partial list is to illustrate the impressive range of demands authors can put on readers' ability to monitor who possesses what information at what times.

This catalog of possible sources for knowledge dissociations makes tacit reference to the concept of *layers*. By differentiating what an author might know from what narrators and characters might know, I was suggesting that a nested structure of shared information exists within a typical narrative. My admission that the catalog was incomplete was mandated in part by Bruce's (1981) analysis, in which he provides several elegant examples of multiple levels of social interaction within otherwise unexceptionable stories. (I am using Clark's [1987] term "layer" rather than Bruce's "level" because I prefer the image of one layer being laid upon another.) In Washington Irving's story about Rip Van Winkle, Bruce detects several layers: "Rip Van Winkle tells a story to his fellow villagers, a county justice, and also to Diedrich Knickerbocker. Knickerbocker writes the story; Irving discovers it and transmits it to us. I enjoy reading the story and appreciate the novelty of the format" (p. 276). More formally, Bruce proposes five layers (p. 277):

Level 0: The real author, Washington Irving, communicates with the real reader.

Level 1: The implied author writes to the implied reader.

Level 2: Diedrich Knickerbocker writes his "history" for his implied reader.

Level 3: Rip Van Winkle tells his story to Diedrich Knickerbocker.

Level 4: Characters in Rip Van Winkle's story tell stories to each other.

With this unexceptional example, Bruce has shown how far authors can multiply layers without making any purposeful effort to confound the reader.

Often authors compact the layering of experience into brief moments within a narrative. In his book *Self-Consciousness,* for example, John Updike manufactures a richly layered world virtually within a single sentence. A chapter entitled "A Letter to My Grandsons" begins, "Dear Anoff and Kwame" (p. 164). Within the chapter (that is, within the letter), Updike relates this anecdote:

At a low time in my life, when I had taken an exit not from my profession but from my marriage, and left your mother and her siblings more in harm's way than felt right, my mother in the midst of her disapproval and sadness produced a saying so comforting I pass it on to you. She sighed and said, "Well, Grampy used to say, 'We carry our own hides to market.' " (p. 211)

Within the experience of the letter (which has already contributed one or two layers), readers must create a layer in which the narrator's mother exists as a speaker, and beneath that the layer in which "Grampy" exists. The multilayering here appears to put the grandchildren into almost simultaneous contact with three or four generations of their family (or, at least, the text informs the reader of this possibility). What this example makes evident, in any case, is how regularly authors include other voices—other intellects—within their narratives. That is the essence of layering.

Developmental research suggests that language users acquire the ability to produce layered stories at a remarkably early age. In a longitudinal study, Wolf and Hicks (1989) demonstrated that children as young as three produce stories that are already richly layered. Their study traced the growth in storytelling ability of children between the ages of one and seven. In children about age three, Wolf and Hicks began to see stories that contained three different layers: a narrative layer through which children provided the skeleton of the story, a layer of dialogue through which the children allowed their characters to speak, and a layer of stage-managing through which the children directly discussed features of the narrative with their audience. The children's stories emerged in *replica-play:* They "played out sequences of events using small toys as actors and turning floors or kitchen tables into theatres" (p. 334). Consider the beginning of a story told by Heather, aged three years and five months (p. 331). The narrative layer is given in plain type; the dialogue layer in italics; stage-managing in boldface:

> (H. plays with a king, queen, and a princess doll, walking
>   each along a table.)
> once upon a time the baby and the mommy and the daddy
> they walked through the forest to find a house and said
> *there's a porch*
> (H. puts the king in the porch, but has trouble fitting the
>   queen in) and then the baby said
> *there's not room enough*
> (H. looks to adult)
> **there's not enough room in this house**
> **can you make the porch bigger**
> **people won't fit in the porch**

Even at age three, Heather is able to enrich her story through a layered presentation of multiple voices. Between the ages of three and six, children become more adept at differentiating voices through linguistic devices. For example, by age four, a child named Jeannie is able to put her narrative layer in the past tense ("they came and heard him and they were his friends," p. 341) and her characters' voices in the present tense ("me too Mommy," "he sure is ugly," p. 340). Jeannie also changes the sound of her voice to perform the roles of a baby and a hippo. Between ages five and six, children achieve, in Wolf and Hicks's term, true *plurifunctionality:* they are able to use each layer "to portray speech, to describe events, to offer commentary" (p. 331). At this point, they are able to present speech indirectly within the narrative layer and to propel the story forward within the dialogue layer. Thus, at an extraordinarily young age, children have great productive control over the use of layering within narrative worlds.

Narratives of multiple layers provide fertile ground for ironic effects. I now focus on irony to examine how shared and un-shared knowledge is monitored in the moment-by-moment experience of narratives. I choose as my definition of irony the one proposed by Fowler (1965) in his *Dictionary of Modern English Usage:*

> Irony is a form of utterance that postulates a double audience, consisting of one party that hearing shall hear and shall not understand, and another party that, when more is meant than meets the ear, is aware both of that more and of the outsiders' incomprehension. . . . [Irony] may be defined as the use of words intended to convey one meaning to the uninitiated part of the audience and another to the initiated, the delight of it lying in the secret intimacy set up between the latter and the speaker. (pp. 305–06)

Fowler's definition captures the experience of being part of the audience that understands the reality underlying Clare's or Desdemona's words and deeds. The readers can feel privileged with respect to the characters who are not in the know. In fact, most treatments of irony incorporate the intuition that there is something "to get," but not all readers will get it. As Booth (1974) put it in his *Rhetoric of Irony,* "There is reason to believe that most of us think we are less vulnerable to mistakes with irony than we are. If we have enjoyed many ironies and observed less experienced readers making fools of themselves, we can hardly resist flattering ourselves for making our way pretty well. But the truth is that even highly sophisticated readers often go astray" (p. 1). The major difficulty in the perception of irony is that speakers (and authors) are not supposed to risk tipping their hand. If an important purpose of irony is to exclude, then speakers must cut common ground as closely as possible to achieve maximal effect. Obvious irony often shades into sarcasm which, in Fowler's terms, has the explicit aim of inflicting pain on an obvious victim—whereas the members of an irony's excluded audience, under this system, are not intended to know they have been victimized. Without this knowledge, the victims of irony may never even attempt to recover the true meaning. Along the lines of Fowler's definition, speakers of ironies almost inevitably perform infelicitous utterances because in most circumstances the expressed proposition will not accurately reflect the speaker's true intentions. To account for these infelicities, Herbert Clark and I (Clark and Gerrig, 1984; see also Grice, 1978) suggested that speakers are engaging in a sort of pretense:

> Suppose S is speaking to A, the primary addressee, and to A', who may be present or absent, real or imaginary. In speaking ironically, S is pretending to be S' speaking to A'. What S' is saying is, in one way or another, patently uninformed or injudicious. . . . A' in ignorance, is intended to miss the pretense, to take S as speaking sincerely. But A, as part of the "inner circle" (to use Fowler's phrase) is intended to see everything—the pretense, S''s injudiciousness, A''s ignorance, and hence S's attitude toward S', A', and what S' said. (p. 122)

Note that this definition covers only those speakers who intend to be ironic. We wouldn't, of course, want to say that Desdemona's utterances are pretense when she speaks highly of Cassio. Iago has, instead, manipulated the context so that Othello perceives an inner circle of which Desdemona isn't even aware. Note, also, that our evocation of pretense differs from that of Searle (1975), who suggested that authors of fictions indulge in the type of pretense that presupposes no intention to deceive. With irony, speakers adhere to both types of pretense. They do, in fact, intend to deceive some segments of their audience. Even so, the hypothesized nondeceptive use of pretense that is common to both accounts suggests that Searle was incorrect to associate readers' recognition of pretense with dissolution of the rules that relate illocutionary acts and the world. Although speakers of irony indulge in pretense, there is no presumption that they do not intend, by doing so, to perform illocutionary acts that have bearing on the world.

The pretense theory was framed largely in response to theories of irony that failed to make appropriate reference to common ground. The *mention theory* of irony (see Jorgensen, Miller, and Sperber, 1984; Sperber and Wilson, 1981) asserts that speakers are not *using* the literal meanings of ironic utterances but rather *mentioning* them—and expressing attitudes toward them—as echoes of earlier speakers. It suggests that when a speaker makes an utterance such as "See what lovely weather it is: rain, rain, rain!" (Jorgensen, Miller, and Sperber, p. 115), she is echoing a weather bureau report and expressing disdain toward the original claim. Mention theory unfortunately fails to account directly for ironies that rely on distributions of knowledge (an omission Sperber [1984] neglects to redress). Consider, once more, Clare's utterance "Maybe I'm allergic to national monuments." Although Clare (by performing this utterance in real-life circumstances) would surely intend it to be ironic, there is no obvious source that she is echoing, nor is it clear what attitude she would be expressing were there an obvious source. It does, on the other hand, seem natural to describe Clare as indulging in pretense. Although Clark's and my pretense analysis of irony does not exhaust the situations that might be described as ironic (see Williams, 1984), it does appear to capture the major act of invention speakers perform when intending their ironies.

What remains to be explicated, however, is how members of the inner circle—the addressees and side-participants—are able to determine that what the speaker said is not exactly what he or she meant and that other hearers would not come to this realization. Traditional theories of irony have often made the determination of ironic meaning appear rather straightforward. Searle (1979) asserts that in making an ironical utterance, "A speaker means the opposite of what he says. Utterance meaning is arrived at by going through sentence meaning and then doubling back to the opposite of sentence meaning" (p. 122; see also Grice, 1975). Searle's definition relies on the distinction between what a sentence means and what a speaker means by uttering that sentence—two types of meaning that clearly diverge in the case of irony. Many instances of irony, however, do not involve any easy "doubling back" from sentence meaning to speaker meaning (see Gibbs, 1984; Sperber and Wilson, 1981). When Clare utters, "I'm going on the wagon for a little while," she doesn't mean "I'm not going on the wagon." The utterance is ironic in the sense that the unknowing are excluded from her true motives. Imagine, similarly, a driver who says to her passenger, "I love people who signal," after being cut off by a driver who has failed to signal (Gibbs, 1984). The driver's utterance is literally true. Irony arises from the way the true statement misapplies in the situation. The passenger is responsible for understanding that the sentiment is true but the use is ironic.

These examples suggest that the understanding of irony requires appreciable sophistication. In fact, empirical research has typically been concerned with specifying the conditions that are best met if addressees are to understand irony easily. Earlier, I described research by Gibbs (1986a) showing that sarcastic indirect requests like "Sure is nice and warm in here" (which was used to mean "Please close the window") were more easily understood than literal uses of the same utterances. Gibbs (1986b) went on to explore the contexts in which sarcasm became more or less comprehensible. (Although this experiment tested sarcasm rather than irony as such, the sarcasm was accomplished via irony. Furthermore, because irony is typically less obvious than sarcasm, difficulty in understanding sarcasm would almost certainly be transferred to irony.) Following Sperber and Wilson's (1981) echoic mention theory, Gibbs suggested that the presence of an explicit antecedent in a story would facilitate comprehension of a sarcastic echo. Consider this story in which the final sarcastic utterance echoes earlier information (Gibbs, 1986b, p. 8):

Gus just graduated from high school and he didn't know what to do. One day he saw an ad about the Navy. It said that the Navy was not just a job, but an adventure. So, Gus joined up. Soon he was aboard a ship doing all sorts of boring things. One day as he was peeling potatoes he said to his buddy, "This sure is an exciting life."

The non-echoic version of the story excluded information about the Navy being an adventure. When this information was absent, readers took more time to understand the utterance "This sure is an exciting life." The antecedent information, in a sense, provided a victim for the sarcasm. Gibbs also confirmed a much-observed asymmetry in sarcastic uses of language. His subjects found it easier to understand the use of positive statements ("You're a fine friend") to express something negative than the use of negative statements ("You're a terrible friend") to express something positive.

Kreuz and Glucksberg (1989) combined echoes and asymmetries to show that they affect not only ease of comprehension but also the extent to which readers will perceive sarcastic intent. Their experimental stories manipulated the presence or absence of a victim—someone whose earlier utterance was being incredulously echoed—and whether the utterance intended as sarcastic was positive or negative. Here, for example, is a use of a negative statement with an explicit victim:

Nancy and her friend Jane were planning a trip to the beach. "It's probably going to rain tomorrow," said Jane, who worked for a local TV station as a meteorologist. The next day was a warm and sunny one. As she looked out the window, Nancy said, "This certainly is awful weather." (p. 377)

Kreuz and Glucksberg required their subjects, through either open-ended questions or direct ratings, to indicate how sarcastic they considered utterances like "This certainly is awful weather" to be. In every case, subjects perceived more sarcasm when a positive statement was used rather than a negative statement (for example, "This certainly is beautiful weather" when the day turned out cold and stormy). However, when the negative statement had an explicit victim, as in the example cited, subjects were more likely to perceive sarcasm than when no such victim was present.

These two programs of research suggest that the ready perception and comprehension of sarcasm rely heavily on the presence of an appropriate victim. In a sense, then, the actual words of the utterance hardly matter. The speaker's true belief is overdetermined by the context: what remains left over is the speaker's attitude toward the victim. Even so, I believe that Gibbs and Kreuz and Glucksberg rely too heavily on the need for an echo. Consider this brief story:

> Bonnie and Tom are driving on a deserted highway late at night. "Tom," says Bonnie, "the tank is empty."
>
> "I know this car," Tom replies. "I can drive fifty miles when it says empty."
>
> Bonnie responds, "That's fine. I've always wanted to spend the night in the car."

Although it's hard to imagine who Bonnie might be echoing, it seems likely that Tom would interpret her utterance as sarcastic. What sets this example apart from most of those studied experimentally is that Bonnie is using sarcasm to make a claim about the future rather than to confirm one about the past—the latter situation being more conducive to echoes. In addition, Bonnie's intended meaning is not only the opposite of what she has said. Although it is likely that she has never, in fact, wanted to spend the night in a car, the more important part of Bonnie's message is her skepticism. I use this example as a way of suggesting that an experimental psychology of irony based on echoes will be of limited generality. A focus on the more enduring aspects of ironic situations—for sarcasm, the identification of a victim—should lead more directly toward a model of meaning recovery in the greater variety of authors' uses of irony that I cataloged earlier in this chapter.

Theories of irony should also be expanded to account for how readers become aware of the outer audience—those other hearers who would not come to a correct understanding of the ironic utterance. The experimental evidence suggests that, at least for adults, the comprehension of irony requires little conscious attention to the literal meaning of the utterance. If a reader would effortlessly come to understand that "Sure is nice and warm in here" means "Please close the window," how would that same reader go on to notice that other hearers would be captured by the literal meaning? Part of the answer might be that language users expect utterances to have particular effects—what Austin (1962) called *perlocutionary effects:* "what we bring about or achieve *by* saying something, such as convincing, persuading, deterring, and even, say, surprising or misleading" (p. 109). What members of the inner circle may generally notice when other hearers do not grasp an ironic meaning is that the utterance did not produce the expected effect: the uninformed did not react the way they would if they shared appropriate knowledge. In more-concrete terms, if someone hearing the utterance "Sure is nice and warm in here" failed to close the window or explain why he or she was not going to do so, we would quickly come to the conclusion that the irony had been lost on that hearer. In literary circumstances, readers often have explicit evidence that an utterance that has ironic resonance for them has failed to affect, for example, a narrative's character in the same way. Recall the way Desdemona unwittingly falls into Iago's trap by continuing to praise Cassio. Although the audience understands the consequences of her actions, evidence is in plain view that Desdemona does not.

Similarly, the tension of suspense tales is often heightened when a character fails to act in accordance with all the information available to the reader, and the difference can be noted. In Ian Fleming's short story "Risico," the reader strongly believes that James Bond is being set up by a beautiful young woman, Lisl Baum. Bond fails to act on that knowledge (despite strong participatory responses of advice) until he is being chased by three gunmen down the beach to which he and Lisl have traveled together. (Were this a movie rather than a short story, the audience might be tipped off to danger by a swell of music on the soundtrack. There, the dissociation of what the characters and the audience know is particularly evident.) I am not trying to suggest that every instance of irony will yield proof within the work itself: in some cases, determinations of ironic intention will be made by virtue of the relative status of literary critics and the inner and outer audiences will be constituted along lines of received wisdom (see Fish, 1989). Even so, we can take it to be an aesthetic strategy for authors that they display explicitly the consequences of being in or out of the know.

I began this section by illustrating circumstances in which readers must attend to the distribution of information known and unknown by the inhabitants of a narrative. My initial claim was that readers have developed the ability to monitor dissociations of knowledge through conversational practice. This skill, after all, is what allows speakers to include side-participants and exclude overhearers. It was exactly because of the focus on inclusion and exclusion that I discussed irony at some length. One conclusion was that irony is best understood when a purpose is evident in the context. A more general conclusion would be that readers best accommodate dissociations of knowledge when the author's intentions with respect to the scheme of distribution become revealed as part of the on-going experience of the narrative.

One of my major goals in this chapter has been to give an account of the experience of language in narrative worlds built up from ordinary processes of language use. I described how Clark and Carlson's (1982) informative analysis of everyday conversation can be extended to cover narrative utterances. In particular, I suggested that authors treat readers as side-participants toward whom they direct sincere informatives. What often matters to readers' experiences of narratives is what knowledge authors take to be in common ground in advance of a text and how they parcel out information within the text. Much of my focus has been on the cognitive processes readers undertake to construct appropriate representations of this knowledge.

The second overarching theme of this chapter has been to begin an assault on taxonomies of narrative experience that make an immediate distinction between fiction and nonfiction. I have suggested repeatedly that examination of the cognitive processes that underlie language experiences make such a division untenable. I fortify this case in the chapters that follow. Having laid out in this chapter an account of how narrative language is experienced, I return in chapter 6 to the effects those experiences have outside the world of the narrative: How is it that nonserious language can have serious effects in the real world?

Some Consequences of Being Transported

At the core of the metaphor of being transported lie readers' subjective reports of having left the real world behind when visiting narrative worlds. In earlier chapters, I provided anecdotal evidence that there are genuine discontinuities of experience associated with these visits. Here, I match experiment to anecdote in an attempt to document these claims, providing case studies of narrative experiences that have most often been explained by reference to special psychological processes. I hope to demonstrate that general and basic aspects of psychological structure give rise to readers' feelings of being transported.

Anomalous Suspense

Chapters 2 and 3 were devoted largely to describing the many ways knowledge from outside of narrative worlds influences the experience of those worlds. Readers who draw inferences or produce participatory responses do so largely by virtue of the information they possess—about restaurants, subways, and so on—apart from the narrative. We take for granted that such knowledge can cross the boundary from without to within the narrative world. I offer this reminder because what is most striking about the phenomenon I illustrate here is that it relies, by contrast, on an apparently strict separation of knowledge between the real world and narrative worlds.

Consider this excerpt from Garrison Keillor's collection *Leaving Home*:

> In Uncle Lew's story, a house burned down on a cold winter night and the little children inside ran barefoot into the snow of 1906—some were pitched out the bedroom window by their father—and all were safe. But although I heard the story dozens of times, whenever he told it again I was never sure they'd all get out. And since these children grew up to be my ancestors, I had an interest in their survival. (pp. 220–21)

Keillor is reporting what I defined in chapter 3 as *anomalous suspense:* he claims to experience suspense with respect to an outcome about which he should not have any uncertainty. Information that might be readily available to him—the children, after all, turn out to be his ancestors—does not, apparently, impinge on his experience of Uncle Lew's story. I presented a similar example in chapter 1 from Doctorow's *World's Fair,* in which Edgar confessed that he regularly believed his Uncle Willy to be in danger; although he knew exactly why he was not, this knowledge failed to penetrate the narrative world.

Anomalous suspense is not restricted to works of fiction. Clive (1989) described how the renowned nineteenth-century historian Thomas Carlyle had the explicit strategy of creating anomalous suspense in his masterful *History of Frederick the Great:*

> [Carlyle's] interventions induce a state of suspense, a feeling that events were not destined to happen as they did; that their course could be changed, as it were in midpassage, by

the historian himself. But since we already know what happened later, we also know that the suspense is artificial. And Carlyle, who *knows* that we know the outcome, is perfectly aware of the artificiality of his device. What happens, in fact, is that, paradoxically, these dramatic interventions on the part of the historian enhance rather than diminish the ground bass of the history, which is that destiny holds sway, and that its course cannot be tampered with. (p. 105)

Modern historians have followed Carlyle's lead in creating suspense even with respect to well-known outcomes. In *The Making of the Atomic Bomb,* Richard Rhodes so painstakingly lays out obstacles to the development of the bomb that the book is incessantly suspenseful. Because many readers have no knowledge of how those obstacles were overcome, much of the suspense is not anomalous. Readers may, for example, have genuine uncertainty about which of several potential designs for the bomb will prevail. Readers should not, however, have uncertainty about the ultimate outcome. Even so, Rhodes presents his history in such a fashion that he creates uncertainty with respect to a range of questions whose answers should be readily available to any educated reader: Is an atomic bomb technologically feasible? Will the United States muster the resources to produce a bomb? Will successful deployment of the bomb end the war? Consider this excerpt:

> Someone had gotten careless and put [Fat Man's] cable in backward. . . . Removing the cable and reversing it would mean partially disassembling the implosion sphere. It had taken most of a day to assemble it. They would miss the window of good weather and slip into the five days of bad weather. . . . The second atomic bomb might be delayed as long as a week. The war would go on. (p. 739)

The ready availability of details of the historical record does little to cut the suspense-generating effect of the tag line "The war would go on." A core feature of the experience of anomalous suspense is that what should be "readily available" (by virtue of solid prior knowledge) is not, in fact, readily available in the experience of a narrative. It may, furthermore, be an author's explicit strategy to engender anomalous suspense as a way of heightening a narrative's emotional impact.

The experience of anomalous suspense, however, does not always rely on an author's explicit intentions or manipulations. As a final example, consider these excerpts from John Steinbeck's journals. Published as *Working Days,* the journals cover the period when he was working on the novel that became *The Grapes of Wrath,* which won the Pulitzer Prize in 1940 and endures as a classic of American fiction:

> If only I could do this book properly it would be one of the really fine books and a truly American book. But I am assailed with my own ignorance and inability. . . . For no one else knows my lack of ability the way I do. I am pushing against it all the time. Sometimes, I seem to do a good piece of work, but when it is done it slides into mediocrity. (June 18, 1938; pp. 29–30)

> [The last chapter] must be just as slow and measured as the rest but I am sure of one thing—it isn't the great book I had hoped it would be. It's just a run-of-the-mill book. And the awful thing is that it is absolutely the best I can do. (October 19, 1938; p. 90)

These excerpts capture the theme of self-doubt that runs through the journals. Steinbeck experiences genuine suspense as to whether he will be able to finish the book and how it will be received. For readers, the experience of suspense *could* be undermined by knowledge from outside the narrative world. Given an appropriate degree of immersion in Steinbeck's narrative, however, anomalous suspense prevails.

Because anomalous suspense is such a compelling aspect of the real-life experience of narratives, I sought to bring it under closer scrutiny by reproducing it experimentally. One immediate difficulty was measuring this type of suspense. In chapter 3, I described research in which the experimenters elicited direct ratings of the amount of suspense subjects were feeling at various times in a text. I considered this direct rating inappropriate for studying anomalous suspense for at least two reasons. First, the phenomenon relies on subjects' remaining immersed in the narrative world; I had little confidence that the subjects would remain sufficiently affected by a story to rate themselves as being in great doubt about Steinbeck's ability to complete *The Grapes of Wrath*. Second, my greatest interest was in exploring the memory ramifications of anomalous suspense. Even if readers confirmed that they were experiencing suspense, that would provide little information on the memory consequences of that experience. I turned, therefore, to a measure that would provide a more direct index of access or nonaccess to information in memory.

In these experiments (Gerrig, 1989b), I required readers to respond true or false to well-known facts about history and current events. Consider this statement:

Charles Lindbergh was the first solo pilot to cross the Atlantic.

Under ordinary circumstances, subjects find it easy to verify that this sentence is true. In an initial experiment, however, I made circumstances less ordinary by writing a brief text that created mild doubt about Lindbergh's flight:

Charles Lindbergh wanted to fly an airplane to Europe. Lindbergh's proposed flight was the subject of much controversy. Newspaper polls showed 75% of all Americans were against the trip. They feared that Lindbergh would kill himself unnecessarily. Even the President tried to discourage the flight.

Note that the suspense here—will Lindbergh fly or not?—is biased toward the counterfactual outcome, but that outcome is never stated (that is, all the assertions could be true components of actual history). My hypothesis was that subjects would get sufficiently caught up in this story so as to find it more difficult than usual to verify the true statement that Lindbergh crossed the ocean.

The subjects in the experiment read one of four versions of each experimental story. For each subject, half of the stories created suspense and the other half were free of suspense. Here, for example, is the No Suspense version of the Lindbergh story:

Charles Lindbergh wanted to fly an airplane to Europe. Lindbergh's proposed flight was the subject of much discussion. No one had ever attempted such a long journey alone. But everyone thought that Lindbergh was the right person to try. Even the President encouraged Lindbergh to make the flight.

Each of the experimental statements was chosen to be solidly within the body of knowledge of college undergraduates: for example, "The North defeated the South in the Civil War," "Neil Armstrong was the first man to walk on the moon," and "Washington, D.C., is the capital of the United States." In each case the grounds for suspense were not very fanciful: the stories suggested that the Civil War might have been ended earlier by a secret treaty that established two separate countries, that Buzz Aldrin was scheduled to set foot on the moon first, and that members of Congress wanted to place the capital in New York or Philadelphia.

Each story also began with or without what I called a *Prior Warning:* in two of the versions, the story began explicitly with the statement that would later be subject to verification. For example, for one Suspense and one No Suspense version, the sentence "Charles Lindbergh was the first solo pilot to cross the Atlantic" began the story rather than "Charles Lindbergh wanted to fly an airplane to Europe." The Prior Warning versions were included to make certain that I was creating suspense with respect to facts known to the subjects. I wanted to be able to attribute impaired verification performance unambiguously to uncertainty created within the experiment rather than to uncertainty inherited from the real world. The Prior Warnings were included to increase confidence in that conclusion.

Subjects in the experiment read a total of thirty-two brief stories on a computer screen. Each story was interrupted after several sentences by a signal from the computer, after which the subjects were required to say true or false to the next statement presented, which reproduced either accurately ("Charles Lindbergh was the first solo pilot to cross the Atlantic") or inaccurately ("Charles Lindbergh was not the first solo pilot to cross the Atlantic") the extraexperimental state of affairs. After performing this judgment, the subjects read another pair of sentences which, in the case of the Suspense versions, returned them to the real-world outcome:

Against all opposition, Lindbergh flew toward Europe. The successful flight made him the hero of all Americans.

For the No Suspense versions, the completion further confirmed the original outcome:

Lindbergh flew to Europe without any difficulties. The successful flight made him the hero of all Americans.

Subjects had little trouble alternating between reading the text and making the verification judgments.

My most important hypothesis was that readers would find it harder to verify the truth of real-world outcomes while reading a story that inspired suspense. That prediction was confirmed: on average, subjects took 2.326 seconds to confirm, for example, that Lindbergh crossed the Atlantic when no suspense was involved, but 2.586 seconds to do so in the presence of uncertainty. The effect was even larger when subjects had to reject the false statement (that is, "Charles Lindbergh was not the first solo pilot to cross the Atlantic"). Overall, subjects took longer to give false responses (mean for the true responses, 2.227 seconds; mean for the false responses, 2.700 seconds), but against that background suspense slowed verification by 130 milliseconds for true responses (2.163 versus 2.293 seconds) and by 374 for false responses (2.514 versus 2.888 seconds). Subjects, therefore, found it particularly difficult to respond "false" to a statement that conformed to their growing representation of the story (for example, that Lindbergh did not make the flight). (A control group of subjects verified the statements without having read any of the stories. On average, they took 2.035 seconds to confirm the true statements and 2.347 seconds to disconfirm the false statements. These control data rule out the possibility that the No Suspense stories speeded subjects' responses rather than, in accord with my hypothesis, the Suspense stories slowing responses.)

Finally, subjects found it considerably easier to verify the statements when they had received a Prior Warning (mean, 2.260 seconds) than when they had not (mean, 2.643 seconds). The effect of Suspense was about the same, however, whether or not Prior Warning was given. With a Prior Warning, Suspense produced a 260-millisecond decrement in verification performance (2.131 versus 2.391 seconds). Without a Prior Warning, the decrement was 238 milliseconds (2.526 versus 2.764 seconds). Thus, although subjects obtained a reliable advantage from an explicit statement of the verification target, that warning failed to enable them to overcome the effect of uncertainty brought about within the narrative world. (Error rates were generally quite low, about 4 percent overall, and paralleled the verification times.)

This pattern of results strongly indicates that readers can be made to experience uncertainty when immersed in brief stories. The increased verification latencies suggest that subjects entertained the implied conclusions of the Suspense stories even when they had information available in memory that directly contradicted these conclusions, and even when that information had been made readily available through Prior Warning. These verification judgments, however, were made immediately after suspense was induced—exactly the circumstances in which we might expect new information to have its greatest effect (see McKoon and Ratcliff, 1988). Furthermore, we could be concerned that the suspense effect was brought about because the target sentences were simply incoherent within a context that suggested an opposite outcome. To allay these concerns, I carried out a second experiment in which the verification judgments were divorced from the context of the new information.

Much of experiment 2 replicated the original suspense experiment. Once again, four versions of each story were used that included or excluded Prior Warning and Suspense. All of the stories, however, ended before the sentences that returned the subjects to reality in experiment 1, and the verification judgments were carried out roughly ten minutes after the subjects finished reading the full set of stories. The subjects were told that the purpose of the experiment was to study the cognitive processes that enable readers to think of titles for brief stories. At the end of each story, a signal from the computer instructed them to "Think of a title for the story." They indicated they had done so by pressing a key on the computer. After reading the set of thirty-two stories, the subjects wrote brief descriptions of someone they knew well as a filler exercise. Finally, they returned to the computer to verify a set of sixty-four sentences that included within it the thirty-two experimental targets. Target sentences appeared in either true or false forms at verification. An analysis of the title times revealed that subjects had taken considerably longer to create titles for stories involving Suspense (mean, 5.093 seconds) than for those with No Suspense (mean, 4.060 seconds). There was no comparable effect for Prior Warning (mean, 4.714 seconds) versus No Prior Warning (mean, 4.443 seconds). These title times suggested that subjects may have used the time to create a title as an opportunity to resolve the anomalous suspense. At the end of the experimental session, I asked the subjects to recall their titles as well as they could, and some of those titles, in fact, directly echoed the grounds for suspense:

> An Early History of the Tonight Show or Heeeeeeeeere's Katherine?
>
> George Washington—the president that almost wasn't.
>
> The Providence Red Sox?
>
> The taking of Paris, Fact or Myth?
>
> Gondolas in Venice: Heading for a romantic crash?

If subjects were using the time in which they thought about appropriate titles as an opportunity to call to mind the genuine outcomes, we would expect the effects of Suspense to be diminished.

Despite this concern, subjects still showed an effect of Suspense on their verification performance (No Suspense, 3.048 seconds, versus Suspense, 3.310 seconds). Once again, this effect was much larger for false responses (3.370 versus 3.853 seconds) than for true responses (2.717 versus 2.816 seconds), and subjects averaged 12.5 percent errors for false responses versus 3.8 percent for true responses. With the delay before verification, however, Prior Warning failed to provide any reliable assistance to performance (No Prior Warning, 3.276 seconds; Prior Warning,

3.074 seconds). The interfering effect of Suspense, then, proved to be longer-lived than the facilitating effect of Prior Warning. Although it seemed as if subjects in experiment 2 might use the "think of a title" task as an opportunity to find their way back to the true outcome, the verification times indicated that, curiously, they failed to do so. Another way to understand this pattern of results would be to suggest that the verification task itself transported the subjects back to the narrative worlds. When the subjects returned to the computer, the very act of reading a statement like "Charles Lindbergh was the first solo pilot to cross the Atlantic" may have reactivated the uncertainty that had been evoked during the first session of reading. What I am suggesting is that the methodology may have contributed to the separation of the real world and the narrative world. What remains intriguing is that (apparently) resolving the suspense in the real world did not attenuate suspense in the narrative world. To reinforce this interpretation, I undertook a third experiment in which suspense was explicitly resolved within the narrative world.

In experiment 3, one third of the stories subjects read in the initial phase of the experiment (while thinking of titles) returned them to the real-world outcome. I accomplished this by using the full Suspense stories from experiment 1, which had, for example, correctly gotten Lindbergh across the ocean. Another third of the stories were Suspense stories without this resolution, and the final third were No Suspense stories. (The three types of stories were made equivalent in length.) Experiment 3 omitted Prior Warning versions because that variable had failed to have a reliable effect in experiment 2. I predicted that the Resolved Suspense stories would lead to verification times on a par with the No Suspense stories: resolving suspense within the narrative world would be roughly equivalent to never creating it at all. This comparison also allowed me to examine a final alternative explanation for the Suspense result. It might be possible that the

Suspense stories produced delayed verification only because those stories introduced a body of new, counterfactual information that would result in a larger memory structure (see Anderson, 1976; Lewis and Anderson, 1976). The Resolved and Unresolved Suspense stories introduced much the same new information. If only Unresolved Suspense impaired verification performance, this would suggest that anomalous suspense is not merely a matter of memory load.

Experiment 3 once again revealed differences in "title times" for the different types of stories. Subjects took the least time to think of titles for the No Suspense stories (mean, 7.655 seconds) and then roughly one second extra each for the Resolved Suspense (mean, 8.665 seconds) and Unresolved Suspense (mean, 9.605 seconds) stories. The pattern, however, was different for verification of the test sentences. Subjects performed virtually identically in the cases of Resolved and No Suspense (3.292 versus 3.335 seconds), but Unresolved Suspense produced a reliable decrement (3.748 seconds). Furthermore, the effect of Suspense was quite robust for both true responses (the mean difference between Unresolved Suspense and the two other conditions was 397 milliseconds) and false responses (the mean difference was 478 milliseconds). This last result contrasts with the earlier experiments. It could be that the explicit resolution of much of the suspense prompted subjects to harbor more-lingering uncertainty toward the situations that were left unresolved. In any case, the robust Suspense effect for both true and false responses supports the hypothesis that suspense is best resolved within the narrative world.

Against this body of experimental results, I now sketch out a theory of anomalous suspense. Most accounts of the phenomenon have made reference to special aspects of the experience of fiction (for example, Skulsky, 1980; Walton, 1978b, 1990). My experiments, because they used nonfictional outcomes, were specifically designed to rule out explanations that rely on fiction-ality. Although Walton (1990) argued implicitly for such a strict separation, it would be extremely unparsimonious to hypoth-esize different cognitive mechanisms underlying fictional and nonfictional anomalous suspense. However, even if we repair these earlier theories by broadening their scope to include nonfic-tion, they cannot give a complete account of the phenomenon. Skulsky (1980), for example, suggested that anomalous suspense arises because readers participate in fictional worlds alongside the characters:

> In some worlds compatible with the truth of the fiction, I myself witness [Oedipus's] suffering or am attacked by a monster or turn a corner to find Pickwick on a London street. (p. 11)

> Where repetition is tolerated, the tolerance is due not to feigned uncertainty but to unfeigned sympathy for the hero—who is always uncertain. Take away the sympathy and you take away the desire to contemplate his uncertain-ties. No amount of pretense will redeem the story. (p. 13)

Skulsky's suggestion has some face validity, for it seems as if readers do feel suspense when they read *Working Days* partially because they identify with Steinbeck's uncertainty. Identifica-tion, however, cannot serve as a general explanation for anom-alous suspense. First, the stories in my experiments infrequently contained characters with whom the readers could feel sympa-thy. In the Lindbergh story, for example, there are no characters who are directly experiencing uncertainty with respect to the outcome. Readers feel as if they are generating suspense on their own behalf. Second, readers often experience suspense with re-spect to potential outcomes to which the characters are oblivious. Carroll (1990) describes a general feature of horror movies in which "suspense accrues as the audience is made aware that the monster is stalking an innocent, oblivious victim" (p. 139). Viewers might feel sympathy for the victims in the sense that they would prefer that they not be killed, but the only feelings of uncertainty present in these stalking scenes are their own. To the extent that these feelings recur across repeated viewings, anomalous suspense occurs. Identification, then, is neither necessary nor sufficient to give rise to this phenomenon.

What I wish to suggest, in fact, is that anomalous suspense arises not because of some special strategic activity but rather as a natural consequence of the structure of cognitive processing. Specifically, I propose that readers experience anomalous suspense because an *expectation of uniqueness* is incorporated within the cognitive processes that guide the experiences of narratives (Gerrig, 1989a, 1989b):

> Because life presents repeated types, but not repeated tokens, readers do not ordinarily have cause to search memory for *literal* repetitions of experiences.

My claim, in its purest form, is that anomalous suspense results from an optimization of cognitive resources: readers should not expend effort seeking out information that can only rarely be present—and those rare circumstances arise exactly because readers can reexperience narratives. The contrast I am trying to make is captured by this aphorism from Bobbie Ann Mason's novel *Spence + Lila* (p. 152):

> Baseball is the same situations over and over, but no two turn out alike. Like crops and the weather. Life.

To understand a baseball game, we need to refer to knowledge we have about typical baseball situations. The only time it makes sense to try to recall how a particular situation will turn out is when we have seen a particular game before. My suggestion is that anomalous suspense arises because our experience of narratives incorporates the strong likelihood that we never repeat a game. Note that this expectation of uniqueness need not be conscious. My claim is that our moment-by-moment processes evolved in response to the brute fact of nonrepetition.

I will refine my claim of an expectation of uniqueness further by drawing parallels to a model that has been developed by Bharucha and Todd (1989; Todd, 1988) in response to a phenomenon similar to anomalous suspense in the experience of works of music. Bharucha and Todd observed that listeners often remain surprised by particular sequences of notes in pieces of music they know well. This observation can be framed as a variation of anomalous suspense, which I call *musical suspense:* listeners' responses within the experience of a piece of music are not undermined by what they know outside that experience. To model this phenomenon, Bharucha and Todd draw a contrast between *veridical* and *schematic* expectancies (see Bharucha, 1987). Veridical expectancies are those a listener builds up by repeated contact with a particular piece of music. Schematic expectancies encode regularities within the overall body of music within a particular culture. In Bharucha and Todd's formulation, musical suspense relies on the different time-course with which veridical and schematic expectancies are generated in experiencing a passage of music.

To support this conclusion, Bharucha and Todd created an explicit computational model of music perception and production using a connectionist formalism. Connectionist models have been developed in a number of domains to demonstrate that apparently rule-governed behavior can emerge from a network of simple units that do not directly represent those rules (see McClelland and Rumelhart, 1986; Rumelhart and McClelland, 1986). Learning in these models is most often described by a mixture of linear and nonlinear equations. The spirit of Bharucha and Todd's model, however, can be captured independent of the mathematical details. What is essential is that, as a function of the input context, the model produces output over a series of units representing notes of the scale. This context specificity enables the network to learn particular melodic sequences in the sense that the appropriate output units are activated at each point in a sequence of notes. This *sequential network* is thus able to reproduce veridical expectancies when acquiring individual melodies.

To model the clash between veridical and schematic expectancies that gives rise to musical suspense, Bharucha and Todd introduce a formalism that allows activation on the output units to approach some threshold criterion with differing speed. Todd (1988) presented a straightforward example to illustrate this property of the model. The sequential network was trained with eight melodies, six of which included the progression of notes D-E. Five of those melodies continued with an A (that is, D-E-A). Only one contained the sequence D-E-G. When the network was tested, it always produced the continuation appropriate to the melodies (recall that the D-E-A and D-E-G sequences were components of longer melodies). The output unit for the A, however, reached threshold much more swiftly than the output unit for the G. The delayed activation of the note G reflects the clash of schematic and veridical expectations.

My account of anomalous suspense also relies on a contrast between types and tokens, or between veridical and schematic expectancies. If we let the notes of a melody represent lines of a story, then Bharucha and Todd's sequential network provides a strong analogy. The schematic ending—the D-E-A sequence—of the Suspense story about Lindbergh's flight, for example, is that he would choose not to go. To verify the veridical ending, readers required extra time, just as the computational model of musical suspense required more time to produce the nonschematic note G. Both the model and my subjects were able to find their way to the correct output, but with a measurable delay. This may not always be the case. If a veridical expectancy is sufficiently weak with respect to overlearned schematic expectancies, it may never achieve a sufficient threshold of activation to affect conscious experience. Thus, if Garrison Keillor's Uncle Lew makes the victims of the fire seem inescapably imperiled, Keillor may forever be caught up in obligatory schematic expectancies. Where does the expectation of uniqueness belong in this account? My suggestion is that it resides in the choice among architectures and equations that link inputs to outputs. What Bharucha and Todd make evident is that they have sampled from a large space of formalisms to assemble their model. Other connectionist models achieve different input-output relationships by virtue of alternative architectures, learning rules, and so on. (Rumelhart, Hinton, and McClelland [1986] review the range of networks and mappings that were implemented in early connectionist models.) Within this class of models, we could imagine devising a network that would preclude the experience of anomalous suspense. To the extent that anomalous suspense, in fact, appears to be nonsensical—why should readers feel suspense about outcomes they have perfect knowledge of?—we can wonder why we didn't evolve toward some other cognitive architecture. Bharucha and Todd's model, therefore, provides insight into how anomalous suspense might emerge from the ordinary structure of cognition, but it does not answer the question of why that particular structure is ordinary. I have evoked the expectation of uniqueness to provide a link between formalism and function. My suggestion is that cognitive processes optimally deliver schematic expectations. Anomalous suspense follows from there.

My more global assertion with respect to anomalous suspense is that it provides evidence that readers who are transported to narrative worlds lose access to the details of the real world. We can now see in what sense that might be true with respect to cognitive mechanisms. One possibility is that immersion in a narrative world will change the time-course with which information becomes available. To the extent that schematic expectancies clash with veridical information, the veridical information—even if it is well established outside the narrative—might be activated only slowly. A second possibility is that the balance of veridical and schematic expectancies, or the degree of immersion, would be such that nonnarrative information would be insufficiently activated to enter consciousness within the experience of a narrative. These two possibilities, which anchor a continuum, capture intuitions about the depth of the experience of anomalous suspense. In some cases, as in my examples from Steinbeck's *Working Days,* the anomalous suspense seems to dissolve quickly (that is, "Maybe he won't finish the book" or "Maybe the book will be a flop" gives way quickly to "This is *The Grapes of Wrath*"). In other cases, as perhaps with Rhodes's *The Making of the Atomic Bomb,* the suspense seems to endure throughout a long narrative. The hallmark of being transported, however, might be that schematic expectancies become relatively dominant: readers treat each story as if it were brand new.

What this account leaves murky is differences among narratives in fostering anomalous suspense. Why do some narratives easily prompt suspense upon repetition whereas others do not? I cannot provide the aesthetic theory that would constitute a full answer to this question. Instead, I want to consider how this issue provides a more narrowly psychological challenge to my developing theory of anomalous suspense. Specifically, I have suggested that anomalous suspense *ought* to be the default: the reexperience of suspense ought to be an automatic consequence of the ordinary experience of a narrative. That some narratives do not produce anomalous suspense appears to provide a strong challenge to this theory. To put this contradiction in an appropriate context, I wish to make an analogy to *capture* phenomena in perception and attention.

Situations are typically labeled as capture when a stimulus automatically demands attention (see, for example, McCormick and Jolicoeur, 1992; Remington, Johnston, and Yantis, 1992) or provokes an inevitable perceptual response (see, for example, Steiger and Bregman, 1981). As such, capture phenomena reveal basic structural properties of attention and perception. Consider a series of experiments carried out by Steiger and Bregman that examined some properties of perceivers' "parsing" of complex auditory signals. (Conversationalists carry out this sort of task when they try to follow one voice among many simultaneous speakers.) Steiger and Bregman began with a stimulus in which a single gliding tone sequence (X) was followed by a complex signal composed of two parallel glides (Y and Z). Subjects' perception of this auditory "scene" differed as a function of the stimulus parameters. In parsing the scene, they sometimes reported hearing an alternation between a pure tone (X) and a fused tone (Y and Z). However, under appropriate circumstances—when, for example, X and Y were in the same frequency range—X would capture Y so that subjects heard two streams with X and Y dissociated from Z. What is important here is that both parsings of this scene follow automatically from the ordinary operation of processes of auditory perception. What produced one or the other percept is the specific auditory properties of X, Y, and Z. The stimulus configuration dictated what would automatically occur.

When I apply the analogy to the domain of narrative, what becomes immediately evident is how little is known about the "dimensions" of narrative experience—that is the theory of aesthetics that remains undeveloped. If we had such a theory, we could manipulate narratives just as Steiger and Bregman manipulated auditory stimuli to determine the exact narrative circumstances under which anomalous suspense arises. From the analogy, however, we gain confidence that the nonincidence of anomalous suspense does not imply that the processes that bring the experience about are not automatic. What is lacking (and I do not consider this a minor omission) is a specification of the stimulus properties that are necessary for readers to be automatically captured by a narrative.

Anomalous Replotting

The hallmark of anomalous suspense is that knowledge from outside a narrative world fails to influence the moment-by-moment experience of the narrative. Anomalous replotting moves one step further by simultaneously displaying both influence and noninfluence (Gerrig, 1989a). Consider this excerpt from Stephen Oates's biography of Abraham Lincoln, *With Malice Toward None*. Lincoln and his wife, Mary Todd Lincoln, are trying to settle their theatergoing plans after Ulysses Grant has turned down an invitation to join them for *Our American Cousin:*

> So what couple to invite? As it turned out, the Stantons
> [the secretary of war and his wife] were unable to go,
> mainly because Ellen Stanton and Mary didn't get along
> either. Also, Stanton worried about Lincoln's theatergoing,
> worried that some deranged rebel sympathizer might take a
> shot at him right from the streets, and beseeched him to
> stay home at night. At lunch, Lincoln told Mary he had
> half a mind not to go, but she thought it important to stick
> with their plans, since they had been announced in the
> newspapers. (pp. 465–66)

When one experiences this passage (and the full context makes this even more the case), it feels almost inevitable that readers will hear a mental voice cry out, "Don't go to the theater!" Oates, in fact, structures the paragraph in a way that seems optimal to elicit this participatory response. What makes this replotting, as I described in chapter 3, is that the reader is actively thinking about what could have happened to change an outcome. What makes this *anomalous* replotting is that the plea for change is emitted within the unfolding narrative before that outcome has been disclosed. If *With Malice Toward None* were not about Abraham Lincoln, readers would have no special reason to wish that the protagonist avoid the theater. "Don't go to the theater!" reveals that readers, in fact, apply special knowledge about Lincoln to shape their preferences. At the same time, however, "Don't go to the theater!" suggests that readers in some way believe that the characters' behavior is not predetermined. There is an odd sort of recursion here: readers are generating preferences that attempt to undo the immutable circumstances that brought about the preference.

In other instances of anomalous replotting, the replotting is apparent only by comparison to the original experience of the narrative, in advance of knowledge of the outcome. My own most vivid instance of this phenomenon centered around the explosion of the space shuttle *Challenger*. In the days following this tragedy, replays of the video footage were virtually inescapable. Even before seeing the videotape for the first time, I knew the outcome, and yet again and again I found myself watching the first few seconds of lift-off and crying out mentally, "Make it!" Unlike the Lincoln case, I had a reason to want the shuttle to "make it" independent of knowledge of the outcome-to-be. What makes this situation anomalous replotting, nonetheless, is what I might call a "loss of innocence" with respect to this desire. I never felt prompted to cry out "Make it!" when watching shuttle footage until I knew that this one shuttle had failed to do so. It felt as if this desire had been called forth by the same knowledge that rendered it impotent.

Note that anomalous replotting can also arise in less tragic circumstances. Fans watching football games, for example, may sometimes find themselves calling out "Catch the ball!" or "Make the field goal!" even when they are watching an instant replay of a failed endeavor. A negative outcome of some minimal intensity does, however, appear to be required. Readers apparently do not spontaneously replot to change the precursors to positive outcomes.

Much of my interpretation of anomalous replotting relies on the belief that the propositions readers entertain—"Don't go to the theater!" "Make the field goal!"—are as genuine as everyday thoughts about future (unknown) events and outcomes. This belief rests on a distinction that can be made in everyday experience between hope and hopefulness. As Ortony, Clore, and Collins (1988) observed, there is often a dissociation between the desirability and the likelihood of prospects for the future. People often genuinely desire an outcome (that, say, they might win a lottery) without believing the outcome to be particularly likely (the odds might be one in a million): they can have hope without being very hopeful. Against this background, the emotional content of the propositions generated through anomalous replotting appear unexceptional. The desirability that the Lincolns not attend the theater is quite high, and we should not be surprised that readers strongly hope for that outcome. What remains to be explained, however, is how readers also appear to retain some hopefulness in the face of perfect knowledge that the likelihood that the hope will be satisfied is zero.

To explain the durability of hopefulness, I want to evoke the same mechanism I used to account for anomalous suspense. Once again, I believe the phenomenon relies on a clash between veridical and schematic expectancies. What is more evident for anomalous replotting, however, is exactly how actively readers are hopeful that they are experiencing a different story. I motivated the "expectation of uniqueness" by noting that under ordinary circumstances readers cannot know outcomes. For anomalous replotting, this has become that much more strongly an article of faith: even though the propositions readers entertain (such as "Don't go to the theater") might be informed by one well-known story, they default to the expectation that outcomes are not restricted until they have actually transpired. Anomalous replotting constitutes a remarkable dissociation of different layers of influence in the ongoing experience of a narrative world.

What I have largely ignored for both anomalous suspense and anomalous replotting is the ways they reveal quirks in the interaction of affect and cognition. In both cases, readers experience emotions—suspense and hopefulness—under circumstances in which knowledge should undermine those affective experiences. In the next section, I consider more systematically the experience of emotions in response to, in particular, fictional narratives.

Emotional Responses to Fictional Narratives

Readers' critiques of fictional narratives almost invariably make reference to the emotions engendered by the experience of the narrative: "I laughed"; "I cried"; "I was really frightened." Such emotional responses, however, have often been characterized as paradoxical, because—or so it has seemed to a variety of theorists—readers should not have emotions about situations they know to be unreal. Consider the argument developed by Colin Radford (1975) in an article entitled "How Can We Be Moved by the Fate of Anna Karenina?" He begins by explicating circumstances in which belief in the unreality of a situation does appear to undermine an emotional response:

> Suppose then that you read an account of the terrible sufferings of a group of people. If you are at all humane, you are unlikely to be unmoved by what you read. The account is likely to awaken or reawaken feelings of anger, horror, dismay or outrage and, if you are tender-hearted, you may well be moved to tears. You may even grieve.
>
> But now suppose you discover that the account is false. If the account had caused you to grieve, you could not con-

tinue to grieve. If as the account sank in, you were told and believed that it was false this would make tears impossible, unless they were tears of rage. If you learned later that the account was false, you would feel that in being moved to tears you had been fooled, duped. (p. 68)

Radford moves swiftly from this observation to the paradox of fiction. If, in fact, unreality should militate against emotional response, how is it that readers regularly experience strong emotions toward characters and situations that are purely authors' inventions:

> What seems unintelligible is how we could have [an emotional] reaction to the fate of Anna Karenina, the plight of Madame Bovary or the death of Mercutio. Yet we do. We weep, we pity Anna Karenina, we blink hard when Mercutio is dying and absurdly wish that he had not been so impetuous. (p. 69)

Radford goes on to examine six solutions to this apparent dissociation in fiction between belief and emotional response. His rejection of all six sets the tone for a literature that has been replete with proposals and counterproposals, assaults and counterassaults (for reviews, see Boruah, 1988; Carroll, 1990; Dammann, 1992; McCormick, 1988; Novitz, 1987; Walton, 1990). In this theoretically rich domain, similar solutions have been independently proposed at various times and have fallen victim to the same disconfirming anecdotes. Rather than review the history of these interactions, I wish to attack an assumption shared by the majority of these theorists. I argue, in particular, that far from being unique, the experience of emotions in response to fictions follows more-general patterns of circumstances in which affect is dissociated from cognition.

To make my case, I consider two aspects of the paradox that I believe to be logically separable. The first is the one on which

Radford focused, which I will call the *nonpenetration* of belief into emotional experience. Pylyshyn (1984) defined *cognitive penetrability* as "the rationally explicable alterability of a component's behavior in response to changes in goals and beliefs" (p. 133). The purest description of this first aspect of the paradox is that beliefs fail to penetrate the mental components that determine readers' experiences of emotions. A reader's belief, for example, that Anna Karenina is a product of Tolstoy's imagination does not derail the feeling of pity. What remains true, even so, is that such a feeling of pity rarely calls forth any action on the part of the reader, whereas real-life emotions often have strong associations with overt behavioral responses. We might expect people who feel pity to try to formulate a plan for alleviating the suffering of the object of pity; or, especially, people who feel fear to attempt to remove themselves from the situation that is making them fearful. Thus, the second aspect of the paradox of fiction is that most readers do not even consider carrying out these more overt behavioral responses.

Consider this opening paragraph from Kendall Walton's essay "Fearing Fictions" (1978b, p. 5):

> Charles is watching a horror movie about a terrible green slime. He cringes in his seat as the slime oozes slowly but relentlessly over the earth destroying everything in its path. Soon a greasy head emerges from the undulating mass, and two beady eyes roll around, finally fixing on the camera. The slime, picking up speed, oozes on a new course straight toward the viewers. Charles emits a shriek and clutches desperately at his chair. Afterwards, still shaken, Charles confesses that he was "terrified" by the slime. *Was* he?

Walton takes the absence of Charles's acting on his fear as strong evidence that he was not, in fact, terrified in the ordinary (real-world) sense: "Even a hesitant belief, a mere suspicion, that the slime is real would induce any normal person seriously to consider calling the police and warning his family. Charles gives no thought whatever to such courses of action. He is not *uncertain* whether the slime is real; he is perfectly sure that it is not" (p. 7). If Walton is correct, emotional responses to fictions *are* penetrated by beliefs: overt behavior is curtailed by the belief that, in this case, the object of fear is not real.

There appears, then, to be a discontinuity even between the experiential and behavioral aspects of emotional responses to fictions. I nonetheless believe it is possible to give a coherent account by demonstrating that neither nonpenetration nor behavioral inhibition is unique to experiences of fiction. I argue, rather, that they reflect fundamental consequences of mental architecture.

Solutions to the paradox of emotional responses to fictions have routinely been predicated on the assumption that the nonpenetration of belief is unique to fiction—and these solutions, therefore, have invoked or invented properties or processes special to the experience of fictions. In this section I challenge this assumption by reviewing other cases in which powerful emotional responses survive in the face of well-represented countervailing beliefs.

Consider this excerpt from Eric Lax's biography *Woody Allen,* in which Allen is describing his feelings while waiting to perform as a stand-up comedian:

> I remember sitting backstage so many times with [Diane] Keaton in Vegas and as soon as we heard Edie Adams going into a certain song, it meant she had one more before I was introduced. I'd start to get tense. It's just Pavlovian. It's so silly, because I knew they loved me, my reviews

were good, they'd booked me in places because they liked me, the people were there to see me, I killed them every night. It didn't matter how far into my engagement I was. It could be a Thursday night my third week there and I'd know I was going to do great because I did great the show before and the night before and the week before. But it still got to me. (p. 247)

Allen has described a paradigmatic experience of the noninfluence of beliefs—however well supported—on emotional experience. At least in his recollection, there was no statement of fact he could produce that ameliorated his anxiety response. (He even nominates as the source of his anxiety Pavlovian conditioning which, as I discuss later, is a solid suggestion.) Clinical psychologists have documented many similar circumstances in which beliefs do not penetrate emotional responses. Consider cases of phobias in which individuals become incapacitated in circumstances that cause nonsufferers only minimal distress. Beck and Emery (1985) characterized phobics as having "dual belief systems": "The phobic person seems to hold simultaneously two sets of contradictory beliefs about the probability of the occurrence of harm when in the situations he fears. When removed from the feared situation, he believes the situation is relatively harmless: the fear he experiences is proportional to the amount of objective risk in that situation. As he approaches the phobic situation, he becomes increasingly anxious and perceives the situation to be increasingly dangerous" (pp. 127–28). Thus, the beliefs that dominate the appraisal of snakes or spiders at a distance are not able to penetrate the mental processes that produce the extreme emotional responses when the objects are at hand. Such clinical instances demonstrate a clear capacity for individuals to experience strong emotions that are not ameliorated by beliefs.

This same capacity exposes itself regularly, if less dramatically, in everyday experience. Consider instances of contamination and disgust that provide dissociations of affect and cognition in even the most stolidly normal individuals. Rozin, Millman, and Nemeroff (1986) carried out an experiment in which participants were asked to report on their food preferences. In one phase of the experiment, subjects were presented with two small glass bottles containing a white powder. The experimenter said:

> Here we have two bottles with powder in them. The powder in both bottles is sucrose, that is, table sugar. These are brand new bottles that we just bought. They never had anything in them but sugar. This bottle (on the subjects' left) has a sucrose label that we put on it. It's a brand new label, that was never on any other bottle. This other bottle (on the subjects' right) has a brand new sodium cyanide label on it [which also said "Poison"]. This label was never on any other bottle and was never even near cyanide. Remember, sugar is in both bottles. (p. 705)

After this introduction, the experimenter prepared sugar-water solutions in two plastic cups using different spoons to add a spoonful of sugar from each bottle to plain water from a pitcher. Subjects were then asked to rate how much they would like to drink from the two cups (on a scale that ranged from "dislike extremely" to "like extremely") and to make an explicit choice between the two. Finally, they took a few sips from the preferred cup and accounted for their choice.

Note that the experimenter went to great lengths to ensure that each subject formed the belief that the cyanide label bore no relationship to the contents of the bottle. Even so, forty-one out of fifty subjects preferred to drink from the cup of water mixed with sugar from the bottle labeled sugar, a proportion considerably different from a half-and-half split. Not surprisingly, subjects also rated themselves considerably more likely to want to drink from the sugar-labeled cup than from the cyanide-labeled cup. When asked to justify their selections, subjects who gave a response almost always made reference to the cyanide label. (Only one suggested that there really might be cyanide in the bottle.) In this situation, therefore, subjects overwhelmingly allowed their behavior to be influenced by emotions that were entirely unsupported by explicit belief. The discomfort caused by the cyanide label won out over the knowledge that the label had no validity.

In another phase of the experiment, Rozin, Millman, and Nemeroff fortified the belief in the invalidity of the cyanide label even further by asking the subjects themselves to put labels on the bottles. The subjects were presented with two bottles and two labels and could pair them off as they saw fit. Even so, they rated themselves as reliably less likely to drink water from the cyanide-labeled cup. Finally, in a separate experiment, Rozin, Markwith, and Ross (1990) allowed subjects to apply their own labels, but in this case the labels read "sucrose, table sugar" and "not sodium cyanide, not poison." Once again, the experimenter prepared two glasses (in this case, of Kool-Aid) using sugar from each bottle. When asked to rate how much they would like to drink from each glass, subjects gave reliably lower ratings to the not-cyanide-labeled glass. Many subjects in this experiment (forty-two of eighty-six) expressed no overt preference between the two glasses, but of the forty-four who did, thirty-five preferred the sugar-labeled Kool-Aid. This experiment presents the nonpenetrability of this class of affective responses in its strongest form: Even with the explicit label that the sugar is *not* cyanide, the fear associated with poison dominated behavior. Rozin and his colleagues (1986) also demonstrated the same pattern of behavior for more purely disgust responses. Subjects were reluctant to drink from a glass of juice in which a sterilized cockroach had been dipped or to eat otherwise desirable fudge that had been formed into the shape of dog feces.

The nonmutability of affect in these experiments can be explained by reference to the likely mechanism through which the emotional responses initially became established. Rozin and Fallon (1987) suggested that many such disgust and fear responses are acquired via classical conditioning (or, as Woody Allen labeled it, Pavlovian conditioning). In Pavlov's seminal experiments, dogs were trained to salivate in response to neutral stimuli such as tones or lights (see Rachlin, 1976). Each neutral, conditioned stimulus (cs) took on meaning because it was paired with an unconditioned stimulus (ucs), such as the presentation of food powder, which elicited, by reflex, salivation. Through repeated pairings of the cs followed by the ucs, the dogs would begin to salivate in the presence of the ucs (the light or tone) alone. Rozin and Fallon suggest that disgust or fear responses may arise through a similar mechanism. Children may come to emit disgust responses to certain objects by virtue of pairings between an otherwise neutral stimulus (cs) and their parents' own disgust responses (ucs). Once the appropriate association has been formed, children will come to feel disgust in the presence of the cs alone.

Note that no part of this process requires any conscious attention to the link that is being formed: neither children nor adults can explain why it is that they find certain objects disgusting. One hallmark of classical conditioning is the noninvolvement of conscious belief. Consider this anecdote (Rozin and Fallon, pp. 29–30):

> Nurses in a children's hospital were inappropriately consuming glasses of juice meant for the children. This problem was handled by serving the juice in new urine-collection bottles. The nurses no longer drank the juice,

even though there was no possibility of a physical trace of urine in this case.

The nurses, but not the children, have a classically conditioned disgust reaction to the collection bottles. This reaction survives countervailing nondisgust beliefs because conscious belief played so little role in the ontogeny of the reaction.

I intend these cases to weigh heavily against the uniqueness of affective responses to fictions. The situations in which people experience strong emotions while possessing explicit knowledge that should undermine those emotions are many and varied. I have presented a classical-conditioning account of disgust to show how some of these situations arise almost entirely outside conscious belief. I believe, in fact, that some subset of the emotional responses to fictions could also be explained as conditioned responses. When the heroine of *Indiana Jones and the Temple of Doom* plunges her hand into an enclosure teeming with large insects, the audience is hard-pressed not to feel reflexive disgust. On the whole, it appears that emotional responses to fictions can be glossed as being experienced under circumstances that activate associations between situations and responses that have been overlearned through day-to-day experience. Under those circumstances, we would rarely expect emotions to be penetrated by belief: only surface features of an appropriate stimulus are required to initiate a train of emotional events.

To reinforce this point, let me conclude this section by describing one psychologist's *law of apparent reality*. On the basis of his review of anecdotal and empirical evidence, Frijda (1988) argued that "emotions are elicited by events appraised as real, and their intensity corresponds to the degree to which this is the case" (p. 352). He was subsequently faulted for failing to consider cases in which fictional—unreal—events elicit emotions (Walters, 1989). In his original defense of this law, however, Frijda (see also Frijda, 1989) made explicit use of dissociations between belief and emotion. He suggested, as I did earlier, that "telling a phobic that spiders are harmless is useless when the phobic sees the crawling animal. Knowing means less than seeing." Furthermore, "when someone steps on our toes, we get angry even when we know that he or she is not to blame. Feeling means more than knowing" (p. 352). What Frijda intends with his law of apparent reality is that what is real for emotional responses is often not informed by other types of belief. The word *reality* is used "to characterize the stimulus properties at hand." That definition goes a long way toward explaining why the case of emotional responses to fiction is not unique but why, also, fictions provide a fruitful domain in which to study emotional processes.

Something appears to be amiss, however, in likening the experience of emotional responses to fictions to other circumstances in which knowledge is dissociated from affect. As Walton (1978b) observed, readers (or, in his original example, horror-movie goers) do not behave as we might expect them to were they genuinely experiencing an emotion. If Charles is truly afraid, he ought to flee the theater. Because he does not, according to Walton, he must be experiencing something besides fear. Walton suggests, in particular, that Charles is participating in a game of make-believe in which he experiences *quasi-fear* of the slime: "The fact that Charles is quasi-afraid as a result of realizing that make-believedly the slime threatens him generates the truth that make-believedly he is afraid of the slime" (p. 14). Walton reaches this conclusion on the basis of an analogy to the make-believe games of children. Just as a child can make-believe that his or her father is a monster poised to attack and scream appropriately, Charles can make-believe that he is imperiled by a danger he knows to be unreal. It is that knowledge of unreality, according to Walton, that keeps Charles in his seat.

The difficulty with Walton's account (or any other theory that makes reference to fiction) is that we would expect the same inhibition of behavior under circumstances of nonfiction. Imagine that the "terrible green slime" was featured in a television documentary on historical incidents of life-threatening terrors. (Within the Hollywood corpus, there are a number of movies that could serve in a less farfetched way as either fact or fiction. Consider movies that document a devastating earthquake or a blazing skyscraper.) If the documentary footage showed the slime advancing on a small community in 1959, we might expect Charles to show the same signs of fear (the shriek, the desperate clutch at his chair) but also the same inaction. We would not expect him to call the police or warn his family. Contrast that with a situation in which a news flash breaks into an ordinary program to announce, once again with video footage, that the slime is quickly approaching the city in which Charles is now sitting. In this case, he would very likely leap into action.

What appears to matter, therefore, is not so much whether the danger is fictional or nonfictional but whether overt action is functional in the circumstances. In fact, what separates the situations of nonaction and action is that only in the latter is Charles the intended addressee of the news bulletin. In the other circumstances, the movie or television documentary makes of him, along the lines of chapter 4, a side-participant—and as a side-participant he is not called to action. (Charles might also take action were he to overhear people talking about the genuine approaching slime. What matters most for action is that Charles not adopt the role of side-participant.)

Let me solidify this analogy by turning back briefly to a situation of language use. Imagine that in one scene of Charles's movie the sheriff asks his deputy, "Do you think I can kill the slime with my gun?" As a side-participant, Charles will be informed by the sheriff's question. He might very well come to the same meaning representation and formulate the same idea for a reply as the deputy (were we to assume the deputy to be processing language in an ordinary fashion)—but Charles would be unlikely to make an overt behavioral response. Similarly, Charles might experience the same emotional response as a character in the movie, but as a side-participant he would be unlikely to perform overt behaviors. Behavioral inhibition follows from side-participation for both the cognitive and affective aspects of the experience.

One notion I am explicitly denying is that Charles's emotional response arises because he directly identifies with the characters (as Skulsky [1980], for example, has argued). Rather, as a side-participant Charles's emotional responses are his own, just as his representations of meaning are his own. Identification with a character might heighten his emotional responses—Charles can choose to imagine how a character might be feeling—but such identification is not necessary or sufficient to explain his responses or the inhibition of overt behavior. Moreover, just as Charles can possess knowledge independent of the characters (see chapter 4), so his emotional responses need not be coextensive with those of the characters.

What I believe we most need to explain Charles's experiences is an account of moment-by-moment aspects of side-participation. We need to determine, for example, in what fashion Charles's knowledge that he is cast as a side-participant (by which I mean his tacit knowledge) modifies his behavior. Consider again Charles's inaction in the face of the fictional or historical slime. One possibility is that his experience of the slime calls forth plans for action (such as "I should warn my family") that are canceled by tacit acknowledgment of side-participation (as in "That action is unwarranted by my role with respect to these events"). We could take as potential evidence for this possibility the occasional situations in which moviegoers find themselves shouting warnings to characters on the screen. A second possibility is that side-participation penetrates the experience of the narrative so that such plans for action are never formulated. Walton (1978b) appears to conform to this latter possibility when he suggests that "Charles gives no thought whatever" to "calling the police and warning his family" (p. 7). (Note, however, that the first possibility does not require conscious awareness that action is being considered.) Both of these models, therefore, receive some phenomenological support. A direct empirical contrast could shed light on narrative experiences of emotions as well as on more-general aspects of mental structure.

A Developmental Perspective on Being Transported

To conclude this chapter, I will describe one study from the developmental literature on children's experiences of narrative worlds. I wish to show the continuity from childhood to adulthood in the experience of being transported (see Singer and Singer, 1990). Consider an experiment in which four- and six-year-old children were brought into a laboratory furnished with some chairs and two large boxes (Harris, Brown, Marriott, Whittall, and Harmer, 1991). When the children first arrived in the room, they were asked to verify that both boxes were empty. The experimenter next described a game to them: "It doesn't matter that the boxes are empty because we are going to play a game of pretend. I expect you're good at pretend games, aren't you?" For different groups of children, the experimenter went on to request that they imagine that one of the two boxes contained either a "nice, white, friendly rabbit" who would want to come out so that the child could stroke him or a "horrible, mean, black monster" who would want to come out to chase the child (pp. 116–17). When the children were asked whether the box was in fact inhabited or whether they were only pretending, twenty-two of the twenty-four younger children and twenty-one of the twenty-four older children answered correctly that they were only pretending. Even so, when the experimenter attempted to leave the room, four of the four-year-olds did not want her to leave because they were afraid of the monster (three of these four had answered correctly that the monster was only pretend). Even when the children and the experimenter verified together that the boxes were still empty, they asked that she not leave the room.

After the experimenter left the room (as she did for the other forty-four children), the behavior of the children with respect to the boxes was clandestinely videotaped. Harris et al. hypothesized that children who believed even fleetingly that the pretend rabbits or monsters might be real would behave differently toward the two boxes. The experimenter left the room so that the children's behavior could not be dismissed as specially designed for an adult. When she left the room, the children were sitting down, although they were told that they need not remain seated. Roughly half the children got up to investigate the boxes. In both age groups, the children approached and touched the box that housed the pretend creature reliably more quickly than they interacted with the neutral box. If they touched only one box, they overwhelmingly chose the box that had been the object of their pretense irrespective of whether they had imagined a rabbit or a monster. When the experimenter returned after two minutes, she asked the children whether they had wondered if the imagined creature was really inside the appropriate box. Roughly half of the children confessed that they had—even though nearly all of them had asserted, just minutes before, that they had only pretended that the creature was there. The majority of the children, in fact, once again denied that an act of pretense could generate a real creature (14 out of 20 four-year-olds and 19 out of 24 six-year-olds), although the remainder asserted that they could bring creatures into existence through pretense. Among the groups of 14 and 19 children, five at each age implied that although they themselves could not transform pretend creatures into real creatures, they believed that others might be able to do so.

These young subjects thus provided a tangle of contrasting behavior and beliefs. As an explanation, Harris et al. suggested at a global level that the children's acts of imagination increased their estimates of the subjective likelihood that they could encounter the fantasy creatures. To account for this shift, the authors proposed two alternative mechanisms. The first mechanism relies on the powerful effect the *availability* of instances in memory has on judgments of the probability of real-world occurrences (Tversky and Kahneman, 1973). Consider the media's tendency to underreport certain classes of risks (for example, deaths from disease) and overreport others (deaths from accidents). Because the media have a strong impact on what is available in memory, adults tend systematically to misestimate the likelihood of different risks of death (Slovic, Fischoff, and Lichtenstein, 1982). The suggestion of Harris et al. was that the children's experience of having imagined a creature in the box would increase the availability of instances in which the box might really contain a creature and thus increase the apparent risk of there really being a creature inside. Against this background, they suggested that a decline in fear of imaginary creatures over development could be explained by "an increasing resistance to such 'availability' effects" (p. 121).

As an alternative mechanism, Harris et al. described the *transmigration* hypothesis. As part of their research, they had demonstrated that children are able to distinguish consistently between fantasy and reality. Even so, they proposed that "children might still remain unsure of the rules that govern transformation between those two realms" (p. 121). Four- and six-year-olds might know that all things are either fantasy or real but fail to understand that no act of mind can bring about a category change. To explain developmental change with respect to this second alternative, Harris et al. proposed that "the decline in children's fear of imaginary creatures would be explicable in terms of their changing conception of the causal links between mind and reality" (p. 122).

Although I find both proposed mechanisms to be inventive explanations for their findings, I believe Harris et al. go astray in taking for granted some implicit notion of grown-up behavior. The processes I have described in earlier sections of this chapter undermine confidence that adults' behavior would seriously depart from the children's. Although I am reasonably certain that adults would be less likely to feel so fearful as to ask the experimenter not to leave the room, I suspect that—were the experiment motivated in an appropriate fashion—adults would explore the creature-filled box just as readily as the children did. Suppose, furthermore, that the adults were asked why they had investigated the box. I am, again, reasonably certain that they would not admit to believing they could bring imaginary creatures into real existence, but I am not at all sure what they would claim instead.

We could, in fact, characterize the phenomenon identified by Harris et al. as an instance of either capture or nonpenetration (or both). The exploration of the (imaginarily) creature-filled box is in many ways comparable to anomalous suspense or anomalous replotting. When subjects become immersed in a narrative world in which the box is occupied, they might find that because attention is so thoroughly captured, knowledge of the box's real-world emptiness is momentarily crowded out of consciousness. This experience also echoes emotional responses to fictions. The parallel is very close when children become so frightened that they ask the experimenter not to leave the room. Even in the case of the friendly rabbit, however, we can imagine that the belief that the creature is not real does not penetrate the curiosity generated by experience of the narrative. I am suggesting, therefore, that Harris et al. have not demonstrated a phenomenon that dissipates with age. Rather, they have exposed a basic aspect of narrative experience that endures through the life span.

In this chapter I have tried to reduce much of what has seemed special about the experience of narratives to the operation of general mental processes and structures. I suggested that anomalous suspense reflects the ordinary dominance of schematic over veridical expectancies—or what I have called the expectation of uniqueness—in many domains of day-to-day experience. I also argued that the emotional responses generated with respect to fictional narratives, as well as the lack of overt behavior, are representative of more-general instances of nonpenetration of belief and side-participation. Finally, I described one developmental study to show perhaps how little our capacity to be transported changes with age. Nothing about my analysis, however, undermines readers' special feeling of being transported. Rather, this repertory of mental processes and structures conspires to produce the unique phenomenology of the experience of narrative worlds.

Narrative Information and
Real-World Judgments

In the *Republic,* Plato suggested that dramatic poets, and the majority of poetry, should be banished from the ideal state. He was concerned especially with the potential of poetry to exert an immoral influence on the populace:

> I am afraid that we shall find that poets and story-tellers are in error in matters of the greatest human importance. They have said that unjust men are often happy, and just men wretched, that wrong-doing pays if you can avoid being found out, and that justice is what is good for someone else but is to your own disadvantage. We must forbid them to say this sort of thing, and require their poems and stories to have quite the opposite moral. (pp. 148–49)

Plato's analysis of poetry mostly resides in the section on education: his concern was that children not be exposed to stories that would adversely influence their moral development. What is most salient in Plato's formulation is his certainty that poems and stories have an effect on their audience. Were that not the case, their content would hardly matter.

This final chapter deals largely with developing a psychological theory to match Plato's certainty that stories matter. I begin by presenting informal evidence that fictional information has real-world effects. Next, I review the types of theories that have most frequently obscured the origins of those effects. I then demonstrate why these theories are unworkable as psychological models of the uptake of fictional information, both with respect to mental representations and to moment-by-moment processing. My general conclusion is that there is no psychologically privileged category "fiction."

Real-World Effects of Fictional Information

In chapter 1, I offered the movie *Jaws* as vivid anecdotal evidence toward the conclusion that experiences of fictional worlds can shape viewers' behavior in the real world. After watching that film, in which a great white shark wreaked havoc on a beach community, many vacationers found themselves facing the ocean with trepidation. Psychologically, the circumstances were reminiscent of the nonpenetration situations I described in chapter 5. The beachgoers were well aware that the proximal cause of their fear was a work of fiction, yet this knowledge did little to allay the fear. Why not? *Time* magazine quoted Bob Burnside of the Los Angeles County Department of Beaches: "I had to force myself back in the water. . . . So have my lifeguards. It has affected them more because they know it can really happen" (July 28, 1975, p. 47). For these lifeguards, *Jaws* did not so much manufacture a fear as present vivid evidence to confirm one that preexisted. Because shark attacks really do happen, it hardly mattered that the reminder was provided in a fictional context. Thus, we need look no further than *Jaws* to confirm that under entirely transparent circumstances, real-world judgments can be affected by fictions.

The majority of fictional effects, however, are likely to be much more subtle. They won't halt readers at water's edge but, rather, will become part of the body of information readers access to make day-to-day judgments. Consider this excerpt from Robertson Davies's novel *The Lyre of Orpheus*. The initial speaker is the character Maria, who is pregnant:

> "I was drinking this [rum and milk] last night when Al and Sweetness were here, and Sweetness was shocked."
>
> "Shocked by rum and milk? . . . What shocked her?"
>
> "She gave me a long, confused talk about what she called the foetal alcohol syndrome; booze in pregnancy can lead to pixie-faced, pin-headed, mentally retarded children. I knew something about that; you have to drink rather a lot to be in danger. But Sweetness is a zealot, and she's deep into the squalor of pregnancy, poor wretch. . . . She is paying the full price nasty old Mother Nature can exact for Al's baby. I just hope it's a nice baby." (pp. 344–45)

Either Davies has gotten his facts wrong, or he has knowingly put incorrect information into Maria's mouth. Although fetal alcohol syndrome is most often associated with heavy drinking, mothers who drink even small amounts of alcohol cam damage the fetus during critical periods of development (see Restak, 1988). What makes this instance of misinformation—with respect, that is, to the real world—even more compelling is that in the novel Maria delivers a healthy child but Sweetness delivers a stillborn. Thus, the book makes a rather dramatic fictional case that women should have a relaxed attitude about drinking during pregnancy.

Fictions often, in fact, depict circumstances in which morally ambiguous behavior is framed within a rhetorical structure that makes it aesthetically pleasing. Often, even blatantly immoral characters are cast in a romantic light. Consider the 1991 film *Bugsy*, in which Warren Beatty plays Benjamin "Bugsy" Siegel, the gangster who "invented" Las Vegas. Here is talk-show host David Letterman's response to the movie ("Late Night," January 9, 1992):

> *Letterman (to audience):* Have you folks seen "Bugsy"? [Audience responds with scattered applause and "yeahs."] See, that's—It's a great movie. You go and you watch that movie and it, it makes organized crime, it really, it puts the fun back in organized crime for me. [Audience laughter.] You know it really does because you're pulling for 'em. You want these, these organized criminals, You want 'em to succeed in the end. And you don't, you don't even mind when they beat people up 'n shoot people. I mean that's the way, you know that's the way movies ought to be for gosh sakes.

Letterman is clearly exaggerating his response to amuse his audience. Even so, he has captured the spirit of *Bugsy*. Siegel should in no sense be a laudable character: the audience sees him commit at least two murders as well as other acts of violence. Once he articulates the dream of Las Vegas, however, the audience is increasingly taken up with the grandeur of his scheme. The great tragedy of the film is that Siegel is murdered by his gangster partners before he can see his dream come true. At the end of the movie, the information appears on the screen that the small amount of money invested by Bugsy and his colleagues has burgeoned into billions of dollars in profit. The audience likely leaves the theater feeling uplifted by this visionary tale: with what consequences, we wonder, for everyday behavior?

The rhetorical power of fiction can also be turned to inculcating less morally ambiguous values. Psychiatrist Robert Coles, in *The Call of Stories* (1989), reports on the success he has had at inspiring students to reflect on their own lives by reflecting on fictional lives. His case studies often reveal moments of startling psychological transformation. For Coles, this is the special power of narratives:

> Novels and stories are renderings of life; they can not only keep us company, but admonish us, point us in new directions, or give us the courage to stay a given course. They can offer us kinsmen, kinswomen, comrades, advisers—offer us other eyes through which we might see, other ears with which we might make soundings. . . . No wonder, then, a Dr. Lydgate [from George Eliot's *Middlemarch*] or a Dick Diver [from F. Scott Fitzgerald's *Tender is the Night*] can be cautionary figures to us, especially to us doctors, can be spiritual companions, can be persons, however "imaginary" in nature, who give us pause and help us in the private moments when we try to find our bearings. No wonder, too, Jack Burden in Robert Penn Warren's *All the King's Men* speaks to all of us who have tried to understand the nature of politics, the possibilities, the terrible temptations. (pp. 159–60)

The students who benefited from Coles's explorations of narratives were usually willing participants, in the sense that they came to expect that the fictions could illuminate their own lives. Culler (1975), in his discussion of the conventions that undergird readers' ability to experience literature, encodes this expectation as the *rule of significance:* one reads a poem "as expressing a significant attitude to some problem concerning man and/or his relation to the universe" (p. 115). This rule of significance is grounded in readers' expectations about authors' intentions: "To write a poem is to claim significance of some sort for the verbal construct one produces, and the reader approaches a poem with the assumption that however brief it may appear it must contain, at least implicitly, potential riches which make it worthy of his attention" (p. 175). Culler's suggestion can be straightforwardly extended to prose to yield the conclusion that everyday readers fundamentally believe that fictions are intended to have real-world significance.

Professional readers also often search for the real-world point of works of fiction. Graff (1981) quotes Richard Ellmann's summary of the theme of James Joyce's *Ulysses* as "casual kindness overcomes unconscionable power" (p. 150). Graff says that Ellmann "surely qualifies as a competent reader" but nonetheless "assumes that Joyce is expressing a certain view of the world and that this view matters both to Joyce and his reader" (p. 150). Graff's greater purpose is to demonstrate that theories of literary criticism that attempt to regulate real-world effects of fiction out of existence fail to capture the real-world activities of competent readers. What I suggest in the next section, in fact, is that theories of the experience of fiction have quite regularly obscured the pathways through which fictions can have good or ill effects on such readers.

Toggle Theories of Fiction

In the face of this widely held belief in the real-world significance of fictions, I wish to review theories that have either denied these effects or made them obscure (see also Woodmansee, 1978). I call this class of theories *toggle theories* to invoke an image of a mental toggle that is thrown one way or the other to accommodate experiences of fiction and nonfiction. The classic toggle image comes from Samuel Taylor Coleridge's *Biographia Literaria*, in which he famously suggested that the experience of poetry requires a "willing suspension of disbelief" (p. 6). This phrase is widely cited to stand for some cluster of special processes that readers are supposed to undertake when they know themselves to be experiencing fiction. If we contrast fiction and nonfiction, the implication is that there is a toggling back and forth between suspension and nonsuspension of disbelief. It was not, of course, Coleridge's intent to provide a theory of moment-by-moment psychological processes, nor can his phrase be casually expanded into such a theory. There is little evidence, for example, that readers can alter beliefs in any important sense by acts of will (see Carroll, 1990). Even so, the "willing suspension of disbelief" has often served as the foundational image on which theorists have built more-modern forms of toggle theories. By referring to this phrase, theorists have accepted as given that the mental processes performed by readers of fiction are special to those experiences—that there is a toggle to be thrown. The great inconvenience of this whole class of theories, however, is that they are often at a loss to account for the real-world effects of fictions. I explore this difficulty by working through some representative theories, all of which, I believe, postulate toggles and are unable to explain the real-world impact of fiction.

The strongest toggle theory—in which fictional information would have no real-world effects—has typically been put forth only as an aesthetic ideal. Consider Graff's (1981) generic characterization of what he calls *anti-assertionist* views:

> [The anti-assertionist's] resistance to permitting literary works to be read as making assertions comes not from any notion that it is not *possible* for such works to be read that way—he concedes, in fact, that many people do read them this way; it comes rather from the conviction that literary works *ought* not to be read as making assertions, that if they are read that way we give encouragement to a philistine or reactionary view of culture. In other words, what is often at issue for the anti-assertionist is the fear that literature will be degraded to the purely utilitarian level to which a practical and commercial society reduces all objects. (pp. 140–41)

Such views call into question the possibility of teaching readers to experience fictional narratives in such a way that they could treat them only as aesthetic objects. (Graff comments that anti-assertionist theories "may be seen either as wishful thinking or as attempts at 'behavior modification' " [p. 160].) The evidence I review in this chapter, however, strongly suggests that the non-toggle nature of the experience of fiction is too deep a property of cognitive structure to be trained into oblivion. Whatever new language games theorists might invent to strengthen the strong toggle ideal will necessarily clash with inherent psychological properties.

Most toggle theories have acceded to the reality of fictional effects on the real world. Rather than argue against such effects, these theories have typically—by postulating a fiction-nonfiction toggle—made the origins of those effects obscure. Consider Searle's (1975) pretense theory of fictional utterances, described in chapter 4. (I take advantage of Searle once again because he did not shroud his theory in ambiguity. Most of the approaches I cited in chapter 4 implicitly merit the toggle label.) At the core of Searle's theory is the claim that authors pretend to perform fictional utterances, and that "the pretended illocutions which constitute a work of fiction are made possible by the existence of a set of conventions which suspend the normal operation of the rules relating illocutionary acts and the world" (p. 326). Here, exactly, is Searle's toggle: there is a theoretical set of conventions that turns on or off in the presence of fiction or nonfiction. Even so, Searle acknowledges that "serious (i.e., nonfictional) speech acts can be conveyed by fictional texts, even though the conveyed speech act is not represented in the text. Almost any important work of fiction conveys a 'message' or 'messages' which are conveyed *by* the text but are not *in* the text." Searle goes on to say that "there is as yet no general theory of the mechanisms by which serious illocutionary intentions are conveyed by pretended illocutions" (p. 332). There is an open admission that fiction has effects. Within the bounds of the theory, however, the mechanism is obscure. Searle makes a final claim that enables me to describe some of the variations among toggle theories. Recall Searle's assertion that "a work of fiction need not consist entirely of, and in general will not consist entirely of, fictional discourse" (p. 332). He offered, as part of his evidence, Tolstoy's "genuine assertion": "Happy families are all happy in the same way, unhappy families unhappy in their separate, different ways." The great difficulty, as I suggested earlier, is in knowing when authors intend their utterances to be taken nonfictionally, particularly when these utterances are buffered through narrators of varying reliability. In the current framework, the concern is easy to label: if there is an all-or-none toggle between fiction and nonfiction, readers must know when to switch the toggle—and by doing so, if Searle is correct, those readers would be switching on and off whole sets of conventions (and thus, presumably, whole sets of cognitive processes).

In response to the seeming impossibility of differentiating fiction from nonfiction moment by moment, other theorists have asserted that readers take every utterance performed within a fictional work as fiction. Beardsley (1981) argues that a strict separation must be maintained between authors and the narrators (or, for poems, "speakers") they create: "If the speaker is not the author then *his* illocutionary actions are not the author's" (p. 304). Only speakers perform utterances within the fictional world. The toggle for Beardsley is thrown as soon as readers come to believe that what they are reading is intended to be a work of fiction. Like Searle, however, Beardsley acknowledges that fictions can be used to have real effects. He offers the case of a poem by Gaston Miron that was intended to fan the flames of Quebec nationalism:

But of course if Gaston Miron reads his poem from a platform during a rally in which thousands of people are petitioning the Canadian government for a redress of grievances, and shouting their resolution to secede from the other nine provinces, then the act of producing a token of *that* text under *those* circumstances will be political, and will generate genuine illocutionary actions. (p. 309)

What remains obscure in Beardsley's theory, however, is how fictional works can have the more mundane effects I illustrated earlier. Beardsley's toggle appears to presuppose that fictions can have an effect only in some specially marked circumstances. But what was special about the circumstances in which the "text" of *Jaws* was experienced so that viewers recalculated the real-world danger of swimming in the ocean? Viewers of the film are not already immersed in a context in which the text contributes to ambient real-world themes. Similarly, what circumstances would prompt Robertson Davies's readers to readjust their beliefs about the prenatal dangers of alcohol? These examples suggest that the circumstances in which fictions can generate "genuine illocutionary actions" are entirely unexceptional. Beardsley must explain how the speech acts "represented" in fiction can have real-world impact as a part of the moment-by-moment flow of a narrative. In the absence of such an account, Beardsley's toggle fails to eliminate the dilemma of nonfiction within fiction.

Let me focus my analysis of toggles more narrowly onto the issue of whether mentions of real-world entities are, in fact, "real" when they appear in fictional works. Did Tolstoy's readers take fictional statements about the Napoleon of *War and Peace* to apply to the historical Napoleon? Do readers confuse Sherlock Holmes's London with the real London? Opinions on these questions have been strongly polarized. Unsurprisingly, Searle (1975) took it to be the case that "most fictional stories contain non-fictional elements: along with the pretended references to Sherlock Holmes and Watson, there are in Sherlock Holmes real references to London and Baker Street and Paddington Station; again, in *War and Peace,* the story of Pierre and Natasha is a fictional story about fictional characters, but the Russia of *War and Peace* is the real Russia, and the war against Napoleon is the real war against the real Napoleon" (p. 330). Responses to assertions like Searle's have often focused on the impossibility, for example, that real people could have met Sherlock Holmes on the streets of London. Adams (1985) suggests that

> since we cannot meet a fictional character—which I think can be taken to be self-evident—we cannot go to any place that would make such a meeting possible. So in the case of the Sherlock Holmes stories, there must be two Londons, each with its own Baker Street, one in our world and one in Sherlock Holmes's world. And since we cannot enter a fictional world and since fictional characters cannot enter our world, fictional characters remain unaware of the real world and are, therefore, unable to talk about it. (pp. 21–22)

These two positions constitute polar claims. In the first view, readers treat Sherlock Holmes's London as the real London and must toggle between pretend referring phrases and real referring phrases. In the second view, the toggle is thrown to separate entirely the understanding of references made in fictions from real-world references. The respective positions of Searle and Adams (used here to represent a generic opposition in the literature) are both developed from strong intuitions about the effects they *ought* to have (that is, what would be rational), as well as the effects that fictions really do have. Because these intuitions lead to opposite conclusions, the safest course is to gather evidence about what readers actually do. In the next section, I describe empirical research about the psychological fate of fictional information.

In this section I have illustrated why toggles pervade theories of the experience of fiction and hinted at why these toggles, in all their manifestations, are unworkable as elements of psychological theories. They have almost inevitably arisen because the taxonomy of readers' experiences has been drawn with the dichotomy between fiction and nonfiction taken as the first, and fundamental, distinction. In the rest of this chapter, I argue that fiction emerges as an experiential category not through a passive and wholesale suspension of disbelief but, rather, through active scrutiny of the particular information proffered in fictions.

The Representation of Narrative Information

In the previous section, I narrowed the focus to Sherlock Holmes's London so that I could quickly identify the core issue for cognitive psychological models of the experience of narratives. In particular, the competing theories largely constitute claims about the way information presented in fictional works is represented in memory. Let us imagine that readers have information already stored in memory about some topic treated in a work of fiction. How, then, is the fictional information stored with respect to this prior (let us suppose) nonfictional information? We could imagine a range of hypotheses, motivated equally by knowledge of anecdotes and notions of rationality. Thus, at one end of the continuum, we might imagine that fictional information's definitional lack of correspondence to the real world would prompt readers to *compartmentalize* it with respect to nonfictional information. If information is entirely compartmentalized, it would not become associated in any way with information acquired from other sources. The types of theories I have characterized as toggle theories most often presuppose compartmentalization.

Anecdotal evidence, however, leads strongly to the prediction of at least some amount of *incorporation* of fictional information into nonfictional knowledge structures. The degree of incorporation would reflect the extent to which the information became associated with preexisting knowledge. When we observe that viewers of *Jaws* were unable to coax themselves into the water by remembering that *Jaws* was a work of fiction, we suspect that some information from the movie had come to wield an influence on real-world judgments.

The question of the relative compartmentalization or incorporation of fictional information has been analyzed in a number of psychological paradigms (Potts and Peterson, 1985; Potts, St. John, and Kirson, 1989). To test some representational consequences of fictional information, Lewis and Anderson (1976) asked a group of subjects to read a series of statements that provided fantasy facts about well-known individuals. Subjects read that "George Washington wrote *Tom Sawyer*" and "Napoleon Bonaparte was from India." The instructions for the experiment specifically emphasized that the statements should be taken as belonging to a fantasy world that included the individuals named. Lewis and Anderson did not want their subjects to memorize the sentences verbatim, so the subjects—with no expectation of a memory test—were simply asked to write continuations for each statement. By the end of the study phase, subjects had read statements associating between zero and four fantasy facts with each of twenty real individuals. Previous research with materials that excluded real-world individuals had revealed a verification time cost for each additional piece of information associated with a particular individual. This result was called the *fan effect* because the memory structures were visualized as multiple pieces of information forming a fan off of a common node. The larger the fan, the greater the decrement in performance (for a review, see Anderson, 1983). Lewis and Anderson sought to determine whether there would be orderly increments in the difficulty of verifying *real* facts about George Washington (for example, "George Washington crossed the Delaware") as a function of learning zero to four new fantasy facts.

The experimental results straightforwardly displayed interference: subjects were slower to verify real facts and made more errors in doing so in proportion to the number of fantasy facts they had read. Lewis and Anderson argued that this result provided evidence for the integration in memory of fantasy and real facts. They acknowledged, however, the alternative possibility that such interference could arise because of subjects' uncertainty about which of two memory structures they ought to search to verify particular statements; they labeled this a *decision-interference* model. In the original study, subjects had verified a list of statements that contained a mixture of real and fantasy facts (both types of statements displayed a fan effect). To examine the decision-interference model, Lewis and Anderson conducted a second experiment in which they had their subjects verify statements either in mixed lists, once again, or in lists of pure fantasy or pure facts. Subjects' decision uncertainty should be minimized when verifying statements on the pure lists. In fact, Lewis and Anderson demonstrated fan effects under all circumstances, including tests on the pure lists of real facts. This result strongly argues for integration of the fantasy facts into preexisting memory structures.

One difference that did emerge, however, between the pure and mixed lists was that verification latencies were considerably shorter when the lists were pure. This result suggests that some aspect of the representation of the new facts allows subjects to constrain memory retrieval. Peterson and Potts (1982) conducted a pair of experiments to determine whether the advantage of pure over mixed lists was a consequence of a fantasy-fact distinction or of an experimental-preexperimental distinction. They required subjects to learn a series of statements using a procedure nearly identical to that of Lewis and Anderson. For different groups of subjects, however, these statements were either fantasy facts of the sort used by Lewis and Anderson or real facts that were simply unknown to the subjects (for example, "Julius Caesar was left handed"). Peterson and Potts replicated the original fan-effect finding that the acquisition of extra facts—whether fantasy or real—resulted in increased verification latencies. They also demonstrated, however, that only the fantasy facts yielded a difference between pure and mixed lists. Peterson and Potts interpreted their results as revealing a distinction between *specific* and *global* integration of information. They suggested that a new piece of information is always integrated with specific preexisting information in memory. It need not, on the other hand, have particularly global consequences in reorganizing memory representations less directly related to the topic. Peterson and Potts suggested that fictional information has specific consequences (that is, readers integrate the fictional fact that Napoleon was from India with other knowledge about Napoleon) but not global consequences (readers do not reorganize other knowledge about India in the way they might if the information were veridical). According to Peterson and Potts, it is the lack of global perturbations that yields the processing advantage of pure over mixed lists for fantasy facts alone.

Lewis and Anderson's results (and Peterson and Potts's replication) rule out models of the uptake of fictional information that suppose total compartmentalization to be obligatory. At the same time, however, the experiments leave open the possibility that fantasy facts retain some degree of representational coherence. This proviso is particularly appropriate given that both sets of experiments quite plainly offer up fictional information in a way that minimizes continuity among the collection of fantasy facts. The benefit of this methodology is that it makes the fictionality of the facts absolutely transparent. If it were possible—automatically or strategically—for readers to isolate individual statements of fiction from nonfiction in memory, they ought to have done so here. The methodology, however, does not afford an opportunity to assess whether, or how strongly, information that constitutes a narrative is drawn together into a coherent representation.

Potts and his colleagues (Potts and Peterson, 1985; Potts, St. John, and Kirson, 1989) invented a new methodology to address this issue. I will illustrate the technique with respect to a passage from Richard Powers's novel *Prisoner's Dilemma*:

> [Walt Disney] informs [Secretary of War] Stimson that if he can't get the ten thousand bodies out [of the Japanese internment camps], he will publicly demand to be arrested. Stimson suddenly recalls the well-known but hitherto conveniently overlooked fact that Walt Disney's grandfather was the offspring of a geisha girl and a midshipman on Matthew Perry's ship *Susquehanna*. Disney is, in short, an American of Japanese Ancestry living in that sensitive national security area, Hollywood. (p. 180)

The bit of fictional information that Walt Disney was of partially Japanese descent (and therefore was in danger of being incarcerated during World War II) is on a par with Napoleon's having been from India (and could probably be treated experimentally as either a fantasy or an actual fact). The research by Lewis and Anderson suggests that this information would be integrated with preexisting knowledge about Disney. To what extent, even so, would it also be maintained as part of a coherent representation of the narrative? Imagine this information represented in memory so that it was completely divorced from the rest of the information in *Prisoner's Dilemma*. When thinking about other aspects of the book, readers would then fail to activate this fact about Disney. If, by contrast, the Disney information were stored together with other information from the book, readers should be able to locate the information when thinking about other aspects of the book.

The methodology of Potts et al. captures these intuitions by requiring subjects to verify story information in one of two contexts: in *story contexts,* the critical statements (which might be something like "Walt Disney is of Japanese descent") are included within a verification list composed of other statements culled from the same story; in *nonstory contexts* the other statements on the verification list did not appear in the original story. To the extent that the statement is represented coherently with other story information—to the extent that the information is compartmentalized with respect to other information in memory—there ought to be a performance advantage when the critical statement is verified in the story context rather than in the nonstory context. If no such advantage accrues, we can conclude that the information has been represented in memory with functional independence from its original story context.

Potts et al. designed their experiments to reveal differences in the degree of compartmentalization or incorporation for factual versus fantasy information. On the basis of intuitions about utility, they predicted that subjects would be, on the whole, more likely to incorporate information that was identified as nonfictional. One important consequence of incorporation is that the information becomes accessible in contexts that depart from the original circumstances in which it was learned. To the extent that incorporation is under strategic control, readers should work harder to have factual information more readily accessible than fantasy information.

In the experiments by Potts et al., subjects read double-spaced texts roughly two or two and a half pages long that introduced information about novel topics. One story, for example, concerned the near extinction of a New Zealand bird called the takahe. Two groups of subjects received different instructions. Subjects in the *artificial* group were told, "Though some of the information in the story may be familiar to you, most of the information is fictional and was constructed for use in the present experiment" (pp. 309–10). In the *real* condition, subjects were told, "Though some of the material may seem unusual, all of the information in the story is true and has been verified using various reference sources" (p. 310). Subjects read the texts three times and answered practice true/false questions after each of the first two readings. After reading the story a third time, subjects verified statements in twelve blocks, half of which created a story context and half of which created a nonstory context. They completed the six blocks of each type as a unit, but half of the subjects performed the story blocks first, and half the nonstory blocks.

The most important prediction of Potts et al. was that the degree of compartmentalization would be greater when subjects believed they were reading artificial materials. Comparisons of performance in the story and nonstory contexts bore out that prediction. Across two experiments, the researchers found that those subjects who believed the materials were artificial obtained roughly a two-hundred-millisecond advantage in the story contexts over the nonstory contexts. When subjects believed the materials were real, no such advantage emerged. The texts were identical: all that could explain the compartmentalization shift was the readers' strategic stance toward what they believed to be real or artificial information.

In a final experiment, Potts et al. began to bring the consequences of compartmentalization into tighter focus by contrasting two classes of representational models. Consider, once again, the possibilities that might ensue when readers encounter story information about Walt Disney. Let us assume that readers already have some organized body of information that can be visualized as connected to a central node representing Disney. ("Nodes" and the "connections" among them are metaphors cognitive psychologists use to refer to organizational properties of memory structures. They circumscribe no physiological claims.) Against this background, one possibility, which Potts et al. called a *structural model,* is that readers would create a new node in memory to represent the story Disney information. Under this model, the degree of compartmentalization would be determined by the strength of the association in memory between the old knowledge concepts and the new story concepts. A second possibility, called a *context-directed search model,* is that the story information about Disney is directly integrated into existing Disney memory structures (that is, no new Disney story node is created), but it also becomes associated with a node in memory that represents the story context. In this model, the degree of compartmentalization is reflected by the relative strength of the associations between the old knowledge nodes and the story node. Thus, if the new Disney information is strongly associated with the story context and only weakly associated with old Disney facts, the information could be more readily accessed through activation of the story context rather than through general world knowledge. The most salient contrast between the two models, therefore, is whether readers form new nodes in memory even when story concepts overlap with nonstory concepts.

To contrast these models, Potts et al. measured the priming relationships between new story information and preexisting nodes. Recall that one of their stories introduced information about a bird called the takahe. According to both models, we would expect readers to set up an association in memory between the concepts "bird" and "takahe." If, however, the structural model is correct, the story "bird" node would be distinct from the preexisting "bird" node and, thus, there would be little direct association between "takahe" and the world knowledge "bird." By contrast, the context-directed search model assumes that there is only one "bird" node; thus, there should be a direct association between the world knowledge "bird" and "takahe." Potts et al. turned once again to story and nonstory contexts to tease apart these predictions. If the structural model is correct, access to "bird" should facilitate access to "takahe" only in story contexts. If the context-directed search model is correct, access to "bird" should facilitate access to "takahe" in both story and nonstory contexts.

Subjects in this third experiment were all led to believe that the texts they were reading were real. Because this belief should have led to a small degree of compartmentalization, this allows for a contrast of the two models in the limiting case. After reading each text three times (and answering a set of forty questions between readings), the subjects were asked to perform a lexical decision task (see chapter 2). As in the earlier experiments, different blocks of trials were arranged to create story and nonstory contexts. Each block contained critical pairs in which a potential source of facilitation (for example, "bird") preceded the new experimental term ("takahe"). The data revealed a performance advantage (on proportion of correct lexical decisions) only in story contexts. Thus, when "bird" preceded "takahe" in a context that did not otherwise activate concepts from the story, subjects obtained no benefit from the story association of the two concepts. Potts et al. take this as strong evidence in favor of the structural model. Readers appear to form new memory nodes to serve as the foci for story information even when those nodes reproduce preexisting concepts. This result is especially striking because subjects were reading the stories as if the information were real, a circumstance that had produced relatively less compartmentalization in the first two experiments. The practice of creating new nodes cannot, therefore, be considered special to fiction.

Potts et al. provided a series of powerful results about the representational fate of factual and fictional story information about topics that were largely new to their readers. Deborah Prentice and I (Gerrig and Prentice, 1991) sought to extend the analysis of Potts et al. to circumstances in which information presented fictionally had direct bearing on familiar topics. Information from *Prisoner's Dilemma* about Walt Disney's lineage provides a striking example of the real-worldness of some fictional information. Most often, however, fictions are relevant to familiar concerns in a gentler fashion. As I noted earlier, readers often approach fictional narratives with the strong expectation that there are lessons to be extracted. Prentice and I were interested in determining the extent to which fictional information can in fact wield an influence on real-world judgments. We predicted that we would find evidence, as Potts et al. had, of some degree of compartmentalization of fictional information but that, even so, aspects of that information would become available in nonstory contexts.

For our experiments, we wrote two versions of a short story introducing some information that was consistent and some that was inconsistent with the real world. The two versions shared a plot in which a group of college students learned from the *New York Times* that a professor at their institution had been kidnapped. As the story progressed, some of these students also fell victim to the kidnappers. At the end of the story, it was revealed that all the events were staged as a birthday surprise for the hero of the tale, Brad Wollip. This plot served as a scaffold for two different types of information: *context details* and *context-free assertions*. Prentice and I defined context details as aspects of the setting that were specific to the particular fictional world. Thus, a novel might name a fictional president of the United States, but no argument within the novel could bear on the identity of the real-world president. Context-free assertions, by contrast, have the potential to transcend their fictional origins. The same novel, for example, might assert or demonstrate the great corruption of the fictional president. Readers might come to believe that real-world presidents are also corrupt.

In some cases, it would be difficult to label a type of fictional information as context-bound or context-free, and different readers might treat the same information differently. The two types of information are best thought of as anchoring a continuum: we could imagine that the continuum of context-freeness would be reflected by a continuum of influence on judgments outside the fictional world. For our initial experiments, however, Prentice and I made a sharp methodological contrast between context details and context-free assertions. We suggested, accordingly, that readers ought to be more affected in their real-world judgments by the context-free assertions than by the context details.

In each of two versions of the story, half of the context details and half of the context-free assertions (eight in each case) were consistent with real-world circumstances at the time the experiments were carried out. The other half created a fictional reality. The portions of each story that accomplished this manipulation were not at all subtle. Half of the subjects, for example, read a passage that confirmed the context-detail that the national speed limit was fifty-five miles per hour (the kidnappers have been arguing about the consequences of that limit):

> "Do you suppose that Congress envisioned these sorts of arguments when they dropped the speed limit to 55 ten years ago?" asked Dane [Brad Wollip's good friend].
> "Right now, I wish the speed limit were much higher than 55," said Abrams [the kidnapped professor], "so that the president and the money could get to us just that much sooner."

The other half read of a fictional change to seventy miles per hour:

> "Do you suppose that Congress envisioned these sorts of arguments when they raised the speed limit to 70?" asked Dane.

"The only good thing about the raised speed limit," said Abrams, "is that it should get the president and the money to us a little bit sooner."

The context-free assertions were all statements easily recognized as true in the real world. One story version, for example, confirmed the belief that penicillin has been beneficial to humankind (Dane is commenting on his frequent use of penicillin):

> "I don't talk about it much—but I can tell you one thing, if that guy hadn't discovered penicillin in his moldy bread, I probably wouldn't have lived long enough to be kidnapped with you today. It certainly has been important stuff for me." He laughed and continued, "When they ask me for the secret of life, I'll tell them *penicillin*." He assumed a tone of voice appropriate to delivery of the "secret of life." "*Penicillin*. A thrill for mankind; a thrill for me."

The other story version suggested that penicillin has done more harm than good (because the passages appear in identical positions in the two versions, the speaker is once again Dane):

> "I've been keeping up on this [research] since I've taken *so* much penicillin for *so* long. Doctors have been noticing for about a decade now that all sorts of birth defects have been on the rise. They couldn't quite figure out why: The only thing that a lot of the babies had in common was that one or the other of the parents had taken penicillin in the year before they were conceived. It didn't even have to be much, either. These scientists are starting to worry that penicillin will turn out to have really bad consequences for humankind."

All of the fictional information, therefore, was relevant to familiar topics. For each subject, half of the information was at odds with day-to-day reality.

In our first experiment, Prentice and I examined the extent to which fictional information of the two types affected judgments about the truth of the statements apart from the fictional setting. To measures these effects, we required our subjects to verify a series of statements presented on a computer monitor. Subjects were led to believe that the verification task constituted a new experiment that required judgments about real-life topics. The verification list included the relevant context details and context-free assertions, as well as filler statements that were not relevant to the previous story but consisted of the same dichotomous types of information. The computer recorded the accuracy and latency of subjects' responses to the statements. These measures allowed us to determine whether readers would find it more difficult to reject statements such as "The speed limit is 70 miles per hour" or "Penicillin has had bad consequences for humankind" after completing a story in which those assertions had been fictionally true.

One hypothesis was that fictional information would have no effect on such judgments and could be wholly compartmentalized with respect to prior knowledge. A second hypothesis was that the two types of information would act identically to interfere with these truth judgments. Readers could briefly find themselves transported to the narrative world so that the fictional context details and context-free assertions would linger equally. The hypothesis Prentice and I preferred, however, was a middle ground reflecting the differing potential utility of the two types of information. Context details cannot, at least in our strict dichotomy, bear on circumstances in the real world. Context-free assertions might. Readers should therefore give more strategic attention to fictional context-free assertions. We predicted, along these lines, that fictional information would have a stronger interference effect on judgments for context-free assertions than on those for context details.

To assess this hypothesis, we compared the judgment times of subjects who had read the experimental stories to those of subjects who read a control story that contained no information relevant to the experimental topics. Against this control baseline, we could gauge the effects of our fictional information. Each subject in the experimental groups read passages that contained information consistent and inconsistent with the real world. Each subject was also asked to verify statements that were consistent and inconsistent. Thus, for each subject (and for each context detail and context-free assertion) we asked, What was the average verification time cost associated with reading information in the fictional world that was inconsistent with the real world? For context details this cost was roughly 78 milliseconds. If subjects read that the speed limit was 70, it took them, on average, an extra 78 milliseconds to respond true to "The speed limit is 55 miles per hour" (which was universally true at the time of the experiment) and false to "The speed limit is 70 miles per hour." For context-free assertions, the cost was 302 milliseconds. (Although the actual statistical analysis was not structured to compare these average costs directly, the patterns of interference for the two types of information were reliably different.) For the context-free assertions, in fact, the entire effect was carried by the responses to inconsistent test statements like "Penicillin has had bad consequences for humankind." Subjects took 600 milliseconds longer to say false to this statement (but only 3 milliseconds longer to say true to the consistent statement) by virtue of having read the inconsistent fictional information.

Overall, the results suggest that, when returning from the narrative world, the readers left context details behind but retained some information about context-free assertions. The different patterns of interference for context details and context-free assertions enabled us to suggest that the fictional information was incorporated into preexisting long-term memory structures. Parallel results might have suggested that subjects were confused within the experiment about the information with respect to which they were intended to make the true/false judgments. However, within a verification list that mixed context details and context-free assertions as well as statements that were and were not relevant to the previous story, we found a strong pattern of interference only for the inconsistent context-free assertions. We believe this result supports the claim that context-free information is of enough potential utility, in contrast to context details, to become globally incorporated into preexisting memory structures.

Our second experiment was designed to demonstrate, even so, that story information of both types retains some features of a representation that is compartmentalized in memory. Prentice and I adapted the technique of Potts et al. (1989) for having subjects make verification judgments of context details and context-free assertions in story and nonstory contexts. We believed, along with Potts et al., that facilitated performance in story blocks would indicate lingering coherence of information in memory. Subjects in this second experiment read only one version of the story from experiment 1, updated somewhat to reflect changes in real-world context details. For the verification phase of the experiment, subjects were required overall to make true/false judgments for sixteen blocks of twenty statements. Eight were story blocks and eight nonstory blocks. Eight were purely context details, and eight context-free assertions. Subjects began with either all of the story blocks or all of the nonstory blocks, but within these groups, context detail and context-free assertion blocks were randomly intermixed. Once again, we had a group of control subjects who performed the verification phase of the experiment without reading the original story.

Our main prediction that subjects would find it easier to verify both types of information in the context of other statements from the story was confirmed. Verification latencies were 365 milliseconds faster when subjects verified context details in story blocks rather than in nonstory blocks. For context-free assertions, the advantage was 565 milliseconds. This difference was even greater when we examined performance for the first group of verification blocks. When subjects verified the statements in the group of eight story blocks first, they did so 719 milliseconds faster than the control group. If the eight nonstory blocks came first, subjects were 409 milliseconds *slower* than the control group. (Note that even without relativization to the control, the verification means were 2.882 seconds when subjects made the story-block judgments first and 3.573 seconds when they made the nonstory-block judgments first.) This pattern of data strongly suggests that story information was stored coherently in memory. What makes this result more surprising, perhaps, is that the story itself was about twenty pages of single-spaced text. The nontarget context-free assertions and context details that were used to constitute the story blocks were sampled more or less randomly from all portions of this long text. We would therefore expect very little facilitation because of direct relationships between individual sentences. Rather, the story-block facilitation must arise because of a more distributed coherence afforded by presence in the story.

The results of this pair of experiments are straightforwardly accommodated within the structural model of Potts et al. Recall that Potts et al. suggested that readers created a new "bird" node to encode story information about birds. Similarly, Prentice and I argued that readers created a new "penicillin" node to serve as the focus for encoding story information about penicillin. In our experiments, we manipulated story content so that the information associated with the fictional nodes would often directly contradict information associated with the preexisting nodes. The details of our data can be explained if we assume that a link is formed between the fictional and the preexisting penicillin concepts. Such a link would enable fictional information to affect real-world judgments as a function of the strength of the association. One way to understand the results of experiment 1 would thus be to posit a weak link between, for example, the fictional and the real-world speed limit, but a stronger link between the fictional and the real-world penicillin. The results of experiment 2 follow naturally from the assumption of new concept nodes. Separate encoding of story information would yield the outcome of compartmentalization.

This review of empirical research leads toward the conclusion that the only representational toggle is between narrative and preexisting information—which may reflect a sort of conservative mental stance toward all new narrative information. Individual elements of narrative accounts are initially drawn together in a coherent form in memory. Even in the case of nonfiction, representations of narrative information appear to begin life stored apart from preexisting knowledge.

Note that other aspects of the representations of narrative information would also probably differ from representations of information gathered through direct experience. Johnson (1988a, 1988b) reviewed the qualitative features that set memories of perceived events apart from memories of imagined events. Memories for perceived events often have more sensory and contextual information than do those for imagined events. On this dimension, it will matter more whether the experiencer of a narrative is watching a movie or reading a book. Whatever differences emerge, however, are likely to apply equally to both fictional and nonfictional narratives. Thus, although some features of narrative representations might allow experiencers to discriminate them from representations of real events, those features will most likely not function as a diagnostic tool to exclude fictional information from real-world consideration.

The empirical evidence leads to a conclusion about Sherlock Holmes's London that is consistent in some respects with the accounts typified by Searle and Adams—if we replace *fiction* with *narrative*. Consistent with Adams, we would expect readers initially to store information about the narrative London apart from information about the real London. Consistent with Searle, however, we would expect that this information could become available to real-world judgments if a sufficiently strong link developed between narrative and real-world knowledge about London. That is, what appears to determine the extent to which the information will affect real-world judgments is the strength of the association between the story concepts and the preexisting world-knowledge concepts. As Potts et al. found, this link may typically be weaker for fictional information than for nonfictional information, but their research provides no hint that this "typical" difference arises from any force but the outcome of strategic processing on the part of readers. Taken as a whole, research on representation has ruled out the possibility that fictional information is obligatorily excluded from determinations of belief.

Narratives and Strategic Formation of Belief

My review of the literature on representation revealed the inherent potential of fictional information to have an influence in the real world. What remains to be shown, however, is under what circumstances that potential is realized. As a first step toward putting this issue in a broader context, I will describe an experiment that shows a direct impact of fictional information on belief—but as a function of the strategic stance readers adopted toward the information.

Recall the experiments that Prentice and I carried out (Gerrig and Prentice, 1990). In those studies, we demonstrated that fictional arguments suggesting, for example, possible ill consequences of penicillin for humankind could interfere with a reader's ability to make accurate judgments about truth in the real world. Prentice, Daniel Bailis, and I (Prentice, Gerrig, and Bailis, 1992) wished to demonstrate, further, that readers would show an influence of that information on overt ratings of their beliefs—but only to the extent that they failed to appraise the information in a fashion that rendered it ineffectual. We used much the same story from the earlier experiments. Scattered within the tale of the professor's kidnapping were discussions of context-free assertions that were half-consistent and half-inconsistent with the real world. After our subjects had read the entire story, we asked them to indicate their agreement with statements like "Penicillin has been a great benefit to humankind" or "Penicillin has had bad consequences for humankind" on a nine-point scale ranging from "strongly disagree" to "strongly agree." Under appropriate circumstances of appraisal, we expected our fictional arguments to have a direct effect on these ratings.

To manipulate appraisal of the information, we began with the intuition that readers would be unlikely to assess the information presented in a story critically if the fictional world was removed from their own. Researchers have, in fact, demonstrated that readers tend to evaluate more critically information relevant to issues that are of personal importance (for reviews, see Johnson and Eagly, 1989; Petty and Cacioppo, 1986). We made the information in the story either more or less important to the person by carrying out a subtle manipulation of the identity of the characters in the story with respect to the readers. Half the subjects read a story set at Yale, half a story set at Princeton. Half of the subjects were Yale undergraduates; the other half were at Princeton.

Our prediction was that our readers would show evidence of change in beliefs only at the "away" school. We argued that a story set at Yale, for example, would prompt Yale students to consider the information much more critically than if the story were set at Princeton. We suggested that critical appraisal—in which, at least in our case, the fictional information was often directly at odds with real-world truths—would lead to a dampening of any persuasive effect. The results of the experiment supported our prediction.

Consider the belief ratings the Yale students gave after reading the Princeton story. If we presented them with a statement of a real-world truth (such as, Penicillin has been a great benefit to humankind) subjects' ratings of agreement were on average 1.25 points lower if the story had made a fictional argument against that truth than if the story had conformed to the real world. When faced with a real-world falsehood (such as, Penicillin has had bad consequences for humankind), subjects gave ratings 0.94 points higher if the story had supported that assertion. Similarly, Princeton students rated truths 1.66 points lower and falsehoods 0.30 points higher in agreement with the fictions put forth in the story. By contrast, students who read the stories set at their home schools did not, on the whole, change their belief ratings in the direction of the story: the Yale students reading the Yale story gave ratings only 0.10 points lower and 0.17 points higher for the truths and falsehoods in the direction of the Yale story. The Princeton students reading the Princeton story gave ratings 1.22 points *higher* for the truths (that is, they agreed more with the true statements when the story had argued otherwise) and 0.01 points lower for the falsehoods. Thus, when the students read the away story, they changed the ratings of their beliefs in accordance with the fictional assertions. When they read the home story, there was either little change or change in a direction opposite to story assertions. The persuasion occasioned by the away story was particularly dramatic given that the subjects' ratings were always moving in a direction that contradicted well-known real-world truths.

In our experiment, greater scrutiny of the arguments ought to have attenuated persuasion, which is why Prentice, Bailis, and I endorsed the personal relevance of the home school story as the force that undermined the fictional arguments. Our results, therefore, support the claim that persuasion by fiction is the *default* outcome: it is only under circumstances encouraging special scrutiny that readers will treat the fictional information in such a fashion that its impact is attenuated. This special effort is needed to overcome the corresponding lack of default marking for fictionality that was revealed in the review of research on representation. The "fictional" label must be strategically appended to representations of information.

This account I have been developing for readers' treatment of fictional information strongly supposes that special effort is required to prevent such information from affecting real-world beliefs. This claim accords well with the account of belief fixation Gilbert (1991) has developed through a repopularization of the work of the seventeenth-century Dutch philosopher Baruch Spinoza. Gilbert begins by suggesting that most modern theories of epistemology have honored René Descartes's distinction between the comprehension and the assessment of ideas. Within Descartes's philosophical system, comprehension is a passive process, but the acceptance or rejection of ideas requires conscious activity: no idea can be labeled as true or false without specific assessment. By contrast, Spinoza argued that the acceptance of belief is an automatic concomitant of comprehension. "Unacceptance" may follow later, but the initial product of ordinary cognitive processing is a belief in the understood propositions.

Gilbert adduces several strands of evidence to support this Spinozan view of belief. He acknowledges that the final representation of false information would probably be identical for both theories: in either case the information would be tagged in some way as not to be believed. The theories, thus, differ only in the types of representations they predict immediately after comprehension. Most important, Spinoza's view would predict that before a stage of unacceptance, all information would be taken as true. To seek evidence of this stage of universal acceptance, Gilbert, Krull, and Malone (1990) devised an experimental procedure in which subjects were interrupted while fixing the truth or falsity of novel propositions. Consider the sentence "A twyrin is a doctor." In a first experiment, such sentences were presented on a computer and followed by a screen signal that read true, or false, or was blank. Subjects were meant to use this signal word to encode the truth or falsity of the original statement. In some cases, however, a five-hundred-hertz tone sounded from the computer shortly after presentation of the truth-value signal. The subjects were required to respond to this signal as quickly as possible by pressing a response button. The Cartesian and Spinozan models of belief formation suggest different consequences for this sort of task. According to the Cartesian account, the interruption should disrupt general post-comprehension processes that tag information in memory as true or false. To the extent that the interruption impairs encoding, its effect should therefore be symmetrical for statements signaled as true or false. The Spinozan account, by contrast, suggests that the interruption should impair processing during a stage at which only false statements need be retagged. The effect of the interruption, therefore, should be localized in memory for the false statements.

To assess the actual effects of the interruption, Gilbert et al. had a second phase of the experiment in which they presented their subjects with a list of statements including the experimental sentences and asked them to label each statement as *true, false, no information* (that is, the statement had been followed by a blank screen), or *never seen*. The pattern of results supported the prediction of Gilbert et al. concerning Spinozan belief formation. For statements followed by a true signal, an interruption had little effect on correct responses: subjects correctly labeled the statement as true 55 percent of the time without an interruption and 58 percent with an interruption. For false statements, however, the interruption yielded a large decrement in performance: correct responses fell from 55 to 35 percent. The interruptions also produced a Spinozan asymmetry for incorrect responses. Without an interruption, subjects were equally likely to misrecall true statements as false (22 percent) and false statements as true (21 percent). With an interruption, however, the number of true statements labeled false fell to 17 percent, whereas the false statements labeled true climbed to 33 percent. Overall, therefore, the interruptions had the effect of revealing exactly the sort of asymmetry predicted by a Spinozan account of belief formation.

In another experiment, Gilbert et al. tested the prediction that simply comprehending a statement would decrease the probability that readers would subsequently label the statement correctly as false. In an initial phase, subjects learned facts about an imaginary animal called a "glark." In a second phase subjects were tested on that knowledge in two different types of trials. In an *assessment* trial, the question "Is the following sentence TRUE?" appeared on the screen followed by a statement that was either true (for example, Glarks have white fur) or false (Glarks have brown fur) with respect to the information acquired in the learning phase. In a *comprehension* trial, the phrase "SPEED READ the following sentence" appeared before either the true or false statement. These two types of trials were included so that Gilbert et al. could test the prediction—in accord with Spinoza's theory—that the mere comprehension of a false statement would subsequently lead subjects to accept it more often as true. The critical comparison, therefore, is between "assessment only" trials, in which subjects encountered statements that had not previously been "merely" comprehended, and "comprehension-then-assessment" trials. In fact, Gilbert et al. found that correct assessments of true propositions rose slightly from 91.6 to 95.9 percent following a comprehension trial. Correct assessments of false statements, however, fell, from 83.1 to 75.5 percent. This pattern of diverging performance follows, once again, from the theoretical premise that comprehension alone leads to belief in the veracity of a statement.

The collected experiments on the representation and use of fictional information also fit well with this Spinozan view. There is, for example, no hint of obligatory tagging for fictional information in the mental representations. This research result conforms to Spinoza's assertion that readers automatically take all information to be valid in the course of comprehension. Furthermore, the Yale-Princeton experiment suggested that there is special effort required to unaccept false information. Thus it appears, just as Spinoza proposed, that conscious appraisal is needed for readers to disbelieve false (or fictional) information.

Within this perspective, many of the paradoxes of the experience of fiction fall away. If readers believe fictional information to be true as an ordinary—and obligatory—consequence of comprehending that information, then there is no real mystery about how fictional information can have a real-world effect. On this view, *fictional information* in fact fails to refer to a category that has any a priori psychological coherence. Information becomes tagged as fictional only as a function of readers' conscious scrutiny. Even then, "fictional" information is unlikely to be represented in memory in a fashion different from any other sort of information readers have worked at disbelieving. The account I am advocating, therefore, replaces a "willing suspension of disbelief" with a "willing construction of disbelief." The net difference is that we cannot possibly be surprised that information from fictional narratives has a real-world effect.

To explore a further aspect of the construction of disbelief, let us return to the viewers of *Jaws,* whose progress into the ocean is stalled. The Spinozan account suggests that beliefs can easily be unaccepted, but *Jaws* viewers may be fully aware that the root of their fears is a work of fiction and still be unwilling to wade into the water. The key to this failure of easy unacceptance lies, I believe, in the sort of claim Bob Burnside made about his Los Angeles County lifeguards: the film "has affected them more because they know it can really happen." Burnside's comment accords with the more general claim that fictions often have their effect because they call forth from memory real-world events and causal possibilities. Even when the import of the original information is canceled out by virtue of its transparent fictionality, the rest of the accessed-belief structure remains intact.

Just such belief perseverance has been demonstrated in a number of circumstances. Ross, Lepper, and Hubbard (1975) showed that subjects made predictions about their own past and future behavior completely in line with discredited information. Subjects in their experiment were asked to examine twenty-five cards that each contained one real and one fictitious suicide note and determine which of the two notes was real. After they made a judgment for each card, they were given immediate feedback about whether they were correct or incorrect. This feedback was entirely rigged: Ross et al. made some subjects feel very successful by telling them that they were correct after each of twenty-four trials. "Average" subjects were told they were correct on seventeen occasions; "failure" subjects only on ten. After subjects worked their way through all twenty-five cards, the experimenters revealed the fictionality of the feedback. They explained that the true purpose of the study was to examine the physiological correlates of success and failure (subjects had been equipped with a recording device at the beginning of the session), which made the false feedback a necessary part of the experiment. The subjects were all required to reiterate their understanding that the feedback had no validity.

Having revealed the false feedback to the subjects, the experimenter mentioned that "the physiological readings might have been influenced by the subject's 'actual performance and perceptions' " (p. 883). With this motivation, subjects were asked to fill out a questionnaire on which they provided a number of performance estimates, such as how they believed they actually did on the suicide-note task and how they might do were they asked to perform a similar task in the future. With great consistency, subjects who had been given success feedback gave more optimistic ratings, the average subjects lower, and the failure subjects lowest of all. For example, success subjects believed their true initial performance was 17.05 (out of 25) correct, average subjects guessed 15.85, and failure subjects guessed 12.75. Actual performance did not, in fact, differ across the three groups. Thus, despite the best efforts of Ross et al. to convince the subjects that the feedback had no validity—and the subjects' apparent understanding that this was so—the effects of the fictional feedback lingered.

Subjects' estimates of their performance can also be affected by feedback that is identified as false *before* they begin a task. Wegner, Coulton, and Wenzlaff (1985) warned half of their subjects ahead of time that they would be getting false feedback. These subjects, who were participating in a suicide-note discrimination task modeled after Ross et al., were told specifically that "the feedback will not be genuine. The feedback you will receive has been predetermined and will not reflect your actual performance on this task. This procedure is used in an attempt to identify how false feedback affects physiological responses during decision making" (p. 342). The other half of the subjects were told that the feedback was false after they had finished the task. For both the "briefing" and "debriefing" subjects, Wegner et al. gave identical success or failure feedback. When the subjects were subsequently asked to make estimates about their true past and future performance, Wegner et al. found that the false feedback had roughly the same effect irrespective of the time of the revelation. For example, the difference between the estimates of actual performance for the success and failure subjects was about four cards for both the briefed and debriefed subjects. Even when subjects knew in advance that the feedback had no validity, they were not able to dampen its effect on their subsequent judgments. Applied to the situation of reading (or watching a movie, and so on), the results of Wegner et al. suggest that even reminding oneself that "This is only fiction" will not generally eliminate the effects of fictional information in the real world. What lingers, in fact, is not the original fictional information but the other belief structures that are brought to mind as a consequence of the original information. Ross and Lepper (1980) identified two categories of psychological propensities that lead to perseverance effects:

Biased search, recollection, and assimilation of evidence. Under most circumstances, people have a bias toward searching memory for information that supports their working hypotheses. In the face of success feedback on the suicide-note task, subjects would be likely to recall other situations in which they performed well on similar tasks. Thus, even when the feedback was revealed as fictional, these subjects would be left with this activated catalog of other successes to influence judgments about their real performance. Even when the revelation precedes the task, the experiences called to mind as the experimenter repeatedly intones "correct" or "incorrect" may come to outweigh knowledge that the feedback is false. The propensity to search memory for supporting evidence does much to explain the experience of viewers of *Jaws.* Once they have called to mind even hazy recollections of genuine instances of shark attacks, it no longer matters much if the original impetus for the memory search is discredited.

The formation of causal explanations and scenarios. Under almost any circumstances, people find it difficult not to create a causal structure to explain some outcome (see chapter 2). This predilection provides an overlapping mechanism to explain perseverance effects. When subjects come to believe that they have been successful at the suicide-note task, they may well construct a causal scenario that would have allowed them to predict such success (for example, "I've spent a lot of time talking to distraught friends"). When the success is revealed as false, this causal explanation will remain in place. The explanation itself can be so compelling that it would have predicted success (or so it seems) independent of the false feedback. Even when the revelation precedes the feedback, subjects might find that the causal explanations compete successfully with the knowledge that the feedback has no validity (a nonpenetration of belief reminiscent of the cases I described in chapter 5). Turning one final time to *Jaws,* we can imagine that viewers relate sharks and swimming in causal scenarios that are easily more compelling than any reminders that the movie itself is fictional.

Certainly when the propensities toward both biased search and causal-scenario construction operate simultaneously, viewers will be loath to unaccept the belief that they should eschew the water's pleasures. Beliefs do not, of course, always persist: Ross et al. (1975) found they could eliminate the effect of bogus feedback on subjects' ratings by providing *process* debriefing that specifically laid out the psychological forces in the situation that led toward perseverance. Readers, however, rarely debrief themselves by reference to psychological processes.

In experimental situations it often appears as if such biases and propensities lead exclusively to errors in reasoning. In fact, the specific examples I have adduced for fiction also constitute circumstances in which the effects of the information would likely be pernicious. The method of argument here parallels the use to which sensory and perceptual illusions are often put: the ordinary, successful operation of the system is laid bare by demonstrations of the circumstances under which it produces nonveridical judgments. However, what keeps these propensities in place—and what, perhaps, has allowed cognitive processes to evolve without a barrier to information from fictions—is the overall normative utility of these mechanisms for guiding mental experience (see Ross and Lepper, 1980). Under most circumstances, the bias that directs people to confirm their hypotheses will help to establish an accurate context in which judgments can be made. Similarly, the strong tendency toward interpreting events via causal scenarios facilitates predictions about future likelihoods.

Lewis (1983; see also Novitz, 1987; Rockwell, 1974; Slater, 1990; Walsh, 1969) provides an analysis parallel to the explanations for perseveration effects that explains why fiction can so often be "a means to truth" (p. 278). Along the lines of biased assimilation, he suggests that readers often have much good evidence for propositions that have gone unstated in real life. When authors of fictions formulate those propositions, they enable readers to gather that evidence: "If we are given a fiction such that the proposition is obviously true in it, we are led to ask: and is it also true *simpliciter?* And sometimes, when we have plenty of unappreciated evidence, to ask the question is to know the answer. Then the author of the fiction has made a discovery, and he gives his readers the means to make the same discovery for themselves" (p. 279). Along the lines of causal-scenario formation, Lewis suggests that fiction can serve to demonstrate causal possibilities. He comments, "I find it very hard to tell whether there could possibly be such a thing as a dignified beggar. If there could be, a story could prove it" (p. 278). This analysis suggests that the very same processes that make the ideas and circumstances of fiction potentially dangerous make them more often tremendously useful.

The utility of fictions was demonstrated most rigorously in a classic work by Hans Vaihinger (1935) in the domain of scientific reasoning. Vaihinger made a fundamental distinction between *hypotheses,* which are "directed toward reality, i.e. the ideational construct contained within [them] claims, or hopes, to coincide with some perception in the future" (p. 85), and *fictions,* which "are never verifiable, for they are hypotheses known to be false, but which are employed because of their utility" (p. xlii). Vaihinger's study is devoted to demonstrating how propositions known to contradict reality can nonetheless have such utility. Much of his method, in fact, consists of displaying happy outcomes of reasoning with fictions. That the products of such reasoning most often appropriately conform to reality leads Vaihinger to emphasize repeatedly that fictions are merely a *"means* to a definite end, in other words . . . they are expedient" (p. 99). He suggests that fictional arguments can yield factual conclusions precisely because they have this quality of expediency. Having served as "transit-points of thought," they "disappear and logically are canceled" (p. 104). In the domain of mathematics, for example, Vaihinger provides instances in which proofs rely on the introduction of fictional elements that are subsequently canceled—their fictionality revealed—to yield valid results. Such examples build confidence that fictions can be introduced with little cost, but the mechanism remains obscure. In many respects, Vaihinger's argument amounts to a claim that we so habitually reason with fictions ("thought of its very nature necessarily develops these fictions" [p. 134]) that we have learned exactly how to do so without ill consequences ("But it cannot be denied that thought obtains its practical success only at the price of its logical purity" [p. 177]).

Vaihinger makes closest contact with the use of aesthetic fictions when he insists that each scientific fiction must justify its own existence: "The criterion of a good fiction is simply its fertility in practical use" (p. 54). Whenever a fiction is sufficiently evocative of real-life experiences, we would expect that its effects linger, however thoroughly readers were cautioned to unaccept the original information. The lack of mental barriers to the influence of information from fictions suggests, once again, that this type of information has provided a positive balance of utility over the period in which our mental processes were shaped.

I began this chapter by providing evidence that information encountered in fictional narratives influences readers' real-world judgments. Against that background, I illustrated a category of toggle theories, which did not deny these effects so much as make their origins obscure. Because these theories presupposed a fundamental psychological distinction between fiction and nonfiction, they were largely unable to explain the identical consequences for readers of these two categories of information. My review of the empirical research on the representation of fictional and nonfictional information revealed that such a fundamental distinction is unsupported: any differences between fiction and nonfiction appeared to be strategic rather than obligatory. I argued, furthermore, that readers' experience of fictional narratives accords well with a Spinozan theory of belief formation in which initial acceptance is a concomitant of comprehension. Within that perspective, information presented in fictions affects real-world judgments because it is initially accepted as true alongside all other types of information. Finally, I suggested that even when readers actively try to discredit fictional information, they may have called to mind other beliefs that will persevere after the fiction itself has been unaccepted.

I will draw together the themes of this book by addressing two questions: What must a reader do to experience a narrative world? and What might a reader do to experience a narrative world?

The answer to the first, which has emerged over the course of these chapters, is that a reader need invest only minimal attention to experience a narrative world. I have identified a collection of psychological processes and structures that make it virtually inevitable that a reader will, with limited conscious effort, enjoy much of the phenomenology of being transported. Consider the "minimalist hypothesis," which I described in chapter 2. McKoon and Ratcliff (1992) articulated this hypothesis to define the classes of inferences that are privileged as automatic in narrative understanding. These classes are "minimal," however, only with respect to the infinite range of possible inferences: they still go a long way toward ensuring that readers will have a rich narrative experience. Because local coherence is assured through the automatic action of cognitive processes, readers' resources are available to elaborate the narrative world in other ways.

The automatic operation of cognitive processes can explain a variety of prominent aspects of narrative experiences. Recall "anomalous suspense," which I described in chapter 5. The question, as Walton (1978b) put it, is how a child "listening to *Jack and the Beanstalk* for the umpteenth time, long after she has memorized it word for word, may feel much the same excitement when the giant discovers Jack and goes after him, the same gripping suspense, that she felt when she first heard the story" (p. 26). My theoretical treatment of anomalous suspense relied on a contrast between *veridical* and *schematic* expectancies (see Bharucha, 1987). In the context of music, veridical expectancies are those a listener builds up by repeated contact with a particular piece of music; schematic expectancies encode regularities within the overall body of a particular culture's music. My overarching claim was that across domains—musical, textual, and so on—moment-by-moment experience is dominated by schematic expectancies. Rather than requiring special-purpose cognitive structures, anomalous suspense emerges as an automatic consequence of the time-course advantage schematic expectancies enjoy with respect to veridical expectancies. Cognitive structure alone, therefore, can explain how suspense may unavoidably survive multiple experiences.

As a final example, consider my claim from chapter 4 that readers adopt a side-participant stance with respect to narrative utterances. My argument was that readers have vast experience being informed by language that is not specifically addressed to them. In the same way that Ed Koch is able to recover meaning effortlessly from utterances Larry Kramer nominally addresses to his dog ("There's the man who murdered all of Daddy's friends"), readers can recover meaning from utterances nominally intended for the various addressees of a text. Once again, no special-purpose structures need be invented to account for the use of language in narrative worlds. Rather, we need a general theory of the processes that enable readers to be such skilled side-participants. In chapter 5, I suggested that such a general account will also help explain how, even when narratives elicit strong emotions, behavioral responses are so straightforwardly inhibited.

On the whole, therefore, I believe that many criterial properties of narrative worlds emerge directly from the ordinary and obligatory operation of basic cognitive processes. I offer this conclusion partially as an antidote to theories that have treated narrative experiences in isolation. In some sense, all a reader must do to be transported to a narrative world is to have in place the repertory of cognitive processes that is otherwise required for everyday experience.

In answer to the second question, even if automatic processes minimize the effort that readers *must* expend to be transported, readers may still indulge in a large and heterogeneous range of optional activities to enhance their experiences of narratives. In chapters 2 and 3, I described a variety of both inferences and participatory responses that are under readers' strategic control. Recall the relationship I described in chapter 3 between suspense and problem solving. I argued that, to the extent that readers effortfully attempt to find solutions to textual dilemmas, their enjoyment will be intensified. It is important to note that although such participatory responses are not obligatory, they need not fall outside the scope of psychological theories. In chapter 3 I presented evidence that p-responses occasioned by readers' preferences can reliably alter their narrative experiences (Allbritton and Gerrig, 1991). An invocation of readers' typical responses to violations of norms (Kahneman and Miller, 1986) allowed accurate predictions to be made about likely, if not automatic, responses to preference situations. A focus on readers' strategies suggests that an author's expertise consists partially in creating circumstances that will reliably prompt readers to undertake optional activities.

I have also suggested that readers might strategically undertake a "willing construction of disbelief." My claim has been that the only experiential distinctions between fiction and nonfiction are those that readers effortfully construct. Throughout this book, I have argued for the unity of fiction and nonfiction. I suggested that there is no processing distinction between the serious and nonserious assertions of nonfiction and fiction. I suggested that a range of phenomena (for example, anomalous suspense and anomalous replotting) regularly occur in response to both fictional and nonfictional narratives. And I suggested that all information is understood as true until some is unaccepted. My general conclusion is that fictions will fail to have a real-world impact only if readers expend explicit effort to understand them as fictional.

Finally, I suggested in chapter 4 that although readers automatically adopt a side-participant stance when they experience a narrative, they might also choose a broader range of activities. Readers could, for example, undertake special analysis of a text based on the beliefs that authors might purposely conceal meanings and that meanings might be hidden from even the authors themselves. Against the background of side-participation, readers can enhance their narrative worlds through various interpretive techniques.

I began this book by announcing my intention to use the metaphor of being transported as a template for discussing a series of topics related to the experience of narratives. In each chapter, I considered salient aspects of the journey to and from narrative worlds. My goal was to explicate the distinct and universal psychological structures that, acting in harmony, create the unique phenomenology of being transported. Through both active participation and passive acquiescence, our lives are enhanced by richly diverse experiences of narratives.

NARRATIVE SOURCES

Barnes, J. (1989). *A history of the world in 10-1/2 chapters.* New York: Vintage International.

Cantor, J. (1977). *The death of Che Guevara.* New York: Vintage.

Carey, J. (1987). *Eye-witness to history.* Cambridge: Harvard University Press.

Clemons, W. (1987, September 28). The ghosts of "sixty million and more." *Newsweek,* p. 75.

Cunningham, M. (1990). *A home at the end of the world.* New York: Farrar, Straus and Giroux.

Davies, R. (1988). *The lyre of Orpheus.* New York: Viking.

DeLillo, D. (1988). *Libra.* New York: Viking.

Doctorow, E. L. (1985). *World's fair.* New York: Fawcett Crest.

———— (1989). *Billy Bathgate.* New York: Random House.

Fleming, I. (1954). *Casino royale.* New York: Macmillan.

———— (1959a). For your eyes only. In *For your eyes only* (pp. 31–74). New York: Charter.

———— (1959b). Risico. In *For your eyes only* (pp. 101–39). New York: Charter.

Jaynes, J. (1976). *The origin of consciousness in the breakdown of the bicameral mind.* Boston: Houghton Mifflin.

Kael, P. (1985). *State of the art.* New York: E. P. Dutton.

Keats, J. (1959). Bright star. In D. Bush (ed.), *John Keats: Selected poems and letters* (p. 198). Boston: Houghton Mifflin.

Keillor, G. (1987). *Leaving home.* New York: Viking Penguin.

Lax, E. (1991). *Woody Allen.* New York: Alfred A. Knopf.

McMurtry, L. (1989). *Some can whistle.* New York: Pocket.

Mason, B. A. (1988). *Spence + Lila.* New York: Harper and Row.

Milton, J. (1965). On time. In D. Bush (ed.), *The complete poetical works of John Milton* (pp. 105–06). Boston: Houghton Mifflin.

Morris, J. (1986). *Manhattan '45.* Oxford: Oxford University Press.

Morrison, T. (1981). *Tar baby.* New York: Alfred A. Knopf.

——— (1987). *Beloved.* New York: Alfred A. Knopf.

Oates, S. B. (1977). *With malice toward none: The life of Abraham Lincoln.* New York: Harper and Row.

Phillips, J. (1991). *You'll never eat lunch in this town again.* New York: Signet.

Powers, R. (1988). *Prisoner's dilemma.* New York: Collier.

Rhodes, R. (1986). *The making of the atomic bomb.* New York: Simon and Schuster.

Roth, P. (1988). *The facts.* New York: Farrar, Straus and Giroux.

Rushdie, S. (1980). *Midnight's children.* New York: Avon.

Russo, R. (1988). *The risk pool.* New York: Random House.

Shakespeare, W. (1965). Sonnet 34. In W. Burto (ed.), *The sonnets* (p. 74). New York: Signet Classic.

Smith, M. C. (1989). *Polar star.* New York: Random House.

Smith, P. J. (1989). *Make-believe ballrooms.* New York: Atlantic Monthly Press.

Steinbeck, J. (1989). *Working days* (ed. R. Demott). New York: Penguin.

Theroux, P. (1989). *My secret history.* New York: G. P. Putnam's.

Toole, J. K. (1980). *A confederacy of dunces.* New York: Grove Weidenfeld.

Updike, J. (1989). *Self-consciousness.* New York: Alfred A. Knopf.

Verlaine, M. J. (1989). *A bad man is easy to find.* New York: St. Martin's.

Walls, J. (1992, January 27). Kramer vs. Koch: To the dogs. *New York,* p. 8.

Welty, E. (1941). *A curtain of green and other stories.* New York: Harcourt Brace Jovanovich.

Wines, M. (1992, January 9). President has intestinal flu, spokesman says—He intends to continue most of schedule. *New York Times,* pp. A1, A8.

REFERENCES

Abelson, R. P. (1981). Psychological status of the script concept. *American Psychologist, 36,* 715–29.

Adams, J.-K. (1985). *Pragmatics and fiction.* Amsterdam: John Benjamins.

Allbritton, D. W., and R. J. Gerrig (1991). Participatory responses in prose understanding. *Journal of Memory and Language, 30,* 603–26.

Anderson, J. R. (1976). *Language, memory, and thought.* Hillsdale, N. J.: Erlbaum.

—— (1983). *The architecture of cognition.* Cambridge: Harvard University Press.

Anderson, R. C., and J. W. Pichert (1978). Recall of previously unrecallable information following a shift in perspective. *Journal of Verbal Learning and Verbal Behavior, 17,* 1–12.

Austin, J. L. (1962). *How to do things with words.* Cambridge: Harvard University Press.

Baillet, S. D., and J. M. Keenan (1986). The role of encoding and retrieval processes in the recall of text. *Discourse Processes, 9,* 247–68.

Bartlett, F. C. (1932). *Remembering.* Cambridge: Cambridge University Press.

Batty, N. E. (1987). The art of suspense: Rushdie's 1001 (mid-)nights. *Ariel, 18,* 49–65.

Beardsley, M. (1981). Fiction as representation. *Synthese, 46,* 291–313.

Beck, A. T., and G. Emery (1985). *Anxiety disorders and phobias.* New York: Basic.

Benton, M. (1982). Reading fiction: Ten paradoxes. *British Journal of Aesthetics, 22,* 301–10.

Berlyne, D. (1971). *Aesthetics and psychobiology.* New York: Appleton-Century-Crofts.

Bharucha, J. J. (1987). Music cognition and perceptual facilitation: A connectionist framework. *Music Perception, 5,* 1–30.

Bharucha, J. J., and P. M. Todd (1989). Modeling the perception of tonal structure with neural nets. *Computer Music Journal, 13,* 44–53.

Bloom, C. P., C. R. Fletcher, P. van den Broek, L. Reitz, and B. P. Shapiro (1990). An on-line assessment of causal reasoning during comprehension. *Memory and Cognition, 18,* 65–71.

Booth, W. C. (1974). *A rhetoric of irony.* Chicago: University of Chicago Press.

———— (1983). *The rhetoric of fiction* (2d ed.). Chicago: University of Chicago Press.

Boruah, B. H. (1988). *Fiction and emotion.* Oxford: Oxford University Press.

Bower, G. B., J. B. Black, and T. J. Turner (1979). Scripts in memory for text. *Cognitive Psychology, 11,* 177–220.

Bransford, J. D., and M. K. Johnson (1972). Contextual prerequisites for understanding: Some investigations of comprehension and recall. *Journal of Verbal Learning and Verbal Behavior, 11,* 717–26.

Bransford, J. D., and N. S. McCarrell (1977). A sketch of a cognitive approach to comprehension: Some thoughts about understanding what it means to comprehend. In P. N. Johnson-Laird and P. C. Wason (eds.), *Thinking: Readings in cognitive science* (pp. 377–99). Cambridge: Cambridge University Press.

Brewer, W. F., and E. H. Lichtenstein (1981). Event schemas, story schemas, and story grammars. In J. Long and A. Baddeley (eds.),

Attention and performance IX (pp. 363–79). Hillsdale, N.J.: Erlbaum.

———— (1982). Stories are to entertain: A structural-affect theory of stories. *Journal of Pragmatics, 6,* 473–86.

Brewer, W. F., and G. V. Nakamura (1984). The nature and functions of schemas. In R. S. Wyer and T. K. Srull (eds.), *Handbook of social cognition* (vol. 1, pp. 119–60). Hillsdale, N.J.: Erlbaum.

Brewer, W. F., and K. Ohtsuka (1988a). Story structure, characterization, just world organization, and reader affect in American and Hungarian short stories. *Poetics, 17,* 395–415.

———— (1988b). Story structure and reader affect in American and Hungarian short stories. In C. Martindale (ed.), *Psychological approaches to the study of literary narratives* (pp. 133–58). Hamburg: Buske.

Brown, R. L., Jr., and M. Steinmann, Jr. (1978). Native readers of fiction: A speech-act and genre-rule approach to defining literature. In P. Hernandi (ed.), *What is literature?* (pp. 141–60). Bloomington: Indiana University Press.

Bruce, B. (1981). A social interaction model of reading. *Discourse Processes, 4,* 273–311.

Bruner, J. (1986). *Actual minds, possible worlds.* Cambridge: Harvard University Press.

Carroll, N. (1990). *The philosophy of horror.* New York: Routledge.

Chiaromonte, N. (1985). *The paradox of history.* Philadelphia: University of Pennsylvania Press.

Chiesi, H. L., G. J. Spilich, and J. F. Voss (1979). Acquisition of domain-related information in relation to high and low domain knowledge. *Journal of Verbal Learning and Verbal Behavior, 18,* 257–73.

Clark, E. V., and H. H. Clark (1979). When nouns surface as verbs. *Language, 55,* 767–811.

Clark, H. H. (1983). Making sense of nonce sense. In G. B. Flores d'Arcais and R. Jarvella (eds.), *The process of understanding language* (pp. 297–331). New York: Wiley.

—— (1987). Four dimensions of language use. In J. Verschueren and M. Bertuccelli-Papi (eds.), *The pragmatic perspective* (pp. 9–25). Amsterdam: John Benjamins.

Clark, H. H., and T. B. Carlson (1982). Hearers and speech acts. *Language, 58*, 332–73.

Clark, H. H., and R. J. Gerrig (1984). On the pretense theory of irony. *Journal of Experimental Psychology: General, 113*, 121–26.

—— (1990). Quotations as demonstrations. *Language, 66*, 764–805.

Clark, H. H., and S. E. Haviland (1977). Comprehension and the given-new contract. In R. O. Freedle (ed.), *Discourse production and comprehension* (vol. 1, pp. 1–40). Norwood, N.J.: Ablex.

Clark, H. H., and C. R. Marshall (1981). Definite reference and mutual knowledge. In A. K. Joshi, B. Webber, and I. Sag (eds.), *Elements of discourse understanding* (pp. 10–63). Cambridge: Cambridge University Press.

Clark, H. H., and E. F. Schaefer (1987). Concealing one's meaning from overhearers. *Journal of Memory and Language, 26*, 209–25.

—— (1989). Contributing to discourse. *Cognitive Science, 13*, 259–94.

Clark, H. H., and D. Wilkes-Gibbs (1986). Referring as a collaborative process. *Cognition, 22*, 1–39.

Clive, J. (1989). *Not by fact alone*. Boston: Houghton Mifflin.

Cohen, T. (1979). Metaphor and the cultivation of intimacy. In S. Sacks (ed.), *On metaphor* (pp. 1–10). Chicago: University of Chicago Press.

Cohn, D. (1978). *Transparent minds*. Princeton: Princeton University Press.

Coleridge, S. T. (1907). *Biographia literaria*. Oxford: Oxford University Press. (Originally published in 1817)

Coles, R. (1989). *The call of stories*. Boston: Houghton Mifflin.

Crittenden, C. (1982). Fictional characters and logical completeness. *Poetics, 11*, 331–44.

—— (1991). *Unreality: The metaphysics of fictional objects.* Ithaca: Cornell University Press.

Crowder, R. G. (1982). The demise of short-term memory. *Acta Psychologia, 50,* 291–323.

Culler, J. (1975). *Structuralist poetics.* London: Routledge and Kegan Paul.

—— (1980a). Literary competence. In J. P. Tompkins (ed.), *Reader-response criticism* (pp. 101–17). Baltimore: Johns Hopkins University Press.

—— (1980b). Prolegomena to a theory of reading. In S. R. Suleiman and I. Crosman (eds.), *The reader in the text* (pp. 46–66). Princeton: Princeton University Press.

Currie, G. (1985). What is fiction? *Journal of Aesthetics and Art Criticism, 43,* 385–92.

—— (1986). Works of fiction and illocutionary acts. *Philosophy and Literature, 10,* 304–08.

—— (1990). *The nature of fiction.* Cambridge: Cambridge University Press.

Dammann, R. M. J. (1992). Emotion and fiction. *British Journal of Aesthetics, 32,* 13–20.

Daneman, M., and P. A. Carpenter (1980). Individual differences in working memory and reading. *Journal of Verbal Learning and Verbal Behavior, 19,* 450–66.

Dell, G. S., G. McKoon, and R. Ratcliff (1983). The activation of antecedent information during the processing of anaphoric reference in reading. *Journal of Verbal Learning and Verbal Behavior, 22,* 121–32.

Denby, D. (1991, September). A guy, a girl, and their guns. *Premiere,* pp. 32–33.

Derrida, J. (1977a). Signature event context. *Glyph, 1,* 172–97.

—— (1977b). Limited inc a b c . . . . *Glyph, 2,* 162–254.

Dooling, D. J., and R. Lachman (1971). Effects of comprehension on retention of prose. *Journal of Experimental Psychology, 88,* 216–22.

Dosher, B. A., and A. T. Corbett (1982). Instrument inferences and verb schemata. *Memory and Cognition, 10,* 531–39.

Duncker, K. (1945). On problem solving. *Psychological Monographs, 58* (5, entire no. 270).

Eaton, M. M. (1973). Liars, ranters, and dramatic speakers. In B. R. Tilghman (ed.), *Language and aesthetics* (pp. 43–63). Lawrence: University Press of Kansas.

———— (1976). On being a character. *British Journal of Aesthetics, 16,* 24–31.

———— (1983). James's turn of the speech-act. *British Journal of Aesthetics, 23,* 333–45.

Fablo, T., and D. F. Polit (1986). Quantitative review of the only child literature: Research evidence and theory development. *Psychological Bulletin, 100,* 176–89.

Fincher-Kiefer, R., T. A. Post, T. R. Greene, and J. F. Voss (1988). On the role of prior knowledge and task demands in the processing of text. *Journal of Memory and Language, 27,* 416–28.

Fish, S. (1980). *Is there a text in this class?* Cambridge: Harvard University Press.

———— (1989). *Doing what comes naturally.* Durham, N.C.: Duke University Press.

Fiske, S. T., S. E. Taylor, N. L. Etcoff, and J. K. Laufer (1979). Imaging, empathy, and causal attribution. *Journal of Experimental Social Psychology, 15,* 356–77.

Fletcher, C. R., and C. P. Bloom (1988). Causal reasoning in the comprehension of simple narrative texts. *Journal of Memory and Language, 27,* 235–44.

Fletcher, C. R., J. E. Hummel, and C. J. Marsolek (1990). Causality and the allocation of attention during comprehension. *Journal of Experimental Psychology: Learning, Memory, and Cognition, 16,* 233–40.

Fowler, H. W. (1965). *A dictionary of modern English usage* (2d ed.). Oxford: Oxford University Press.

Frank, M. G., and T. Gilovich (1989). Effect of memory perspective on retrospective causal attributions. *Journal of Personality and Social Psychology, 57,* 399–403.

Freud, S. (1964). *Leonardo da Vinci and a memory of his childhood* (trans. A. Tyson). New York: W. W. Norton. (Originally published in 1910)

———— (1965). *The interpretation of dreams* (trans. J. Strachey). New York: Avon Books. (Originally published in 1901)

Frijda, N. H. (1988). The laws of emotion. *American Psychologist, 43,* 349–58.

———— (1989). Aesthetic emotions and reality. *American Psychologist, 44,* 1546–47.

Funder, D. C. (1987). Errors and mistakes: Evaluating the accuracy of social judgment. *Psychological Bulletin, 101,* 75–90.

Garnham, A. (1987). *Mental models as representations of discourse and text.* Chichester, Eng.: Ellis Horwood.

Garrod, S., E. J. O'Brien, R. K. Morris, and K. Rayner (1990). Elaborative inferencing as an active or passive process. *Journal of Experimental Psychology: Learning, Memory, and Cognition, 16,* 250–57.

Genette, G. (1990). The pragmatic status of narrative fiction. *Style, 24,* 59–72.

Gerrig, R. J. (1989a). Reexperiencing fiction and non-fiction. *Journal of Aesthetics and Art Criticism, 47,* 277–80.

———— (1989b). Suspense in the absence of uncertainty. *Journal of Memory and Language, 28,* 633–48.

Gerrig, R. J., and D. W. Allbritton (1990). The construction of literary character: A view from Cognitive Psychology. *Style, 24,* 380–91.

Gerrig, R. J., and M. R. Banaji (1991). Names and the construction of identity: Evidence from Toni Morrison's *Tar baby. Poetics, 20,* 173–92.

Gerrig, R. J., and R. W. Gibbs, Jr. (1988). Beyond the lexicon: Creativity in language production. *Metaphor and Symbolic Activity*, *3*, 1–19.

Gerrig, R. J., and D. A. Prentice (1991). The representation of fictional information. *Psychological Science*, *2*, 336–40.

Gibbs, R. W., Jr. (1984). Literal meaning and psychological theory. *Cognitive Science*, *8*, 275–304.

———— (1986a). Comprehension and memory for nonliteral utterances: The problem of sarcastic indirect requests. *Acta Psychologia*, *62*, 41–57.

———— (1986b). On the psycholinguistics of sarcasm. *Journal of Experimental Psychology: General*, *115*, 3–15.

———— (1989). Understanding and literal meaning. *Cognitive Science*, *13*, 243–51.

———— (1990). Comprehending figurative referential descriptions. *Journal of Experimental Psychology: Learning, Memory, and Cognition*, *16*, 56–66.

Gibbs, R. W., Jr., and R. J. Gerrig (1989). How context makes metaphor comprehension seem "special." *Metaphor and Symbolic Activity*, *4*, 145–58.

Gibson, W. (1980). Authors, speakers, readers, and mock readers. In J. P. Tompkins (ed.), *Reader-response criticism* (pp. 1–6). Baltimore: Johns Hopkins University Press.

Gilbert, D. T. (1991). How mental systems believe. *American Psychologist*, *46*, 107–19.

Gilbert, D. T., D. S. Krull, and P. S. Malone (1990). Unbelieving the unbelievable: Some problems in the rejection of false information. *Journal of Personality and Social Psychology*, *59*, 601–13.

Goodman, N. (1978). *Ways of worldmaking*. Indianapolis, Ind.: Hackett.

Gow, G. (1968). *Suspense in the cinema*. London: A. Zwemmer.

Graesser, A. C., S. E. Gordon, and J. D. Sawyer (1979). Recognition memory for typical and atypical actions in scripted activities:

Tests of a script pointer + tag hypothesis. *Journal of Verbal Learning and Verbal Behavior, 18,* 319–32.

Graff, G. (1981). Literature as assertions. In I. Konisberg (ed.), *American criticism in the poststructuralist age* (pp. 135–61). Ann Arbor: University of Michigan Press.

Grice, H. P. (1957). Meaning. *Philosophical Review, 66,* 377–88.

———— (1968). Utterer's meaning, sentence-meaning, and word-meaning. *Foundations of Language, 4,* 1–18.

———— (1975). Logic and conversation. In P. Cole and J. L. Morgan (eds.), *Syntax and semantics,* vol. 3, *Speech acts* (pp. 41–58). New York: Academic Press.

———— (1978). Further notes on logic and conversation. In P. Cole (ed.), *Syntax and semantics,* vol. 9, *Pragmatics* (pp. 113–28). New York: Academic Press.

Hancher, M. (1977). Beyond a speech-act theory of literary discourse. *MLN, 92,* 1081–98.

Harris, P. L., E. Brown, C. Marriott, S. Whittall, and S. Harmer (1991). Monsters, ghosts and witches: Testing the limits of the fantasy-reality distinction in young children. *British Journal of Development Psychology, 9,* 105–23.

Holland, N. N. (1988). *The brain of Robert Frost.* New York: Routledge.

Intraub, H., R. S. Bender, and J. A. Mangels (1992). Looking at pictures but remembering scenes. *Journal of Experimental Psychology: Learning, Memory, and Cognition, 18,* 180–91.

Intraub, H., and M. Richardson (1989). Wide-angle memories of close-up scenes. *Journal of Experimental Psychology: Learning, Memory, and Cognition, 15,* 179–87.

Iser, W. (1978). *The act of reading.* Baltimore: Johns Hopkins University Press.

———— (1980). The reading process: A phenomenological approach. In J. P. Tompkins (ed.), *Reader-response criticism* (pp. 50–69). Baltimore: Johns Hopkins University Press.

——— (1989). *Prospecting: From reader response to literary anthropology.* Baltimore: Johns Hopkins University Press.

Johnson, B. T., and A. H. Eagly (1989). Effects of involvement on persuasion: A meta-analysis. *Psychological Bulletin, 106,* 290–314.

Johnson, J. T. (1986). The knowledge of what might have been: Affective and attributional consequences of near outcomes. *Personality and Social Psychology Bulletin, 12,* 51–62.

Johnson, M. K. (1988a). Discriminating the origin of information. In T. F. Obtmanns and B. A. Maher (eds.), *Delusional beliefs* (pp. 34–65). New York: Wiley.

——— (1988b). Reality monitoring: An experimental phenomenological approach. *Journal of Experimental Psychology: General, 117,* 390–94.

Johnson-Laird, P. N. (1983). *Mental models.* Cambridge: Harvard University Press.

Jones, E. E., and R. E. Nisbett (1971). The actor and the observer: Divergent perceptions of the causes of behavior. In E. E. Jones, D. E. Kanouse, H. H. Kelley, R. E. Nisbett, S. Valins, and B. Weiner (eds.), *Attribution: Perceiving the causes of behavior* (pp. 79–94). Morristown, N.J.: General Learning Press.

Jorgensen, J., G. A. Miller, and D. Sperber (1984). Test of the mention theory of irony. *Journal of Experimental Psychology: General, 113,* 112–20.

Jose, P. E. (1988). Liking of plan-based stories: The role of goal importance and goal attainment difficulty. *Discourse Processes, 11,* 261–73.

Jose, P. E., and W. F. Brewer (1984). Development of story liking: Character identification, suspense, and outcome resolution. *Developmental Psychology, 20,* 911–24.

Kahneman, D., and D. T. Miller (1986). Norm theory: Comparing reality to its alternatives. *Psychological Review, 93,* 136–53.

Kahneman, D., and A. Tversky (1982). The simulation heuristic. In D. Kahneman, P. Slovic, and A. Tversky (eds.), *Judgment under uncertainty: Heuristics and biases* (pp. 201–08). New York: Cambridge University Press.

Kermode, F. (1983). *Essays on fiction.* London: Routledge.

Kintsch, W. (1974). *The representation of meaning in memory.* Hillsdale, N.J.: Erlbaum.

——— (1978). Comprehension and memory of text. In W. K. Estes (ed.), *Handbook of learning and cognitive processes,* vol. 6, *Linguistic functions in cognitive theory* (pp. 57–86). Hillsdale, N.J.: Erlbaum.

Kintsch, W., and T. A. van Dijk (1978). Toward a model of text comprehension and production. *Psychological Review, 85,* 363–94.

Krauss, R. M., and S. Glucksberg (1969). The development of communication: Competence as a function of age. *Child Development, 40,* 255–56.

——— (1975). Social and nonsocial speech. *Scientific American, 236,* 100–05.

Krauss, R. M., and S. Weinheimer (1964). Changes in reference phrases as a function of frequency of usage in social interaction: A preliminary study. *Psychonomic Science, 1,* 113–14.

——— (1966). Concurrent feedback, confirmation, and the encoding of referents in verbal communication. *Journal of Personality and Social Psychology, 3,* 343–46.

——— (1967). Effect of referent similarity and communication mode on verbal encoding. *Journal of Verbal Learning and Verbal Behavior, 6,* 359–63.

Kreuz, R. J., and S. Glucksberg (1989). How to be sarcastic: The echoic reminder theory of verbal irony. *Journal of Experimental Psychology: General, 118,* 374–86.

Labov, W. (1972). *Language in the inner city: Studies in the black English vernacular.* Philadelphia: University of Pennsylvania Press.

Lakoff, G. (1987). *Women, fire, and dangerous things: What categories reveal about the mind.* Chicago: University of Chicago Press.

Lakoff, G., and M. Johnson (1980). *Metaphors we live by.* Chicago: University of Chicago Press.

Lamarque, P. (1991). Review of *Mimesis as make-believe*. *The Journal of Aesthetics and Art Criticism, 49*, 161–66.

Lee-Sammons, W. H., and P. Whitney (1991). Reading perspectives and memory for text: An individual differences analysis. *Journal of Experimental Psychology: Learning, Memory, and Cognition, 17*, 1074–81.

Lewis, C. H., and J. R. Anderson (1976). Interference with real world knowledge. *Cognitive Psychology, 8*, 311–35.

Lewis, D. (1978). Truth in fiction. *American Philosophical Quarterly, 15*, 37–46.

——— (1983). Postscripts to "truth in fiction." In D. Lewis, *Philosophical papers* (vol. 1, pp. 276–80). New York: Oxford University Press.

Lucas, M. M., M. K. Tanenhaus, and G. N. Carlson (1990). Levels of representation in the interpretation of anaphoric reference and instrument inference. *Memory and Cognition, 18*, 611–31.

McCabe, A., and C. Peterson (eds.) (1991). *Developing narrative structure*. Hillsdale, N.J.: Erlbaum.

McClelland, J. L., and D. E. Rumelhart (1986). *Parallel distributed processing* (vol. 2). Cambridge: MIT Press.

McCormick, P. A., and P. Jolicoeur (1992). Capturing visual attention and the curve tracing operation. *Journal of Experimental Psychology: Human Perception and Performance, 18*, 72–89.

McCormick, P. J. (1988). *Fictions, philosophies, and the problems of poetics*. Ithaca: Cornell University Press.

MacDonald, M. (1954). The language of fiction. *Proceedings of the Aristotelian Society, 27*, 16–184.

Mackie, J. L. (1980). *The cement of the universe: A study of causation*. Oxford: Clarendon Press.

McKoon, G., and R. Ratcliff (1981). The comprehension processes and memory structures involved in instrumental inference. *Journal of Verbal Learning and Verbal Behavior, 20*, 671–82.

———— (1988). Contextually relevant aspects of meaning. *Journal of Experimental Pyschology: Learning, Memory, and Cognition, 14,* 331–43.

———— (1992). Inference during reading. *Psychological Review, 99,* 440–66.

Maclean, M. (1988). *Narrative as performance.* London: Routledge.

Mandelker, S. (1987). Searle on fictional discourse: A defence against Wolterstorff, Pavel and Rorty. *British Journal of Aesthetics, 27,* 156–68.

Mandler, J. M. (1984). *Stories, scripts, and scenes: Aspects of a schema theory.* Hillsdale, N.J.: Erlbaum.

Mani, K., and P. N. Johnson-Laird (1982). The mental representation of spatial descriptions. *Memory and Cognition, 10,* 181–87.

Margolin, U. (1987). Introducing and sustaining characters in literary narrative: A set of conditions. *Style, 21,* 107–24.

Miller, A. G., and T. Lawson (1989). The effect of informational option on the fundamental attribution error. *Personality and Social Psychology Bulletin, 15,* 194–204.

Miller, D. T., and S. Gunasegaram (1990). Temporal order and the perceived mutability of events: Implications for blame assignment. *Journal of Personality and Social Psychology, 59,* 1111–18.

Monti-Pouagare, S. (1988). Dramatic suspense in the *Oedipus* plays of Sophocles and Dryden and Lee. *Classical Bulletin, 64,* 7–8.

Morson, G. S. (1987). *Hidden in plain view: Narrative and creative potentials in "War and peace."* Stanford: Stanford University Press.

Nell, V. (1988). *Lost in a book.* New Haven: Yale University Press.

Newell, A., and H. Simon (1972). *Human problem solving.* Englewood Cliffs, N.J.: Prentice-Hall.

Novitz, D. (1987). *Knowledge, fiction and imagination.* Philadelphia: Temple University Press.

O'Brien, E. J., S. A. Duffy, and J. L. Myers (1986). Anaphoric inference during reading. *Journal of Experimental Psychology: Learning, Memory, and Cognition, 12,* 346–52.

O'Brien, E. J., and J. L. Myers (1987). The role of causal connections in the retrieval of text. *Memory and Cognition, 15,* 419–27.

O'Brien, E. J., P. S. Plewes, and J. E. Albrecht (1990). Antecedent retrieval processes. *Journal of Experimental Psychology: Learning, Memory, and Cognition, 16,* 241–49.

O'Brien, E. J., D. M. Shank, J. L. Myers, and K. Rayner (1988). Elaborative inferences during reading: Do they occur on-line? *Journal of Experimental Psychology: Learning, Memory, and Cognition, 14,* 410–20.

Ohmann, R. (1971). Speech acts and the definition of literature. *Philosophy and Rhetoric, 4,* 1–19.

——— (1973). Literature as art. In S. Chatman (ed.), *Approaches to poetics* (pp. 81–107). New York: Columbia University Press.

Ortony, A., G. L. Clore, and A. Collins (1988). *The cognitive structure of emotions.* Cambridge: Cambridge University Press.

Owens, J., G. H. Bower, and J. B. Black (1979). The "soap opera" effect in story recall. *Memory and Cognition, 7,* 185–91.

Pavel, T. G. (1981). Ontological issues in poetics: Speech acts and fictional worlds. *Journal of Aesthetics and Art Criticism, 40,* 167–78.

——— (1986). *Fictional worlds.* Cambridge: Harvard University Press.

Perrig, W., and W. Kintsch (1985). Propositional and situational representations of text. *Journal of Memory and Language, 24,* 503–18.

Peterson, S. B., and G. R. Potts (1982). Global and specific components of information integration. *Journal of Verbal Learning and Verbal Behavior, 21,* 403–20.

Petty, R. E., and J. T. Cacioppo (1986). The elaboration likelihood model of persuasion. In L. Berkowitz (ed.), *Advances in experimental social psychology* (vol. 19, pp. 123–205). Orlando, Fla.: Academic Press.

Pichert, J. W., and R. C. Anderson (1977). Taking different perspectives on a story. *Journal of Educational Psychology, 69,* 309–15.

Plato (1974). *The republic* (trans. D. Lee). New York: Penguin.

Polanyi, L. (1989). *Telling the American story.* Cambridge: MIT Press.

Porter, D. (1983). Backward construction and the art of suspense. In G. W. Most and W. W. Stone (eds.), *The poetics of murder* (pp. 327–40). San Diego: Harcourt Brace Jovanovich.

Potts, G. R., and S. B. Peterson (1985). Incorporation versus compartmentalization in memory for discourse. *Journal of Memory and Language, 24,* 107–18.

Potts, G. R., M. F. St. John, and D. Kirson (1989). Incorporating new information into existing world knowledge. *Cognitive Psychology, 21,* 303–33.

Poulet, G. (1980). Criticism and the experience of interiority. In J. P. Tompkins (ed.), *Reader-response criticism* (pp. 41–49). Baltimore: Johns Hopkins University Press.

Pratt, M. L. (1977). *Toward a speech act theory of literary discourse.* Bloomington: Indiana University Press.

—— (1981). The ideology of speech-act theory. *Centrum, 1,* 5–18.

Prentice, D. A., R. J. Gerrig, and D. S. Bailis (1992). Persuasion by fiction. Unpublished manuscript.

Prince, G. (1980). Introduction to the study of the narratee. In J. P. Tompkins (ed.), *Reader-response criticism* (pp. 7–25). Baltimore: Johns Hopkins University Press.

Pylyshyn, Z. W. (1984). *Computation and cognition.* Cambridge: MIT Press.

Rachlin, H. (1976). *Introduction to modern behaviorism* (2d ed.). San Francisco: W. H. Freeman.

Radford, C. (1975). How can we be moved by the fate of Anna Karenina? *Proceedings of the Aristotelian Society, 49,* 67–80.

Ratcliff, R., and G. McKoon (1978). Priming in item recognition: Evidence for the propositional structure of sentences. *Journal of Verbal Learning and Verbal Behavior, 17,* 403–18.

Remington, R. W., J. C. Johnston, and S. Yantis (1992). Involuntary attentional capture by abrupt onsets. *Perception and Psychophysics, 51,* 279–90.

Restak, R. M. (1988). *The mind.* New York: Bantam.

Rieger, C. J. (1975). Conceptual memory and inference. In R. C. Schank (ed.), *Conceptual information processing* (pp. 157–288). New York: Elsevier.

Rock, I. (1983). *The logic of perception.* Cambridge: MIT Press.

Rockwell, J. (1974). *Fact in fiction.* London: Routledge and Kegan Paul.

Ross, L. (1977). The intuitive psychologist and his shortcomings: Distortions in the attribution process. In L. Berkowitz (ed.), *Advances in experimental social psychology* (vol. 10, pp. 174–214). New York: Academic Press.

Ross, L., T. M. Amabile, and J. L. Steinmetz (1977). Social roles, social control, and biases in social-perception processes. *Journal of Personality and Social Psychology, 35,* 485–94.

Ross, L., and M. R. Lepper (1980). The perseverance of beliefs: Empirical and normative considerations. In R. A. Shweder and D. Fiske (eds.), *New directions for methodology of behavioral science: Fallible judgment in behavioral research* (pp. 17–36). San Francisco: Jossey-Bass.

Ross, L., M. R. Lepper, and M. Hubbard (1975). Perseverance in self-perception and social perception: Biased attributional processes in the debriefing paradigm. *Journal of Personality and Social Psychology, 32,* 880–92.

Rozin, P., and A. E. Fallon (1987). A perspective on disgust. *Psychological Review, 94,* 23–41.

Rozin, P., M. Markwith, and B. Ross (1990). The sympathetic magical law of similarity, nominal realism and neglect of negatives in response to negative labels. *Psychological Science, 1,* 383–84.

Rozin, P., L. Millman, and C. Nemeroff (1986). Operation of the laws of sympathetic magic in disgust and other domains. *Journal of Personality and Social Psychology, 50,* 703–12.

Rumelhart, D. E. (1980). Schemata: The building blocks of cognition. In R. J. Spiro, B. C. Bruce, and W. F. Brewer (eds.), *Theoretical issues in reading comprehension: Perspectives from cognitive psychology, linguistics, artificial intelligence, and education* (pp. 33–58). Hillsdale, N.J.: Erlbaum.

Rumelhart, D. E., G. E. Hinton, and J. L. McClelland (1986). A general framework for parallel distributed processing. In D. E. Rumelhart and J. L. McClelland (eds.), *Parallel distributed processing* (vol. 1, pp. 45–76). Cambridge: MIT Press.

Rumelhart, D. E., and J. L. McClelland (1986). *Parallel distributed processing* (vol. 1). Cambridge: MIT Press.

Rumelhart, D. E., and A. Ortony (1977). The representation of knowledge in memory. In R. C. Anderson, R. J. Spiro, and W. E. Montague (eds.), *Schooling and the acquisition of knowledge* (pp. 99–135). Hillsdale, N.J.: Erlbaum.

Ryan, M.-L. (1980). Fiction, non-factuals, and the principle of minimal departure. *Poetics, 9,* 403–22.

Schama, S. (1989). *Citizens.* New York: Alfred A. Knopf.

Schank, R. C. (1975). *Conceptual information processing.* New York: Elsevier.

Schank, R. C., and R. P. Abelson (1977). *Scripts, plans, goals and understanding.* Hillsdale, N.J.: Erlbaum.

Schober, M. F., and H. H. Clark (1989). Understanding by addressees and overhearers. *Cognitive Psychology, 21,* 211–32.

Searle, J. R. (1969). *Speech acts.* Cambridge: Cambridge University Press.

—— (1971). What is a speech act? In J. R. Searle (ed.), *The philosophy of language* (pp. 39–53). Oxford: Oxford University Press.

—— (1975). The logical status of fictional discourse. *New Literary History, 6,* 319–32.

—— (1977). Reiterating the differences: A reply to Derrida. *Glyph, 1,* 198–208.

—— (1979). Metaphor. In A. Ortony (ed.), *Metaphor and thought* (pp. 92–123). Cambridge: Cambridge University Press.

Sharkey, N. E., and D. C. Mitchell (1985). Word recognition in a functional context: The use of scripts in reading. *Journal of Memory and Language, 24,* 253–70.

Singer, D. G., and J. L. Singer (1990). *The house of make-believe*. Cambridge: Harvard University Press.

Sirridge, M. (1987). Donkeys, stars, and illocutionary acts. *The Journal of Aesthetics and Art Criticism, 45,* 381–88.

Skulsky, H. (1980). On being moved by fiction. *Journal of Aesthetics and Art Criticism, 39,* 5–14.

Slater, M. D. (1990). Processing social information in messages: Social group familiarity, fiction versus nonfiction, and subsequent beliefs. *Communication Research, 17,* 327–43.

Slovic, P., B. Fischhoff, and S. Lichtenstein (1982). Facts versus fears: Understanding perceived risk. In D. Kahneman, P. Slovic, and A. Tversky (eds.), *Judgment under uncertainty: Heuristics and biases* (pp. 463–89). New York: Cambridge University Press.

Snow, M. E., C. N. Jacklin, and E. E. Maccoby (1981). Birth-order differences in peer sociability at thirty-three months. *Child Development, 52,* 589–95.

Sperber, D. (1984). Verbal irony: Pretense of echoic mention? *Journal of Experimental Psychology: General, 113,* 130–36.

Sperber, D., and D. Wilson (1981). Irony and the use-mention distinction. In P. Cole (ed.), *Radical pragmatics* (pp. 295–318). New York: Academic Press.

Spilich, G. J., G. T. Vesonder, H. L. Chiesi, and J. F. Voss (1979). Text processing of domain-related information for individuals with high and low domain knowledge. *Journal of Verbal Learning and Verbal Behavior, 18,* 275–90.

Stanislavski, C. (1936). *An actor prepares*. New York: Theatre Arts.

Steiger, H., and A. S. Bregman (1981). Capturing frequency components of glided tones: Frequency separation, orientation, and alignment. *Perception and Psychophysics, 30,* 425–35.

Stern, L. D., R. G. Dahlgren, and L. L. Gaffney (1991). Spacing judgments as an index of integration from context-induced relational processing: Implications for the free recall of ambiguous prose passages. *Memory and Cognition, 19,* 579–92.

Sternberg, M. (1978). *Expositional modes and temporal ordering in fiction*. Baltimore: Johns Hopkins University Press.

Storms, M. D. (1973). Videotape and the attribution process: Reversing actors' and observers' points of view. *Journal of Personality and Social Psychology, 27*, 165–75.

Stroop, J. R. (1935). Studies of interference in serial verbal reactions. *Journal of Experimental Psychology, 18*, 643–62.

Suleiman, S. R. (1980). Introduction: Varieties of audience-oriented criticism. In S. R. Suleiman and I. Crosman (eds.), *The reader in the text* (pp. 3–45). Princeton: Princeton University Press.

Suleiman, S. R., and I. Crosman (eds.) (1980). *The reader in the text*. Princeton: Princeton University Press.

Tetlock, P. E. (1985). Accountability: A social check on the fundamental attribution error. *Social Psychology Quarterly, 48*, 227–36.

Todd, P. M. (1988). A sequential network design for musical applications. In D. Touretzky, G. Hinton, and T. Sejnowski (eds.), *Proceedings of the 1988 connectionist models summer school* (pp. 76–84). San Mateo, Calif.: Morgan Kaufmann.

Tolstoy, L. (1968). *War and peace* (trans. A. Dunnigan). New York: New American Library. (Originally published in 1869)

Tompkins, J. P. (1980a). An introduction to reader-response criticism. In J. P. Tompkins (ed.), *Reader-response criticism* (pp. ix–xxvi). Baltimore: Johns Hopkins University Press.

Tompkins, J. P. (ed.) (1980b). *Reader-response criticism*. Baltimore: Johns Hopkins University Press.

Trabasso, T., and L. Sperry (1985). Causal relatedness and importance of story events. *Journal of Memory and Language, 24*, 595–611.

Trabasso, T., and P. van den Broek (1985). Causal thinking and the representation of narrative events. *Journal of Memory and Language, 24*, 612–30.

Trabasso, T., P. van den Broek, and S. Y. Suh (1989). Logical necessity and transitivity of causal relations in stories. *Discourse Processes, 12*, 1–25.

Tversky, A., and D. Kahneman (1973). Availability: A heuristic for judging frequency and probability. *Cognitive Psychology, 5,* 207–32.

Vaihinger, H. (1935). *The philosophy of "as if"* (trans. C. K. Ogden). London: Routledge and Kegan Paul Ltd.

van den Broek, P. (1988). The effects of causal relations and hierarchical position on the importance of story statements. *Journal of Memory and Language, 27,* 1–22.

van Dijk, T. A. (1977). Semantic macro-structures and knowledge frames in discourse comprehension. In M. A. Just and P. A. Carpenter (eds.), *Cognitive processes in comprehension* (pp. 3–32). Hillsdale, N.J.: Erlbaum.

——— (1980). *Macrostructures.* Hillsdale, N.J.: Erlbaum.

van Dijk, T. A., and Kintsch, W. (1983). *Strategies of discourse comprehension.* New York: Academic Press.

Walsh, D. (1969). *Literature and knowledge.* Middletown, Conn.: Wesleyan University Press.

Walters, K. S. (1989). The law of apparent reality and aesthetic emotions. *American Psychologist, 44,* 1545–46.

Walton, K. L. (1978a). How remote are fictional worlds from the real world? *Journal of Aesthetics and Art Criticism, 37,* 11–23.

——— (1978b). Fearing fictions. *Journal of Philosophy, 75,* 5–27.

——— (1983). Fiction, fiction-making, and styles of fictionality. *Philosophy and Literature, 7,* 78–88.

——— (1990). *Mimesis as make-believe.* Cambridge: Harvard University Press.

Watson, D. (1982). The actor and the observer: How are their perceptions of causality different? *Psychological Bulletin, 92,* 682–700.

Wegner, D. M., G. F. Coulton, and R. Wenzlaff (1985). The transparency of denial: Briefing in the debriefing paradigm. *Journal of Personality and Social Psychology, 49,* 338–46.

Williams, J. P. (1984). Does mention (or pretense) exhaust the concept of irony? *Journal of Experimental Psychology: General, 113,* 127–29.

Wimsatt, W. K., and M. C. Beardsley (1954a). The intentional fallacy. In *The verbal icon* (pp. 3–18). Lexington: University of Kentucky Press.

———— (1954b). The affective fallacy. In *The verbal icon* (pp. 21–39). Lexington: University of Kentucky Press.

Wolf, D., and D. Hicks (1989). The voices within narratives: The development of intertextuality in young children's stories. *Discourse Processes, 12,* 329–51.

Woodmansee, M. (1978). Speech-act theory and the perpetuation of the dogma of literary autonomy. *Centrum, 6,* 75–89.

Wright, E. F., and G. L. Wells (1985). Does group discussion attenuate the dispositional bias? *Journal of Applied Social Psychology, 15,* 531–46.